Fundamentals of
Social Research Methods

An African Perspective

THIRD EDITION

Claire Bless
Craig Higson-Smith

First edition by C. Bless and P. Achola
published in Lusaka, Zambia, in 1988.

Second edition 1995
Reprinted 1997

Third edition 2000

© Juta Education (Pty) Ltd
PO Box 24309, Lansdowne 7779

This book is copyright under the Berne Convention. In terms of the Copyright Act 98 of 1978, no part of this book may be reproduced or transmitted in any form or by any means (including photocopying, recording, or by any information storage and retrieval system) without permission in writing from the publisher.

ISBN 0 7021 0000 0

Typesetting by Zebra Publications, Cape Town
Cover design by Warren Nelson, Cape Town

Printed and bound in South Africa by
Creda Communications, Eliot Avenue, Eppindust 2, Cape Town

Preface

The first edition of *Fundamentals of Social Research Methods: An African Perspective* developed out of a need for an accessible textbook on social research methods and application within an African context. It was observed that many African government, non-government and private-sector organizations were beginning to attach greater value to social research and the information that it provides. As a result, more and more people entering the workplace were expected to be able to design and implement their own problem-centred research projects and to evaluate the research work of others. Thus, the original edition of this book was written as a resource for the non-professional researcher and the student of research methods. This group includes university students, government administrators, business managers, social workers, educationists and any other people interested in conducting social research. The contents of this book find direct application in a wide variety of fields, including agricultural extension, public health, community development and regional planning, to mention only a few. It will also assist social scientists who, although familiar with the research process, would like to refresh some aspects of their knowledge.

Further, the first edition was designed to fill a particular gap in the available literature on social research methods. Not only did it have to be particularly African in focus — and there are few enough texts on social research methods that take such a perspective — but it had to be aimed at a level which was accessible to people new to social research. With the group of students and lecturers in mind, this book was written and organized in a way that conforms to the syllabi of social science methods courses in many African universities. It is not appropriate for use by advanced social researchers, who should consult specialized literature.

In the past decade there have been important shifts in the political, economic and social contexts of African countries, as well as in the social research methods used in these countries. Such changes have transformed the requirements of social research and placed new demands upon those responsible for training new researchers. With these needs in mind, the second edition was produced so that students and teachers of research methods, who find the book useful, might remain up to date in their understanding of social research methods. This third edition takes the process forward by dealing in greater depth with community-centered research, and by further updating the theory, methods, techniques and examples contained within the text.

The reader should be aware that the term "social sciences" is used here in the widest sense to include all sciences referring to society and social issues. Thus it embraces such disciplines as sociology, economics, political science, psychology, as well as education. Throughout the book, examples drawn from diverse fields are used. Many illustrations are drawn from actual research done in Africa. These include studies sponsored by the UNDP, UNESCO, as well as international and local non-government organizations. Some examples come from conferences, workshops and discussions between social scientists of various disciplines involved in developmental work within the SADC region.

The text strives to present, in a clear and concise way, the fundamentals of research methods in the social sciences. In this sense, the various topics are not necessarily covered exhaustively and the examples given are perhaps not extensive. At the very least, the text is a concise introduction which should be expanded, diversified, further elaborated and deepened by lecture notes and supplementary readings.

Further, it is worth stating that we, the authors, believe that the ultimate aim of social science methodology is to enhance the quality of research results, thereby contributing to the day-to-day lives and circumstances of people. Thus, we aim to provide the reader with the information and skills needed to conduct a research project. For this reason, the topics essentially follow the steps of the scientific process. Each chapter begins with a general overview of the content followed by a set of outcome-based guidelines designed to assist both the learner and teacher. Each chapter ends with exercises which allow the learner to evaluate his or her own progress.

Chapter 1 opens with a discussion of the usefulness of the scientific method for acquiring knowledge as opposed to other ways used by human beings to understand their environment.

In Chapter 2, the main features of science (particularly the social sciences) and the intrinsic relationship between fact and theory are discussed. This helps to clarify the necessary components of research projects. Some broad ethical considerations have been added to this chapter in the third edition.

Chapter 3 focuses on the identification of research problems, as well as on ways to find adequate references and techniques for carrying out an extensive review of literature. Also discussed are sources of background information which constitute an important part of building a complete understanding of the problem at hand.

Chapter 4 is fundamental for anyone who really wants to reach a clear formulation of the problem. It expands on how to identify all the variables at stake; how to understand their interrelationship; how to measure them; and how to express the problem in terms of testable hypotheses.

Chapter 5 presents the various types of research. It looks at quantitative and qualitative research, applied and basic research, as well as descriptive, exploratory, correlational, and explanatory research methods. The section on evaluation research has been removed from chapter five and a more developed version can be found in the new Chapter 6.

Chapter 6 is a new chapter dealing with many aspects of community-centered research. This chapter includes needs assessments, feasibility studies, diagnostic, formative and summative evaluation, programme monitoring, as well as participatory and action-research.

Chapter 7 deals with research design and includes a discussion of the focus of research, the unit of analysis and the time dimension. In addition this chapter covers the most commonly used pre-experimental, quasi-experimental and experimental research designs.

A detailed account of sampling theory is presented in a concrete manner in Chapter 8. The reader is introduced to various probability and non-probability sampling methods. Not only are the inadequacies and dangers inherent in some of these methods discussed, but also how to choose the most appropriate technique.

Chapters 9 and 10 deal with data collection. Various aspects of this process are considered, ranging from the distinction between the scales of measurement to concrete guidelines on how to construct an adequate questionnaire. Attention is given to the properties of a good instrument of measurement and the different biases that can arise from a faulty collection of data. The section on focus groups in Chapter 10 has been extensively rewritten in line with the growing use of this technique in many spheres of social research. Despite many problems, focus groups have the advantage of being empowering of research participants and well suited to many African cultures.

Chapter 11 deals with the development and assessment of valid and reliable research instruments.

Chapter 12 presents a discussion of the process of drawing conclusions from the results of a research study and ways in which those findings may be communicated (including research report writing) and applied. Particular attention is given to the implications of bias in social research.

Chapter 13 is the new closing chapter of the textbook. It looks more broadly at the various role players in the world of social research and the need for social researchers to maintain the highest levels of quality in all their work.

A further important addition to the third edition is the glossary at the end of the book to assist learners who may have forgotten the meaning of terms introduced earlier. At numerous points in the text the reader is referred to a complementary book which looks at the methods of quantitative data analysis. This book by Claire Bless and Ravinder Kathuria is entitled *Fundamentals of Social Statistics: An African Perspective,* and was published by Juta in 1993.

We would like to thank Dr Paul Achola for his contribution to the original version. Although the two chapters authored by him in the first edition have been completely rewritten, his constructive criticisms expressed at the time of first publication are still relevant. Unfortunately, all efforts to consult him about the later editions have been unsuccessful. Many welcome comments and encouragements have come from other colleagues, among them, Dr K Myambo (Zimbabwe), Dr A Maleche (Botswana), Dr H Lemba and Mr D Mulenga (Zambia), Prof S E Migot-Adholla (Kenya), Ms H Shale (Lesotho), Ms Tina Uys (South Africa) and Dr Beth Stamm (United States of America). The authors hope to receive comments for further improvements from readers, especially students.

CLAIRE BLESS
CRAIG HIGSON-SMITH

Johannesburg
January 2000

Contents

Preface ....*iii*

1. *The Different Methods of Acquiring Knowledge* 1
   - Chapter objectives 1
   - Non-scientific methods of acquiring knowledge 1
   - The scientific method and its properties 3
   - Properties of scientific research 5
   - Exercises 6

2. *The Scientific Method Applied to Social Reality* 7
   - Chapter objectives 7
   - The distinction between natural and social sciences 7
   - Interrelationship between facts and theory 8
   - From facts to theory: problem, hypothesis and model 10
   - Ethical scientific research 11
   - Steps in scientific research 12
   - Exercises 13

3. *Problem Conception and Background Information* 15
   - Chapter objectives 15
   - Sources and identification of research problems 15
     - Sources of research topics 15
     - Identifying a research problem 16
   - Literature review 19
     - The purpose of the review 20
     - The literature sources 20
     - The reviewing techniques 21
   - Other background information 22
   - Exercises 23

4. *Variables and Hypothesis Formulation* 25
   - Chapter objectives 25
   - Formulation of the problem 25

Contents

- Identification of the variables.. 26
- Conceptual and operational definitions 31
- Hypothesis formulation 33
- Exercises 35

5. *The Types of Research*.. 37
   - Chapter objectives 37
   - Ways of classifying research 37
   - Quantitative and qualitative research 38
   - Basic and applied research 38
   - Different objectives of social research 39
     - Exploratory and descriptive research............................ 41
     - Correlational and explanatory research........................ 42
   - Exercises 44

6. *Community-centred Research* 45
   - Chapter objectives 45
   - Research and community projects 45
   - Needs assessment 45
   - Feasibility studies 47
   - Project monitoring 48
   - Project evaluation.. 49
     - Diagnostic evaluation 50
     - Formative evaluation 51
     - Summative evaluation 52
     - Some concluding comments on evaluation 55
   - Participatory research 56
   - Action-research... 56
     - Using action-research in developing countries 60
   - Exercises 61

7. *Research Design* 63
   - Chapter objectives 63
   - What is research design?... 63
   - The focus of research 64
   - The unit of analysis.. 64
   - The time dimension 66
   - Types of research design 67
   - Pre-experimental designs 67
     - One-shot case study 67
     - Pre-test/post-test design 68
     - Intact group comparison design 69

© Juta & Co Ltd

Fundamentals of Social Research Methods

- ■ Quasi-experimental designs 70
  - □ Contrasted group design 70
  - □ Time-series design...71
- ■ Experimental designs 73
  - □ Pre-test/post-test control group design 74
  - □ Post-test only control group design..................................75
  - □ Factorial designs 76
- ■ Developing a research design 77
- ■ Sources of bias in research design..78
  - □ History and maturation 78
  - □ Regression towards the mean..78
  - □ Test effect 79
  - □ Instrumentation 79
  - □ Experimental mortality 79
  - □ Reactive effects 79
  - □ Selection bias 80
- ■ Validity of research design 80
  - □ Internal validity 80
  - □ External validity 80
  - □ Relationship between internal and external validity.............81
- ■ Exercises..82

8. *Sampling* 83
   - ■ Chapter objectives..83
   - ■ The purpose of sampling and types of sampling 83
   - ■ Main sampling concepts 85
     - □ A well-defined population 85
     - □ The sample 86
   - ■ Types of probability sampling..87
     - □ Simple random sampling 87
     - □ Interval or Systematic Sampling.....................................88
     - □ Stratified random sampling 89
     - □ Cluster or multi-stage sampling 90
   - ■ Types of non-probability sampling......................................92
     - □ Accidental or availability sampling 92
     - □ Purposive or judgemental sampling.................................92
     - □ Quota sampling 92
   - ■ Other types of sampling 93
     - □ Sampling with or without replacement 93
     - □ Independent versus related/dependent samples 93
   - ■ Sample size 93
   - ■ Sampling errors and related problems 94
   - ■ Exercises...95

Contents

9. Data Collection: Basic Concepts 97
- Chapter objectives 97
- Facts, data and measurement 97
- Scales of measurement 98
- Relationship between type of research and method of data collection......... 99
- Ethical considerations related to data collection: The rights of research participants 100
  - Right to privacy and voluntary participation 100
  - Anonymity 100
  - Confidentiality 101
- Exercises 101

10. Techniques of Data Collection........................... 103
- Chapter objectives 103
- Observation... 103
- Interviews and questionnaires 104
  - Comparison of the different techniques 106
  - Advantages and disadvantages of unstructured or semi-structured interviews.. 107
  - Advantages and disadvantages of structured interviews.............. 108
  - Advantages and disadvantages of mailed questionnaires 109
  - Focus groups... 110
- Constructing a questionnaire..................................... 113
  - The questions.. 116
  - Editing the questionnaire..................................... 120
- The experimental techniques..................................... 121
- The record method or unobtrusive measures....................... 123
- Exercises 124

11. Reliability and Validity of Measurements................. 125
- Chapter objectives 125
- Reliability 126
  - Test retest reliability... 127
  - Equivalent-form reliability.................................... 128
  - Split-halves reliability.. 128
  - Item analysis... 129
- Validity 130
  - Content validity.. 131
  - Criterion-related validity..................................... 132
  - Construct validity 133
  - Face validity 133
- Balancing reliability with validity 134
- Exercises 135

12. *Interpretation of Results and Writing a Research Report* *137*
    - Chapter objectives. 137
    - Data analysis 137
    - Interpreting the findings: detection of possible errors. 138
        - Types of error and mistake 138
    - Drawing conclusions. 140
    - Generalizing research findings 140
    - Suggestions and recommendations 141
    - Types of report formats 141
    - Organization of a research report 142
        - Introduction 142
        - Method 143
        - Results. 143
        - Discussion. 143
        - References or bibliography 143
        - Abstract and appendices. 144
    - Reporting style. 144
    - Exercises. 145

13. *Concluding remarks* *147*
    - Chapter objectives. 147
    - The research world 147
    - Objectivity and values. 148
    - The role of research-funding institutions 150
    - Highest quality research 151

Glossary. *153*

Bibliography. *158*

Index *161*

CHAPTER 1

The Different Methods of Acquiring Knowledge

In this chapter the major methods of acquiring knowledge are presented. Some methods are more accurate and reliable than others and the scientific method has clear advantages. The need to adopt a scientific approach as the most adequate and reliable method becomes obvious as its properties are described in detail.

CHAPTER OBJECTIVES

Learners who have completed this chapter will be able to:
- Describe in detail the various methods by which human beings acquire knowledge, including the scientific method.
- Compare the scientific method with other means of acquiring knowledge.
- Describe and contrast probabilistic and deductive reasoning.
- Discuss the issue of reductionism in social science research.

NON-SCIENTIFIC METHODS OF ACQUIRING KNOWLEDGE

There are many ways of acquiring knowledge and the least mentally developed human being, the child, does not need to carry out sophisticated research in order to develop some understanding of the world around it. One of the first sources of knowledge for the child are the parents, the "authorities" in all spheres of knowledge. This **method of authority** is not only depended upon by children but very commonly by each of us when we rely on the knowledge and "wisdom" of prominent people who are recognized as having a better grasp of their environment than ordinary people. Thus the statements of these "qualified" people are rarely questioned or challenged. On the contrary, the knowledge imparted by them is usually accepted as absolute and a certain amount of faith is placed in these authorities as sources of knowledge. Elderly people in a village who, because of their age, have had more opportunity to accumulate experience in a society where formal education is minimal, are often placed in this position. Other examples would be kings in feudal societies, heads of churches, or, in modern societies, technocrats who are regarded as highly specialized persons in a particular field of knowledge. It is to be noted that such a situation is not without danger. Once individuals are placed in such a position of authority, they will usually rely on particular strategies to justify and preserve their position. This can be done by masking one's own ignorance with impressive rituals, by using a very specialized way of expression (professional jargon), or by emphasizing the uniqueness of one's position ("it is true because I, the minister, say so"). Very often this method allows individuals to hide the superficiality of their knowledge, its underlying ideology and other weaknesses in their argument.

A variation of this "method of authority" is the **mystical method**, where the correctness of the knowledge is assumed to reside in a supernatural source. In this case the "knowledge producers" are regarded as authorities due to their ability to transmit the truth or knowledge imparted to them by supernatural forces.

Whether one's authority to knowledge is recognized because of one's position or because of one's presumed supernatural powers, one's credibility is strongly related to the level of education and general knowledge of the audience. But growing children recognize that their parents do not have the answers to all problems and that they even give dubious explanations at times. In the same way, the authority and mystical modes of acquiring knowledge lose influence when better, alternative explanations can be found. The history of natural sciences is full of examples of mystical explanations being replaced by scientific ones. Who, for example, would still believe that the earth is flat or that it is the centre of the solar system? Some centuries ago, this was a dogma of the Catholic Church accepted by all Christians as the truth!

The foregoing two approaches to knowing are mainly based on faith. In contrast, the rationalistic and the empirical methods which none the less constitute extreme opposites do not attribute special aptitudes to particular persons, but differ in the importance that they give to reasoning and observation.

The **rationalistic method** is based on human reason. Human beings have the ability to think logically or reason, and thus to discover laws through purely intellectual processes. The basis of knowledge is correct reasoning which enables one to know what must be true by principle. A good example is pure mathematics where laws and principles are discovered without relying on any reality but on the basis of axioms. Observation of reality, collection of facts, using the five human senses, are unnecessary. Although this approach to knowledge has had some success in the natural sciences, it has made little progress in the social sciences. This may be because human beings are not rational in the way that the rationalistic method requires.

The opposite of the rationalistic method is the **empirical method**, where facts observed in nature are the foundation of knowledge. Objectivity of observation is emphasized and only what is observable, what can be perceived by our senses, constitutes knowledge. A piece of wood floats on water while a piece of iron does not. For an extreme empiricist, knowledge stops there, since the reason for the difference cannot be observed. Interpretations of observations and speculation about relationships between facts introduce subjectivity and are therefore seen as distortions of the data.

But critics of both the rationalistic and the empirical methods are justified in asking: What are facts without the establishment of a relationship between them, without an explanation for their connection in time and space? And, of what use is a theory which is totally divorced from reality? Obviously, these two extreme methods are inadequate for the acquisition of knowledge, although each one has advantages. The **scientific method**, as described below, is a synthesis of the rationalistic and the empirical methods.

Finally and for the sake of completeness, one should also mention the existence of other methods like the ones used in philosophy, theology or aesthetics. However, the field of investigation and application of these methods is qualitatively different from that of science and thus beyond the scope of this book. The differences will become clear

THE SCIENTIFIC METHOD AND ITS PROPERTIES

To illustrate how the scientific method integrates the above-mentioned two methods, the process of knowing is examined.

The first step to knowing is a *description* of the object, relationship or situation. The object of the study must be accurately depicted. Here, evidently, the empirical method of objective observation must be used. Thereafter, an *explanation* or statement of the relationship between the described facts, should be expressed, where possible in the form of a law. The explanation is thus the result of a reasoning process using the rationalistic method, and leads to the formulation of a natural or social law. In turn, the stated explanation should permit a *prediction* of future events under well-defined conditions. In other words, the explanation should allow one to foretell the occurrence of some event. But to ensure that this explanation or law will enable prediction, the correctness of the explanation must be tested. This is achieved by confronting it with reality as perceived by the five human senses, using the empirical approach. Correct explanations leading to the ability to predict events should yield intelligent *intervention* which enables changes to occur that improve a situation.

e.g.

An objective description of the role of women in the agricultural sector in Zambia in the 1980s reveals that it was an insignificant one. One explanation for this is that it was virtually impossible for women in Zambia to access bank loans for agricultural projects. From this description it was possible to predict that, without intervention, the role of women in the country's agricultural economy was unlikely to grow. Based on this knowledge, strategies could be developed to intervene effectively in order to improve the participation of women in the Zambian agricultural sector.

A science can be defined as a building of knowledge obtained by use of a particular methodology, the scientific one. The scientific method of acquiring knowledge, also called scientific research, is a systematic investigation of a question, phenomenon, or problem using certain principles. *All different sciences are united not by their different subject matter but by their common method, the way knowledge is acquired.* There is a tendency to confuse the content of science with its methodology.

Astrology and divination are not non-scientific because of their aims but because of their methods. The purpose of establishing a relationship between the position of the stars, or the clairvoyance of a diviner and the course of human destiny may be scientific, if a scientific method is used. Some issues, such as the existence of God, whether a person is good or bad, or any issue related to moral values, do not allow for scientific investigation. It thus becomes imperative to specify the main characteristics of the scientific method in order to differentiate it from other methods.

Science assumes the following:

1. *The existence of natural and social laws.* Science presumes order and regularity in natural and social events. Without this assumption some of the main aims of scientific research, such as explanation, prediction and the possibility to act on nature would not be attainable. These laws are assumed to exist independently of the observer and they describe the way phenomena interact or social events occur.

2. *Laws can be discovered by human beings.* Scientific research assumes that although human beings are part of nature and are themselves subject to its laws, they can discover those laws. We obey biological laws determining the growth of our body, psychological laws determining the development of intelligence, sociological laws of organization of society, as well as economic and political laws.
3. *Natural phenomena have natural causes.* No supernatural powers are necessary to grasp the cause of events and no unexplainable supernatural forces are needed to explain the way nature functions. Classical examples, so often found even nowadays, where this assumption is not met, are the use of religious beliefs to explain physical phenomena. For example, some people may regard thunderstorms as an expression of anger of the gods, or they may regard a hurricane's damage as God's wrath on a sinful city, or they may attribute the natural death of a person to displeased ancestors.
4. *Knowledge and truth are founded on evidence.* Numerous examples show how invention of new instruments of investigation and new approaches to studying a problem can lead to new advances in science, showing how relative the previous knowledge was. Famous examples of such advances include the invention of the electron microscope in biology, the theory of relativity in physics, and cross-cultural comparisons in social sciences.
5. *Scientific statements must be distinguished from common-sense statements.* Common sense is often characterized by contradictory statements. "Absence makes the heart grow fonder" and "Out of sight, out of mind" are opposing statements of common wisdom. Clearly, both are possible in different situations and neither is appropriate to all situations. Common sense statements are the result of non-scientific observations in that they do not take into consideration the different variables at stake. The weakness of the approach is that the preconditions for the validity of the statements are not specified due to lack of systematic investigation. This illustration emphasizes once more the empirical aspect of science which relies on experience and observation of the real world.
6. *Scientific observation is objective.* Objectivity here means that the description of reality does not reflect the subjective views of the researcher, but rather corresponds to the description made by anyone examining the same reality. The more accurate a description is, stating measurable properties for instance, the greater the objectivity of the observation. A tree can appear to be tall to someone used to grassland and short to someone used to woodland. But stating that the tree measures three metres in height should find confirmation by anyone able to measure this tree with the same measuring instrument.
7. *Scientific observation is systematic.* All possibilities are considered one at a time, in a logical order. Natural sciences allow the best illustration of systematic observation. In chemistry, for example, different substances can be mixed two at a time, under the same conditions and same proportions, to observe their reaction. On the other hand, when investigating the effects of two different painkillers, it would be confounding to prescribe these two pills to patients with different medical backgrounds or to give the two medicines to the same patient at the same time. What could one conclude with confidence if the ailment disappears? A researcher who gives a medicine to people suffering from different ailments in order to test the effect of that medicine is not being scientific. If a patient recovers,

the researcher is unable to determine whether the positive result was due to the particular medicine or to the nature of the original illness. Since the method was not systematic, the results are ambiguous.

Unfortunately, it is not always possible to observe systematically every phenomenon or all of its aspects. Most often some characteristics remain unknown so that the explanation and, as a result, the prediction cannot be accurate. In fact, one can only predict that an event will take place if one knows *all* the conditions and circumstances which cause the event. In the social sciences in particular, it is very rare to be in possession of all information leading to the occurrence of a certain phenomenon and thus to explain with *certainty* this phenomenon. One has to content oneself with a *probability* statement, asserting that if some given conditions are satisfied the event will occur more often than if some of these conditions are not. Explanations that concede some uncertainty are called **probabilistic explanations**.

Given precise initial conditions, the trajectory of a falling stone can be predicted with certainty. Given some initial genetic, physical, socio-economic information about a new-born baby it is not possible to predict with certainty the personality, intelligence, and physical condition of the same child at 5 years of age. Too many unmeasurable factors are involved. One can only predict that, coming from a middle-class family, the child will in all probability enjoy a good education and a good diet, and will generally have good opportunities to develop its intellectual potential adequately.

Statements of the type "All men are mortal. X is a man. Therefore X is mortal," predict a fact with certainty. X will die. There is no doubt about it: the result has been obtained by deduction from the two premises. However, the age X will reach cannot be predicted with certainty. One can only assess that he will probably not reach the age of 100 and that the probability that he will die before the age of 50 is larger than the one of his reaching 70 years. In fact, life insurance companies function on the basis of life expectancies which are probabilities of the time of death obtained through generalisation from many observations.

In short, the object and the method of investigation will determine the type of causation which can be expressed, and thus the type of prediction.

PROPERTIES OF SCIENTIFIC RESEARCH

Methods that are accepted today as being appropriate for scientific research have a long and complex history. The details of this history fall outside of the focus of this text. However, it is appropriate to mention some of the most important characteristics of scientific research.

1. Scientific research is *empirical* since the aim is to know reality. Each step is based on observation, be it when collecting the basic facts or when testing the explanation, assessing the value of the prediction or the result of an intervention.

2. Scientific research is *systematic* and *logical*. Not only must the observation be done systematically but a certain logical order must be followed all along. Logical prediction cannot be made before a description has been given and an explanation of the observed phenomena has been found. One cannot prepare a questionnaire to gather all data necessary for a study, before having clear ideas on the type of information needed. An analysis of the different variables involved must be undertaken prior to the formulation of the questions to be answered by the respondents.

Fundamentals of Social Research Methods

3. Scientific research is *replicable* and *transmittable*. Since the observation is objective and the explanation logical, anyone placed in exactly the same circumstances can observe the same event and make the same reasoning, leading to the same explanation and prediction. Moreover, it is possible to communicate each step of the research and to transmit the acquired knowledge. The usual way of doing this is to present the research and its results in a report or an article published in a journal.

4. Scientific research is *reductive*. To grasp the main relationships of laws, the complexity of reality is reduced. All details which are not essential or which have little influence on the process under investigation are omitted.

e.g.

When the quality of a blanket is being investigated, the material of the blanket must be analysed since its property of conserving warmth depends on whether it is made of cotton or of wool. But the colour of the blanket has little relevance to its warmth conserving function and need not be considered. Thus, only the necessary properties are taken into consideration.

In social sciences, by controlling for many variables, one nearly always reduces the complexity of reality. One presupposes that the variables which have not been taken into consideration have little effect on the issue in which one is interested.

e.g.

For instance, when studying the loan facilities available to women for small-scale agricultural projects, one rarely takes into account the personality of the policy makers or that of the loan recipients. The economic and social factors at stake are so much more important that one would want to gather information on the type of project, the type of crops to be produced, the size of the field and quality of the soil, the availability of fertilizer and labour power, transport and market conditions, perhaps also the age and marital status of the woman, the number of dependants who would help her and her health condition as far as it might affect her work. But individual characteristics such as her personality traits are considered to be of little relevance for the study under consideration. They are discarded in order to maintain a certain level of generality in the study.

Reductionism or the method of considering only the essential and necessary properties, variables or aspects of a problem is not to be confused with the philosophical concept of reductivism.

EXERCISES

1. What is meant by "replication of scientific research"? What are the preconditions for replication and why is it important?
2. Explain the difference between probabilistic and deductive explanations. Give examples of each.
3. Analyze, using your own example, the positive and negative aspects of research being reductive.
4. Identify a social science research project which illustrates the four steps of research: description, explanation, prediction and intervention.

CHAPTER 2

The Scientific Method Applied to Social Reality

This chapter explores science as an active, purposive reflection about the objective world and its laws. The source of knowledge is the outside world upon which people must act in order to understand it. There is an interaction between the action of people on nature and society, and theory, the set of explanations. The starting point and basis of scientific knowledge is the direct contact of the person with the environment. This superficial knowledge is deepened, generalized and expressed in the form of theory. Facts and theory interrelate at each step of the learning process. This is reflected in the research process which expresses the systematic scientific method.

CHAPTER OBJECTIVES

Learners who have completed this chapter will be able to:
- Compare and contrast the social and natural sciences.
- Analyse the relationship between facts, theory and observation.
- Discuss the broader ethical concerns of research.
- Describe the process of scientific research.

THE DISTINCTION BETWEEN NATURAL AND SOCIAL SCIENCES

Research usually arises from some need, so that it has a particular purpose to fulfil. Natural sciences deal with investigations into the properties and laws of natural phenomena. The development of natural sciences is at times determined by the needs of production, commerce and industry. This explains the development of astronomy which was indispensable to pastoral and agricultural peoples. Geometry was necessary for navigators. Mechanics was developed because of the need for large building operations. In the modern period, the development of chemistry, physics and the biological sciences is directly related to the demands of expanding industries. On the other hand, social sciences deal with investigations into the properties and laws of *social* phenomena. Their development has its roots in the need for general management and control of social affairs. The development of both types of sciences depends more or less on the needs, values, aspirations and other characteristics of the particular society in which it takes place. Thus, many countries in Africa show greater concern for developing techniques to reduce the spread of malaria than they do for research into heart transplants.

Social sciences, however, are much more affected by some properties of the society than are the natural sciences. Moreover, the actual objects of investigation and research

© Juta & Co Ltd

problems of the social sciences introduce new methodological difficulties. For ethical reasons, for instance, some experiments cannot be done on human beings and some variables cannot be controlled. Generally, there are so many uncontrolled factors due to the complexity of social reality that exact laws can rarely be found. Thus, most results are expressed as probability statements, a fact which is itself a reflection of some level of doubt. A physicist can express the laws of electricity with a formula and predict with certainty when an electric bulb will glow. A sociologist can only predict that under certain circumstances unemployment leads to an increase in crime. This textbook concentrates only on the social sciences.

Finally, one should be aware of the controversy which developed in the sixties, but which is still unresolved, about the adequacy of scientific methods in studying social phenomena. The defenders of "social sciences" argue that social disciplines can be correctly understood as "natural sciences of individuals in society", not qualitatively different from the well established natural sciences. The differences between natural and social sciences demand an adjustment of the natural sciences methods to social reality. The methods and techniques must be modified and adapted according to the characteristics of social processes, but they are the correct ones for a successful understanding of social issues and the building of theories.

On the other hand, many people argue that the rigid scientific method is often incapable of grasping the fluidity of many social phenomena. These arguments are determined largely by the school of thought to which the critics belong. Their reluctance to consider social disciplines as sciences extends from the analysis of some failures of the empirical, scientific approach to the extreme of denying the existence of laws in social reality. Since the aim of this book is to introduce the reader to *empirical social science methods*, the first approach has been adopted here. However, the ever-present dangers of an over dependence on the methods of natural science and the inadequate, mechanistic, transfer of those methods on to the social sciences are emphasized repeatedly throughout this book.

INTERRELATIONSHIP BETWEEN FACTS AND THEORY

As mentioned earlier, science is based primarily on facts. Our fundamental knowledge is **perceptual knowledge**, that is, information about the environment perceived through our senses. Only external, superficial relations between information acquired by our senses are known. Perception by itself is only one basis of knowledge. On its own, however, perception falls short of knowledge. One may know that green fruits are not ripe and should not be eaten but what about watermelons? **Rational knowledge**, based on judgement, provides explanations or reasons for the relationships between facts, and hence a deeper understanding of reality. Thus, a description of facts can only be complete when both the direct information given by our sense as well as the deeper understanding based on reasoning and judgement, are taken into account. There exists, therefore, a fundamental relationship between **facts**, defined as empirically verifiable observations, and **theory**, as the explanatory framework.

- *Facts give rise to theory* since they raise a need for explanation of the observed phenomena. Observation of reality, even by pure curiosity, can lead to systematic research and thus to the formulation of a general explanation or theory. Facts, the corner-stone of knowledge, are not the product of just any kind of random observation, but should be *selective* and *meaningful*.

The Scientific Method Applied to Social Reality — Chapter 2

- *Theory serves as an orientation for the gathering of facts* since it specifies the type of facts to be systematically observed. If a theory stipulates that the failure of co-operative unions is related to the absence of particular managerial skills among the members, the observations will focus on the existence or absence of these skills, rather than to the size of the union, the age and sex of its members, or the climatic conditions under which the members live.

- *Facts allow a researcher to confirm, disprove, improve or formulate a theory.* Facts lead to a redefinition or clarification of theory. A scientific explanation must be subjected to empirical testing to determine whether it corresponds to observed reality. This means in practice that a theory allows a researcher to predict some facts. If the predicted facts are not observed during experiment or investigation, the theory is disproved and will need improvement or reformulation. Moreover, if some observed phenomena do not coincide exactly with the theoretical predictions, the theory must be reformulated. For example, if a theory states that delinquency is a consequence of poverty, the existence of many delinquent middle-class children disproves the theory. Reformulation should lead to an improved understanding and more adequate explanation of delinquency.

- *Theory allows for a classification and conceptualization of facts.* It summarizes and provides explanations as to how facts relate to each other.

- *Theory predicts facts.* For example, under certain conditions the law of supply and demand predicts the existence of an illegal market much in the same way as the laws of astronomy predict the occurrence of an eclipse of the sun.

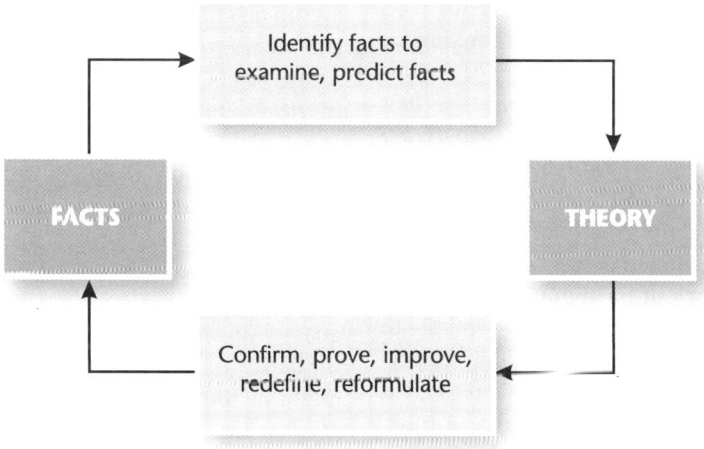

Figure 2.1
Relating facts and theory

FROM FACTS TO THEORY: PROBLEM, HYPOTHESIS AND MODEL

As mentioned before, there exists a fundamental relationship between facts and theory. This relationship is expressed through a succession of steps. Facts raise questions. These questions can in turn be condensed into a **problem** which is then given a temporary solution, yet to be tested, which is called the **hypothesis**. This step is not fortuitous but is related to a large framework, a more general building of knowledge, the underlying **theory**. Thus a hypothesis, a tentative explanation for certain facts, will become part of a theory as soon as it is verified, that is, confirmed by sufficient evidence.

Other forms of thinking that make the transition from empirical to theoretical knowledge possible are analogy and model-building. **Analogy** is a correspondence between a phenomenon or event that has been studied already and another phenomenon or event which resembles the first but has not yet been studied. Analogy permits one to draw conclusions based on the similarities between objects in certain of their properties. Comparing these objects or facts which have been identified as analogous allows one to infer some properties of the less well-known objects. For example, the first aeroplanes were built in analogy to flying birds. Moreover, many explanations of social phenomena are based on analogy to biological processes like the growth of organisms. In understanding human behaviour, an analogy to animal behaviour is often used. Since it is much easier and more morally acceptable to experiment on animals, comparative psychology will study animals subjected to great stress (fear, hunger, lack of sleep) and infer, by analogy, some knowledge about human behaviour under the same conditions.

In **model-building** one object or phenomenon, the well-known one, serves as the model. Here certain properties of the object have been singled out, represented in their pure, simplified form and then studied in the absence of the actual object. Ideal models are formed with the help of particular symbols. For instance, a commonly used model is the representation of certain properties of the earth's surface by geographical maps. Fine lines represent rivers, different colours represent vegetation or altitude, circles of different size represent towns of various size. Of course, each map is a simplification of the object it describes and only represents some of its properties with symbols. In social sciences one finds models of underdevelopment, such as Gunder Frank's model of the centre and the periphery, or models describing the nature of a certain society, like the stratification model used by Evans-Pritchard in his anthropological studies of some African societies.

Analogy and model-building are therefore quite similar ways of discovering some properties of an object or phenomenon by utilizing the existing knowledge of another object or phenomenon. The advantage of model-building is its reductive property, that is, only the main characteristics are considered. The characteristics which do not affect the process under study are ignored and the properties of the model can then be studied in the absence of the original object of study. A geographer can study the properties of a particular region through the use of adequate maps, and without actually travelling to that region.

Of course, the utility or danger of analogy and model-building depends on the adequacy of the analogy or model. The similarity of two chosen objects or events might be too superficial, the model could be an over-simplification of reality, both leading to fallacious results.

The relationship between facts, problems, hypotheses, models and theory is summarized in figure 2.2.

The Scientific Method Applied to Social Reality | Chapter 2

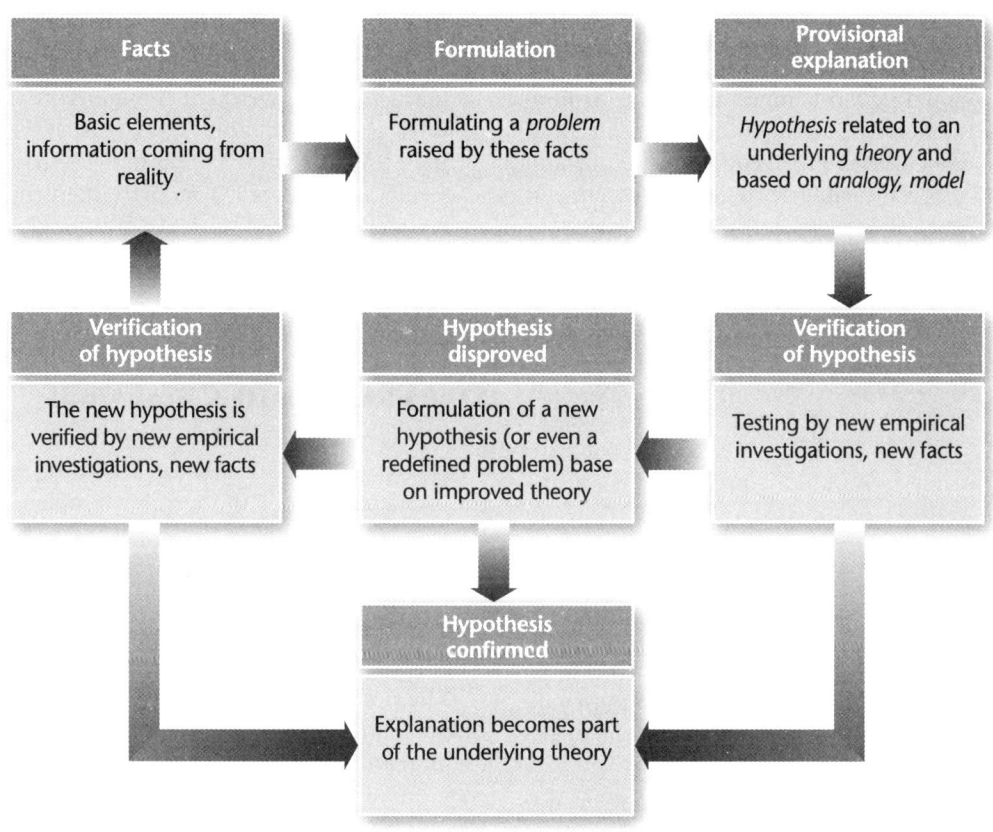

Figure 2.2
The process of knowledge acquisition

ETHICAL SCIENTIFIC RESEARCH

Scientific research can be loosely defined as the translation into practice of the relationship between facts and theory presented above in order to acquire specific information. Accurate information is an important resource. For this reason scientific research is a source of power which can be used and abused. This is reflected in the amount of money that politicians spend to obtain accurate information about public feeling on particular social issues. For almost every new finding that social research produces, there are people who stand to gain from it and there are people who might lose because of it. Thus, both the process and results of research require strict ethical choices and careful thought on the part of the social researcher. Four issues are looked at in more detail.

1. *Highest quality practice*. Internationally, the quality of social research is extremely variable. Unfortunately, poorly performed social research devalues all social research. It is therefore important that social researchers are properly trained,

Fundamentals of Social Research Methods

supported and supervised while they are still inexperienced. It is very important that researchers critically review their own values and biases (see Chapter 12 and 13). Most important is the requirement that methodologies, results and conclusions are recorded in detail and made available to peer review. Only if one knows exactly how a piece of research was conducted can the results be evaluated.

2. *Building capacity of all sectors of the community.* In some cases social research methodology is seen as being beyond the reach of the majority of people. Although it is true that some sophisticated techniques require a degree of specialized knowledge, virtually all problems can be usefully tackled using the methods laid out in this volume. It is important that a wider range of people learn how to conduct useful research so that they can benefit directly from these techniques and judge more accurately the value of research in which they have an interest.

3. *Relevance.* The question of the relevance of research is a controversial and political one in many circles. However, since the resources needed to support social research are somewhat scarce it is safe to say that researchers should aim to make a useful contribution to society. While it is true that people disagree on what is useful and what is not, all social researchers should ask themselves what contribution their work is making to society. This topic is covered in more detail in later chapters.

4. *Promulgation of results.* Too often important research findings are lost because of the manner in which findings are presented. It is part of the researcher's responsibility to make the results available in a form that it usable by the people who can benefit from it. In some cases publication in a journal is sufficient to achieve this. In other cases, the people who are most likely to benefit from the study are unlikely to ever read a scientific journal. In these cases it is required that researchers find other ways of making their findings known. If promulgation of results is not handled properly then the research is unlikely to make a difference to society and the previous point about relevance becomes meaningless.

STEPS IN SCIENTIFIC RESEARCH

The research process in social sciences, although subjected to variation according to the particularities of the research problem, has a constant frame expressed in the form of a loose timetable. Some steps must be performed before others can take place. This book analyses each of the components of the scientific research process in turn.

The best research results are based on a careful planning of the whole process. Here a useful plan of action for research is given. It is by no means the only one. Depending on the subject matter of the research, flexibility must be introduced. Literature review, for instance, is an ongoing process which can be useful at different times. Also, some steps may be ignored when some specific methods of research are used. For instance, case studies seldom require statistical analysis. The last step, writing the report, is in fact a summary of the whole research.

The research process generally involves the following steps.

1. Selection and formulation of the research problem:
   (*a*) selecting a topic for research: identification of the problem;
   (*b*) formulating the research problem;
   (*c*) acquiring knowledge on current theory and research: literature review;

(d) identifying and defining the variables;
(e) defining concepts and establishing operational definitions;
(f) formulating the hypothesis.
2. Development of research method:
   (a) choice of research design;
   (b) description of the samples;
   (c) sampling procedures.
3. Data collection:
   (a) construction of the research instrument;
   (b) actual data gathering.
4. Analysis of data:
   (a) data processing;
   (b) statistical analysis.
5. Interpretation of results.
6. Conclusions and recommendations.
7. Writing the research report.

EXERCISES

1. Describe the differences between natural and social science. In what ways are they similar?
2. Outline three examples that illustrate the relationship between facts and theory.
3. Find two examples of models or analogies used in the social sciences, and not mentioned in this book.
4. Select a social science article and identify the broad ethical issues that the researcher should consider.

CHAPTER 3

Problem Conception and Background Information

This chapter describes how to start a research project, how to identify and formulate the problem and which factors to take into account before embarking on the project. The aim of gathering background information on theories and facts, in particular by literature review, is explored. Some guidelines are given on how to find information, as well as on how to review and abstract articles.

CHAPTER OBJECTIVES

Learners who have completed this chapter will be able to:
- Initiate their own research project.
- Identify and formulate a research problem.
- Search for literature and compile a literature review.

SOURCES AND IDENTIFICATION OF RESEARCH PROBLEMS

Although social reality provides innumerable questions, selecting a research problem is a delicate task. Out of the great variety of queries arising from the environment, one has to sort out those that are appropriate to scientific investigation. Only general guidelines on how to choose and formulate a research problem can be stated, including some criteria which should be satisfied for a successful research project. The difficulty of providing precise directives for the selection of research questions arises from the diversity of possible topics and their sources.

Sources of research topics

1. Observation of reality
The most evident source of research topics is contact with the external world and direct observation of it. Many of the world's great scientific advances are due to pure observation.

2. Theory
Theory is another source of research problems. If a theory is correct, one expects a certain phenomenon to occur in a particular situation. Research is necessary to verify the correctness of the assertion that the particular situation will occur. In psychology, Piaget's theory of cognitive development links the passage through different stages of reasoning to maturation rather than to education. If this is the case, there should be no essential differences in the cognitive development of school children and children who have never received any formal education. Neither should there be major differences between people of different cultures in this

© Juta & Co Ltd

respect. Thus, this theory suggests many research topics.

3. Previous research

Previous investigations often inspire new studies. This may be due to contradictions between results or concerns with the procedures used. Or, it may be due to ambiguous results in need of further exploration. Finally, it might be useful to repeat earlier studies with different groups of participants. For instance, it may be suggested that some findings and interpretations are biased by the way data has been collected. Children may be handicapped when asked to perform some tasks, not because of their lack of skill, but because of their difficulty in grasping the instructions given in an unfamiliar language. Thus, new research should be undertaken where either a non-verbal task is used or where the instructions are given to all children in their mother tongue.

4. Practical concerns

Very often research stems from concrete problems encountered in the everyday life of a certain community. For instance, if students with tertiary education qualifications experience difficulty finding employment, the relationship between the content of courses being offered by the tertiary education institute, and the demands of the job market should be investigated.

5. Personal interest

Sometimes, research projects are undertaken as a result of the personal interest of the researchers. In this case, the relevance of the research to the broader community should be considered.

Identifying a research problem

In the identification of a research problem one can distinguish three steps in narrowing the range of interest. These are the selection of a topic area, the selection of a general problem, and the reduction of the general problem to one or more specific, precise and well-delimited questions. In general, the sources of a research problem are to be found in a combination of direct observations and experiences, theory, previous investigations and practical concerns, mentioned before.

The choice of the topic area may be dictated by various factors: intellectual or academic (the social organization of cockroaches; topic: comparative social psychology), practical interest (the queuing at bus-stops; topic: urban public transport), or personal interest (why do I forget so quickly what is taught in lectures; topic: learning, motivation, memory), or, it could be purely accidental. Nowadays topics of research are strongly influenced by social conditions. It may be "fashionable" to conduct research into a particular area during a particular period (such as issues concerning women and the handicapped emphasized by the United Nations Decade for Women and the Year of the Disabled). The final two decades of the twentieth century have produced an enormous wealth of research on HIV and AIDS. As Africa enters the twenty-first century more and more emphasis is given to issues of war and public violence. Social and financial incentives play an unavoidably important role in the choice of the subject matter for investigation.

Within the topic area a general problem is chosen. Again, the problem could be mainly of scientific and intellectual interest or revolve around a practical concern. The need might be for more information about a particular issue or it might be to explain the relationship between existing facts.

e.g.

A study of the use of oral contraceptives in an African population might aim at determining how many women use this form of contracep-

Problem Conception and Background Information — Chapter 3

tion, taking into account women from different geographic areas (urban vs rural women), income levels, levels of education, age, number of children alive, and so on. A different study in the same area might aim to explore the relationship between the use of oral contraceptives and the health of women in the country. The first study aims to describe a phenomenon in greater detail, the second to understand the relationship between different variables. Both could be aimed at developing interventions in the health sector.

Both of these studies would involve very extensive research due to the enormous variety of variables involved. While the contraceptives themselves may influence the health of women directly, it is also likely that women's health will be indirectly affected by the fact of having fewer pregnancies. Also, how the contraceptives affect women's health is likely to be influenced by the age, nutritional status, and many other factors.

Very often social research involves a large number of different variables and can be extremely complex. Thus, after a general problem has been identified, one still has to find ways of reducing it to a specific and manageable research question.

A research question must be such that it can be handled in a single study or divided into a number of subquestions to be dealt with in separate studies. One way of doing this is to list the different answers to the general problem and to express them in the form of questions.

e.g.

Topic area

Instability of marriages

Research problem

What is the relationship between the level of industrialization in an African country and the rate of divorce?

Question

What factors might be influencing divorce?

Possibilities include:

1. age of partners at time of marriage;
2. differences in religious affiliation between partners;
3. employment status of partners;
4. type of employment (industrial sector, informal sector, commercial sector, self employed, etc.);
5. type of marriage (customary or statutory);
6. method of selection of partner (arranged marriage, individual choice);
7. difference in the education levels of partners;
8. difference in the socio-economic class of partners;
9. financial situation of the family.

Point 1 can, for instance, be expressed in the form of a specific, well delimited and unambiguous research question:

Are marriages between very young people (say, under 23 years) less stable than those between older people?

Point 8 could be formulated as:

(a) Does the rate of divorce vary between different socio-economic classes?

or

(b) Is divorce more frequent in the higher socio-economic class than in the working class?

(Note that in the formulation 8(b) only two groups of the population are considered and expectations are expressed regarding what the difference will be. Thus this formulation is more precise and the study more delimited than 8(a).)

It is a very common mistake of research novices to underestimate the extent of a research problem and to undertake investigations far beyond the time and money available to them, as well as beyond their ability. As a general rule, inexperienced researchers are advised to reduce the research topic to as simple a question as possible. Chapter 4 provides further guidelines on how to achieve this.

A very important issue in the search for and identification of a research problem is that not every topic can be transformed into a research project. The first and most fundamental constraint is that only problems which are empirically based, that is, which deal with observable reality, can be investigated by means of the scientific method. This excludes all problems concerned with subjective issues such as value or moral judgements. Questions like "Are civilized, twentieth century human beings better than people living in the Middle Ages?", "Is politics a dirty business?" and "Is black beautiful?" implicitly or explicitly contain subjective judgments. It is, however, possible to investigate scientifically whether the members of a certain community share the opinion that politics is a dirty business or that black is beautiful. The relationship between the belief that black is beautiful and other beliefs, behaviours, or political views can also be studied.

Another very important constraint to be borne in mind when choosing a research problem is that, although the problem relates directly to empirical reality, the feasibility of data collection may be doubtful or impossible. For this reason the proof of the existence or non-existence of God cannot be studied by scientific means. In other cases, data collection could harm the participants or interfere too much with their private lives. One cannot, for instance, separate a child from its parents when trying to examine the effects of lack of parental care. In addition, any project based on longitudinal study of over twenty or forty years is in acute danger of never being achieved, as the researcher or the respondents may die during this long period and with them the project.

Based on what has been mentioned above, a well-chosen problem should satisfy as many as possible of the following criteria:
1. be timely;
2. relate to a practical problem;
3. relate to a wide population;
4. relate to an influential or critical population;
5. fill a research gap;
6. permit generalization to broader principles of social interaction or general theory;
7. sharpen the definition of an important concept or relationship;
8. create or improve an instrument for observing and analysing data;
9. provide possibilities for a fruitful exploration with known techniques; and
10. have implications for a wide range of practical problems (relevance).

As mentioned in Chapter 2 the relevance of research must be judged in terms of the extent to which it facilitates intervention which leads to an improvement in society. This point has a particular connotation in developing countries where, in the past, the aim of research often did not correspond to the interests of the people or the country. Too often academic researchers prefer to choose their topics of investigation for academic ambition, rather than for their social relevance.

Finally, before going ahead with the actual study, a researcher should check whether the following more general criteria are satisfied.
1. *Empirical testability*. The question must refer to empirical facts and be answerable through the observation of reality. The question should not be based on subjective factors, such as moral and ethical judgements or cultural beliefs. Scientific research cannot answer such questions.
2. *Feasibility*. This refers to whether or not the proposed study is manageable, taking

into account the available time, financial means, the size of the sample and the method or instrument of collecting data. Another hindrance to research feasibility is that the questions the researcher needs to ask may be too personal or too emotionally loaded to be answered honestly by the respondents.

e.g.

It may not be possible within a month to investigate the attitude of nurses towards patients in all the clinics of a large town, neither would it be possible without sufficient funds for transport to move conveniently from one clinic to another. On the other hand, if one wants to restrict the research to psychiatric nurses with at least ten years experience, the sample available in a single town may be too small.

3. *Critical mass*. This refers to the breadth, or scope of the research. Is the problem so narrow, specific, or trivial that it is not worthwhile pursuing?

e.g.

When investigating the use of various methods of contraception it may not be of much use to ask female university professors only whether or not they use contraceptives. Such a focus would be too narrow and almost trivial, as female university professors constitute a negligible part of the population of an African country, with quite specific properties.

4. *Interest*. This refers to the motivation of the researcher to carry out the proposed research. Since conducting a research project is a long and demanding task, strong motivation is essential. Motivation which is only external (like the need to carry out a research project as part of a course on research methodology) will often lead to a deficient, biased research outcome. If, on the other hand, the choice of topic is dictated by a deep-seated interest, the quality of the research is likely to be positively influenced by such interest.

5. *Theoretical value*. The importance of the theoretical relevance of research has already been reflected in many of the criteria given for a well-chosen problem. The general idea can be summarized by the question of whether or not the research will contribute to the advancement of knowledge in a particular field of research and how useful this knowledge will be for the further development of that field.

6. *Practical value*. This refers to the relevance of the research results to society. What changes will the results effect in the actual life situation of those studied? How can the study results be adapted to the present situation so as to improve it? Are practitioners likely to be interested in the results?

In conclusion, note that, although ideas on how to proceed in choosing a research problem should have been clarified by the guidelines given above, the function of a research problem, to be discussed in the next chapter, constitutes a new step in the research process. But this step cannot be meaningfully realized before the literature related to the problem has been carefully studied. A literature review often helps to clarify the question under investigation by showing how it is embedded within the already available facts and theories.

LITERATURE REVIEW

In order to conceive the research topic in a way that permits a clear formulation of the problem and the hypothesis, some background information is necessary. This is obtained mainly by reading whatever has been published that appears relevant to the research topic. This process is called the literature review. Although acquaintance with different theories and models as well as research results takes place, by necessity, before a clear statement of the problem can be formulated, a literature review is an ongoing process. This is the case not only because the relevant research results can be published at any time but also because, in the course of research, new aspects and problems arise requiring new information.

In conducting a literature review, the following three broad issues should be kept in mind: the purpose of the review, the literature sources and the reviewing techniques. Each of these are examined in detail.

The purpose of the review

Why is a literature review necessary? What is to be gained? What should one look for? The purpose of the review of existing literature is one or a combination of the following.

1. To sharpen and deepen the theoretical framework of the research. That is, to study the different theories related to the topic, taking an interdisciplinary perspective where possible.
2. To familiarize the researcher with the latest developments in the area of research, as well as in related areas. In particular, the researcher should become acquainted with the problems, hypotheses and results obtained by other researchers in order not to duplicate efforts but to widen and deepen them. Previous results are a starting point for new research.
3. To identify gaps in knowledge, as well as weaknesses in previous studies. That is, to determine what has already been done and what is yet to be studied or improved.
4. To discover connections, contradictions or other relations between different research results by comparing various investigations.
5. To identify variables that must be considered in the research, as well as those that prove irrelevant. This finding is often a result of the comparison of different investigations.
6. To study the definitions used in previous works as well as the characteristics of the populations investigated, with the aim of adopting them for the new research. Often some definitions are found to be correct and unbiased so that they can be adopted for the new investigation along with other basic characteristics of the population. In so doing, homogeneity between research projects is gained which will allow for an easier comparison of the results obtained in different studies.
7. To study the advantages and disadvantages of the research methods used by others, in order to adopt or improve on them in one's own research.

It should be noted that although a literature review is essential, it also carries some dangers. One may be influenced by the results of previous research, or one may accept without criticism their chosen characteristics and explanations so that one fails to discover new possibilities and to observe without preconceptions or expectations. One may develop the tendency to emphasize mainly what has been brought to one's attention or to work within an already established framework, instead of exploring new approaches.

The literature sources

Where is the information to be found? How does one locate the relevant articles, books and reports? The most common problem when starting a literature review seems to be the identification of relevant sources. Often the impression is created that nothing has as

Problem Conception and Background Information — Chapter 3

yet been written on the chosen topic and the multiplicity of non-relevant literature can be overwhelming. To overcome this problem, the following procedure can be adopted.

1. To start with, information centres, subject abstracts, indexes or reviews should be consulted. The easiest starting point is the indexing system of a library in which different aspects of a topic would be noted. A listing of relevant books and articles could thereby be established. A discussion with the desk librarian could be useful for particularly difficult topics. Another very useful source of information is the abstract or index of the area under investigation. For instance, the Sociological Abstracts will provide researchers with a brief summary of all published articles in different areas of sociology. Bibliographies (such as the *International Bibliography of the Social Sciences*) and indexes (such as the *Book Review Index*) list citations necessary to find literature on specific topics.

2. Professional journals (such as the *Review of Economics and Statistics*; *Psychological Bulletin*) present book and article reviews and are therefore also good sources. Moreover, the new trend is the development of computerized clearing houses on particular topics (such as education or health) which will provide up-to-date surveys of existing literature on a specific topic. For instance, for education issues a researcher could rely on the *Educational Resources Information Centre* (ERIC) which is a major source of documents on education, classified under different topics like rural education, early childhood education, and so forth.

3. Another growing source of information for those with computer access is the Internet. Here it may be possible to identify conference groups, journals and lists relating to the research problem. When searching the internet a researcher is able to limit the search by language (for example, including only English language materials), or by date (for example, including only research published later than 1985), or by form (for example, including only journal articles). Similarly one is able to search in general or subject specific sources. ANANZI (http://www.ananzi.co.za)is a good search facility for South African and African materials. Another potentially useful facility is YENZA (http://www.nrf.ac.za/yenza) which offers assistance in literature reviewing through the internet and links to various resources including libraries of academic institutions.

4. The researcher should discuss the research problem with other social scientists who have experience in the area of the research problem.

5. Once an initial list of books and articles has been established, the next step is to expand the search in a more direct way. Whereas the initial list may cover a wide range of information, the new selection should focus more precisely on the present research problem. In the process of reading the material on the initial list, the most relevant items should be selected and their bibliography and references used to detect new sources of more precise information. In particular, it is useful to consult journals cited in articles since this starts a "snowball" process, providing the researcher with a great number and variety of sources of information.

The reviewing techniques

How does one review and abstract relevant literature? Of the publications identified for reading, a certain number will be selected as being particularly relevant for the proposed research and they should be reviewed for use

© Juta & Co Ltd

in the study. The question revolves around the type of information which should be abstracted from these publications and how to present it. Reviews and abstracts should contain the following information:

1. full reference, including topic or title, name(s) of author(s), name of journal or book in which the publication appears, and date and place of publication;
2. purpose and hypothesis, which should include a summary of the problem, indicate the hypothesis to be tested, and the variables included;
3. methodology, comprising a description of the population, the sample, the design, the instruments of measurement and the method(s) of data analysis; and
4. findings and conclusions, which should incorporate a summary of the results and their interpretation(s), whether the hypotheses have been confirmed, the implications stated and the consequences suggested by the author(s).

The importance of a wide, comprehensive literature review cannot be emphasized enough. Because of the complexity of social issues, an interdisciplinary approach is encouraged. An economic issue always has some sociological, political and psychological aspects which are more or less evident and of relevance. How much is the productivity of a factory related to such economic variables as input, level of technology and style of management? How much is due to motivational factors, learning procedures and the political leaning of the trade union? Moreover, some theoretical reasoning in one science can be applied by analogy in another science.

OTHER BACKGROUND INFORMATION

Although consulting scientific literature is an essential means of acquiring necessary background knowledge for starting a research project, it is not the only one. Much vital information and many personal experiences have never been published, making it necessary to talk to people. Useful background information can be obtained in direct discussion with people involved in a similar issue. Hopefully, these are people who have accumulated experience from which the researcher can learn. Nurses, relating their experiences, methods and difficulties in introducing family planning to the rural population, telling anecdotes or describing the reactions of women, will offer a variety of useful information to the health researcher. A conversation with a foreman or trade-union official may give a labour-economics researcher insights into working conditions, worker morale and salary structures.

Information on a research problem can also be obtained by direct observation of, or even participation in, a relevant situation. Sharing the life of villagers can deepen the understanding of their problems and aspirations and open new perspectives on the type of research question to raise, or how to formulate the problem, taking into account the concrete background.

In conclusion, after a thorough literature review, the researcher should have acquired an overview of the various theories and models which could be adopted for the particular research. The scientist should then be in a position to identify the theoretical framework (and model, if any) on which the research will be based. Moreover, an overview of other research done on the topic should have been gained, leading to a deeper analysis of all relevant studies.

Problem Conception and Background Information — Chapter 3

EXERCISES

1. Analyse the empirical testability of the "healing properties of the mystical components of traditional medicine".
2. How would you proceed to collect the necessary background information on the research topic mentioned in 1 above? Under which topic of the subject catalogue would you start your search for relevant literature? Whom would you contact for further information?
3. Choose an area of personal interest and formulate a research question which meets the criteria specified in this chapter.
4. Why is it important that the researcher conduct a literature review before starting a research project?
5. Choose a research report in a social science journal and review it, using the guidelines given in this chapter.

CHAPTER 4

Variables and Hypothesis Formulation

The purpose of this chapter is to highlight the fact that, after formulating the problem under study, an adequate statement of the research hypothesis is necessary. This step cannot be achieved unless all relevant variables have been identified and classified. Moreover, hypotheses require that all concepts have been given conceptual and operational definitions. The latter are used to measure the variables so defined.

CHAPTER OBJECTIVES

Learners who have completed this chapter will be able to:
- Formulate a research problem
- Identify the various variables associated with a research problem.
- Appropriately define and operationalize variables.
- Formulate testable hypotheses.

FORMULATION OF THE PROBLEM

First the research problem must be identified and reduced to a workable form. Then the gathering of background information by literature review and other means helps clarify the position of the problem within the theoretical framework and the already available results. Only then is the researcher in a position to formulate the research problem. As often stated, a well-formulated problem is already a half-solved problem. A research problem is expressed as a general question about the *relationship between two or more variables*. Since the issue of how to reduce and sharpen a problem has been extensively dealt with, the issue of formulation is elaborated here.

Returning to the example of the development of women's co-operatives in Zambia (see Chapter 1), the following research problems could be formulated:
- How adequate are the credit and funding facilities offered to women's cooperatives?

Here the main variables are the financial needs of the co-operative and the financial facilities available to it.

Alternatively, the problem could be:
- Is the involvement of the women's co-operative members (in terms of time available and regularity at work) related to family obligations?

In this problem, one variable is the extent to which a woman has to spend time and effort to satisfy her family obligations (pregnancy, child care, household chores, as well as time and attention demanded by her husband and social environment). Another variable is the time spent by a woman at the co-operative, including the regularity of her work habits.

The formulation of a problem introduces the necessity of defining clearly all the concepts used and of determining the variables and their relationships. This is covered in the next sections.

IDENTIFICATION OF THE VARIABLES

Suppose that a problem has been formulated in a way that relates two or more variables. It may be relevant to ask such questions as: "Which are these variables and how are they related? Do they all have the same importance? Do they all vary at the same time?" In some cases the researcher might expect a **causal relationship** to exist between variables, where a variation in one results in a variation in the other.

e.g.

When analysing the credit facilities available to women co-operatives, one would suppose that access to credit facilities depends on many factors. For instance, this access could be easier if men and not women were in charge of co-operatives or if the organizations were not co-operatives but private, individual enterprises. In the examples given, availability of credit facilities would depend on the sex of the requesting and managing persons or on the type of business. Thus there is a causal relationship between these variables and the availability of credit facilities.

In some other cases, two or more phenomena take place simultaneously and it is not possible to determine that one is the cause of the other. They might both vary in the same way because they are both under the influence of a third variable. In this case the two variables are said to be **correlated**.

e.g.

The availability of books in the university bookshop may fluctuate with the number of lecturers in the School of Humanities and Social Sciences. But their positive association, that is, the fact that a large stock (or small stock) of books in the bookshop coincides with periods of well-staffed (or under-staffed) departments in the School, can be explained by the variation in the financial situation of the university on which both factors depend. But essentially they do not affect or cause each other.

More will be said on correlational and explanatory research in Chapter 5. For the moment it is useful to define a variable and to bear in mind the difference between a variable and a constant.

A **variable** is an empirical property that is capable of taking two or more values. If a property can change in value or kind, it can be regarded as a variable. If a property cannot take more than one value, it is a **constant**.

e.g.

Consider a crowd gathered at a sports stadium. The people are of different sexes, different age-groups, different social backgrounds, from different residential areas, and so on. All these differences are concepts of sex, age, social background, place of residence, etc. which have been given particular values. They are thus converted into variables with different levels. The variable "sex" has two levels or two different values that it can take, namely "male" and "female". The variable "age" can take many more values, such as "below 20 years", "21–30 years" or any number between 0 and 100. But all the people gathered could have

Variables and Hypothesis Formulation

some common property, something that is constant. They may all be citizens of the same country or they may all have come to the stadium to watch the same event, that is, they may all share the same interest. Such concepts are constants.

Variables may have particular roles in a certain problem. Some variables may be the ones influencing other variables, determining the values of these affected variables. These are the independent variables (indicated by IV). Other variables may be subject to other causes so that their values are influenced by the values of other variables. These are the dependent variables (indicated by DV). Independent and dependent variables are the two most important types of variable. They constitute the core of the problem. As the names indicate, both are tied to each other by a certain relationship: the variations in one (the dependent variable) are a function of the variations in the other (the independent variable). Put another way, changes in the IV *cause* changes in the DV.

e.g.

It is well known that the height of a child (DV) depends on its age (IV). To prove this assertion, a researcher will have to take many children of different ages, say 1, 3, 5, 9, 12 and 15 years old, and measure their respective heights. In so doing, the independent variable "age" will be given different values or levels by the researcher. In other words, the researcher manipulates the independent variable. Then the corresponding measured values of the other variable, the height of each child, will be compared to the age. A certain regularity should become evident: the height of the child (DV) should vary according to the age (IV), or younger children should be shorter than older ones. Obviously, it is not because a child measures 98 cm that she is 5 years old, but rather she is 98 cm (small) because of being only 5 years old.

In a more abstract and precise way, the definitions of these two types of variables are given below.

The **independent variable** is that factor which is measured, manipulated, or selected by the researcher to determine its relationship to an observed phenomenon which constitutes the dependent variable.

The **dependent variable** is that factor which is observed and measured to determine the effect on it of the independent variable; that is, it is that factor that appears, disappears, diminishes or amplifies, in short, varies as the experimenter introduces, removes or varies the independent variable.

e.g.

Regarding the problem mentioned in the previous section about the possible causes for divorce, the independent variable, which is the age of the partners at the time of marriage, is given two sets of values: married when under 23 years of age and married when 23 years or older. The researcher, when selecting the subjects, will categorize them, using this criterion. Then, by measuring the values taken by the dependent variable, that is, the stability of the marriage measured in terms of the number of years without divorce, the researcher will be able to draw a conclusion about the effects of marrying young on divorce rates.

The following example clarifies and illustrates the definitions.

e.g.

The output in number of bags of maize per hectare (dependent variable) may be a function of the quantity of fertilizer used (independent variable). The researcher will manipulate the last variable by choosing different levels or quantities of fertilizer to be used per hectare and will then measure the output in maize per hectare for each level of the independent variable. The output of maize is clearly expected to vary according to the amount of fertilizer used.

Another kind of variable is the moderator variable. In the simple example of the relationship between the age and height of children, a researcher could argue that other factors also influence the height of a child. These include the child's sex, the height of parents, and the quality of the child's diet. These additional variables affecting the dependent variable are called moderators. In other words, the **moderator variable** is that factor that is measured, manipulated, or selected by the researcher to discover whether or not it modifies the relationship between the independent and dependent variables. Since moderator variables share some of the characteristics of independent variables (in that they are measured and manipulated by the researcher to observe the effect on the dependent variable) they can be thought of as "secondary independent variables".

e.g.

To return to the sociological example about the causes of divorce, the economic circumstances of a couple or the birth of a child shortly after marriage could be moderator variables. If the couple is economically self-reliant or if it is tied by the birth of a child, the negative or adverse effects of the youth of the couple on the stability of the marriage could be attenuated. The necessity to care for a new-born might strengthen the ties between a very young couple who may otherwise have felt the need for an early divorce.

Another example makes this clear.

e.g.

In the economic example of maize output per hectare, the moderator variable could be the amount of water available. Using a system of irrigation which allows the experimenter to manipulate the amount of water supplied per hectare, one could study the effect of different quantities of water on the output, where the amount of fertilizer used is the same. In other words, knowing that the output (dependent variable) will increase as a function of the use of fertilizer (independent variable), it must be checked how this increase is accelerated or decelerated by the amount of water used (moderator variable).

Most of the phenomena studied in social sciences cannot be explained by the effect of only one independent variable. The variation of one factor can usually only *partly* account for the variation in the dependent variable. More of the variation will be explained or accounted for by introducing secondary independent and moderator variables. But, the simultaneous variation of many variables will make an assessment of the role of any one particular variable impossible.

e.g.

A researcher is interested in the health of young children in a particular community and how it is affected by the fact that a new clinic has been opened in the area. A comparison of children's health before and after the opening of the new clinic reveals a general improvement. However, the researcher also notes that the average income of families in the communities has risen during the past year. In this case it is extremely difficult to tell whether the improvement in child health is due to the improved health care facilities or the improved economic situation of parents.

Variables and Hypothesis Formulation — Chapter 4

Social researchers overcome this kind of problem through the *control* of certain variables. **Control variables** are those factors which are controlled by the researcher to cancel out or neutralize any effect they may otherwise have on the observed phenomenon. For instance, when measuring the height of children as a function of their age, one should control for their health condition since malnutrition has a negative effect on growth. Practically, it means that children of the same nutritional background (control variable) but different ages (independent variable) should be compared on the basis of their height (dependent variable). Note that, depending on the aim of the research, the quality of the diet given to children or the health condition of the children could be considered as a moderator variable.

e.g.

In the example concerning the causes of divorce, the role of culture could be controlled for by choosing only couples belonging to the same ethnic group; or the role of education could be neutralized by selecting couples with similar levels of education. In the maize production example, the quality of the soil or meteorological conditions could be controlled for by choosing only sample hectares under cultivation in the same area.

Two other variables, both somehow related to the independent variable, often play an important role. The **antecedent variable**, as indicated by its name, appears before the independent variable and determines it. Looking at the example of the maize output per hectare, the independent variable, which is the quantity of fertilizer used, may be strongly influenced by the financial situation of the farmer who can or cannot afford to buy as much fertilizer as he/she would like to. Thus the research could have been to analyse the output of maize as a function of the wealth of the farmer. Note that if the antecedent variable is held constant, the relationship between independent and dependent variable still exists. (One selects only farmers of the same economic position, but who utilize different quantities (but the same quality) of fertilizers. The output of maize will still vary.) Conversely, if the antecedent variable is allowed to take different levels but the independent variable has a fixed level, the dependent variable will not vary. The **intervening variable** is, in some ways, the opposite. It is a consequence of the independent variable and it determines the variation of the dependent variable. It falls between the independent and dependent variables, so that, if it is held constant, the latter will not vary.

e.g.

If the use of fertilizer has, as a consequence, the need for more weeding (which is a time-consuming activity proportional to the quantity of fertilizer used), the intervening variable could be the time needed for weeding. If this time is held constant, there will not be a significant variation of the output of maize, since the crop would have been harmed by the lack of weeding. One would also consider the quantity of fertilizer used as an intervening variable when the independent variable is the financial situation of the farmer.

It is useful to think of antecendent, independent, moderator, intervening and dependent variables as being connected in a causal chain or network. It is part of the social researcher's function to explore these various causal links. However, the researcher should also be watchful for accidental connections and extraneous variables. An **extraneous variable** is a variable that influences both independent and dependent variables, giving the false impression of a relationship between them.

Fundamentals of Social Research Methods

e.g.
Often people who are afraid of hospital treatment will comment that, for the same age group, the death rate in hospitals is much higher than outside hospitals. Although nobody will contest this statement, can one infer from this co-variation (being admitted to hospital and dying) that one is the cause of the other? Or, are they both due to a third variable, the ill-health of people admitted to hospital?

e.g.
The different types of variable are illustrated with a last example. The research of a sociologist focuses on the effect of background sound on employees' performance of clerical tasks in a large enterprise.

1. The independent variable is the sound environment and has four levels:
   (a) total silence;
   (b) incoherent street noise;
   (c) classical music, and
   (d) modern popular music.
2. The dependent variable is the work performance of a group of employees in a clerical task.
3. Moderator variables might include the type of task (simple or complex), the age of the employee (below 25 years, 25–40 years, more than 40 years), and the cultural background of the employee (African or Western).
4. The control variable is sex, since it is presumed that male and female employees perform differently in clerical tasks. Thus, the sample is constituted only of women.
5. The antecedent variable is the acoustics of the offices and includes the type and height of the ceiling, size of the hall, the arrangement of the furniture, and the existence or otherwise of a carpet. Background noise will be influenced by these factors.
6. The intervening variable is the stress or the soothing effect of the sounds and has two levels: stressful and soothing.

Figure 4.1 illustrates the relationship between these variables.

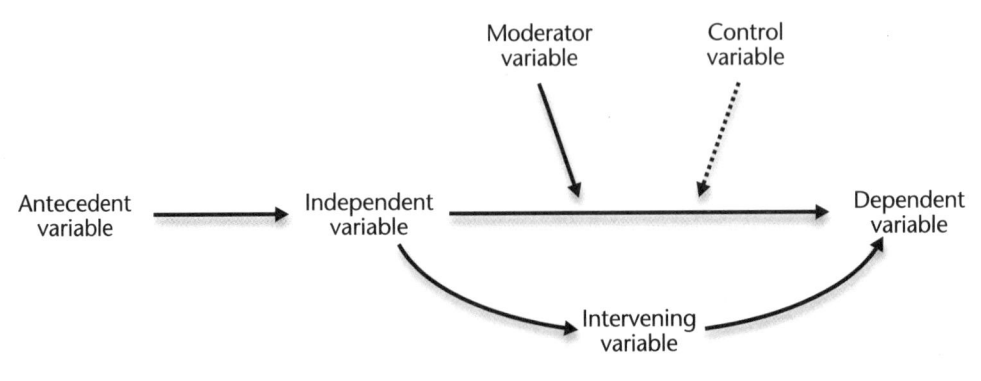

Figure 4.1
Relationship between variables

The importance of correctly identifying these six types of variables for any research problem should be fully understood. No hypothesis can be formulated and no problem resolved unless a clear analysis of all relevant variables has been performed.

Note that the relationship between two variables, one being independent and the other dependent, is only related to the specific problem under investigation. In other circumstances, the independent variable could be depending on another one, or the dependent variable could be considered as determining the variation of other variables.

e.g.

The instability of marriage or the rate of divorce, which is the dependent variable in the sociological example, could become an independent (or moderator) variable in a study investigating the impact of marriage instability on performance at work. Moreover, the independent variable (age at time of marriage) could become a dependent variable when investigating the impact of education or of residential area on age at marriage. It could be asked: "Do people with secondary school education marry later than people with primary school education?" or "Is the age at time of marriage of the urban population higher than that of the rural population?"

Lastly, having identified all the variables, criteria must be established whereby their different values may be measured. In other words, the variables must be defined in a way that allows a systematic and accurate description of their variation.

CONCEPTUAL AND OPERATIONAL DEFINITIONS

Verbal communication among human beings would be impossible without the existence of words expressing concepts. When one speaks of a table or a tree, of patience or of efficiency, one uses words to describe the empirical world, something which exists, in an abstract way. People share a general idea or a concept of what a table is, allowing all objects considered as table to be classified under this category, even if they differ in shape, colour or material. The same is true for more abstract concepts such as who is a patient person or what is an efficient organization.

The main functions of concepts are, firstly, to facilitate communication among human beings. Secondly, concepts aid in the classification of the elements of reality and their generalization. By observation of some plants, one may distinguish between particular characteristics and thus classify one plant as "tree", another as "flower". The concept "tree" can be applied, by generalization, to all other plants sharing the same characteristics. Thirdly, in research, concepts are the building blocks of theories. The concepts of assimilation and accommodation are corner-stones of Piaget's theory of cognitive development; the concepts of supply and demand constitute fundamentals of classic economic theory.

But for concepts to be useful they must be defined in a clear, precise, non-ambiguous and agreed-upon way. For an exchange of views to take place, the participants must "speak the same language". They must attribute the same meaning to the concepts they use. This is particularly important in research.

The two types of definition useful for our purpose are conceptual and operational definitions. A **conceptual definition** is the definition of a concept in terms of a set of other concepts. Thus a courageous person is a brave person, or a person able to control fear in the face of danger, or a person who remains calm in the face of threatening events. A hungry person is someone who needs food. Since concepts are still to be defined by other concepts, they form a chain until one encounters primitive terms. These primitive terms, like colours, sounds and odours, cannot be defined in terms of other concepts. Instead, their meaning is conveyed by direct experience, such as blue like the sky, hot like fire and hard like rock. Concepts like sky, fire and rock used in this analogy are things that one has seen or experienced.

A conceptual definition cannot be true or false, but it may or may not be useful for communication. Below are some properties which conceptual definitions should have in order to be useful.

1. *A conceptual definition must denote the distinctive characteristics of that which is defined.* It must include all things belonging to this class, but only these things. For example, defining a fish as an animal living in water would include whales and shrimps which are not fish.
2. *A conceptual definition should not be circular.* In other words, it should not describe something by using the same concept. For example, an impatient person should not be defined as a person lacking patience.
3. *A conceptual definition should be stated positively*, expressing the properties shared by the objects and not the properties they lack. For example, a book cannot adequately be described as being an object without specific colour and weight.
4. *A conceptual definition should be stated in clear and unequivocal terms* to avoid different interpretations. For example, defining a substance as being a drug could lead to two interpretations: medicinal or narcotic.

Even a very well-formulated conceptual definition does not fulfil the need of a researcher who wants to assess the existence of some empirical phenomenon. This is the function of an **operational definition**. Thus an operational definition does not only give precise indications as to what the fundamental characteristics of a concept are, but it also gives precise indications about how to observe or even measure the characteristics under study. Stated in another way, an operational definition is based on the observable characteristics of an object or phenomenon and indicates what to do or what to observe in order to identify these characteristics. Instead of defining a hungry person as a person needing food, a researcher who finds it difficult to assess the existence of this need will prefer one of the following definitions: a person who has been deprived of food for 24 hours; a person who can eat a loaf of bread in less than 10 minutes, or a person whose blood-sugar level is lower than a specified level. Although these three definitions seem quite different, they share a common property: they indicate a way of observing and measuring the phenomenon under investigation. If a researcher wants to be convinced that a certain person is hungry, any one of these three methods can be chosen and other researchers will agree that the person is hungry on the basis of the given definition.

Clearly, a concept may be described by more than one operational definition. Depending on the aim of the research, an adult can be defined as "physically grown to full size and strength" (biological approach), as "economically self-reliant" (economic approach, excluding students and unemployed) or as "enjoying the right to vote" (legal approach, relative to the country's constitution). Some constraints, like the unavailability of direct information or the need to obtain information through secondary sources will influence the way concepts are operationalized. For instance, if one cannot assess the wealth of research participants by direct evaluation of their income, one can define their wealth by what is observable in their way of living: residential areas, ownership of houses, ownership of luxury items like cars, television sets, stereo sets and furniture. A particular operational definition may even be unique for the particular situation or research for which it has been conceived.

Within the multiplicity of possible operational definitions, three types can be constructed, as seen in the above example of a

Variables and Hypothesis Formulation

hungry person. The first type is an operational definition which indicates the operations that must be performed in order for the phenomenon under study to occur. For example, to make sure that the participant will be a hungry person, the researcher should deprive the participant of food for 24 hours. The second variant is an operational definition which indicates how a particular person or object possessing the characteristics under study will operate or act. Thus a person who, when presented with a loaf of bread, will eat it in less than 10 minutes could be defined as being hungry. If a person takes more than 10 minutes to eat the loaf one can assume that this is not the case. The third variety is an operational definition which indicates some intrinsic properties of a person or phenomenon which possesses the characteristics under study. For instance, by measuring some property of a person, in this case the level of sugar in the blood, one can assess whether or not the person is hungry (low or high blood-sugar levels).

The more unique an operational definition is, the more useful it is since it discriminates accurately between elements which possess the characteristics under investigation and those which do not. In short, the most important feature of operational definitions is their ability to indicate measuring devices or assessment techniques to determine the level of the variables so defined. In our operational definitions of a hungry person, the first definition required the measurement of the period a person has not eaten; the second definition relied on the time needed for a person to eat a loaf of bread, and the third definition suggested the measurement of blood sugar levels. By comparison, the initial conceptual definition of a hungry person — one who needs food — did not indicate how the person's need for food should be measured.

HYPOTHESIS FORMULATION

Essentially, research problems are questions about relationships among variables and **hypotheses** are tentative, concrete and testable answers to such problems. In other words, a hypothesis, which is a suggested answer to a problem, has to be tested empirically before it can be accepted and incorporated into a theory. If a hypothesis is not supported by empirical evidence, it must be rejected and the researcher is obliged to suggest another one. In this sense, the role of hypotheses is not only to suggest explanations for certain facts or problems but also to guide the investigation. The following are the main characteristics of usable hypotheses.

1. *A hypothesis must be conceptually clear.* All variables identified must be clearly described, using operational definitions.

2. *A hypothesis should have empirical referents.* This property is an essential feature of a scientific approach to problems. It is fulfilled as soon as operational definitions have been found for all the concepts appearing in the statement of the hypothesis. Particular care should be taken to avoid moral judgements, attitudes and values. Expressions like "good", "bad", "ought to", "should" and the like are not scientific.

3. *A hypothesis must be specific.* This property reflects the fact that the range of the problem must be narrow enough to allow a precise, well-delimited investigation. If the problem is too wide, the hypothesis will be too general and thus not testable. Again, good operational definitions will safeguard against this pitfall. A hypothesis such as "peasants are more prejudiced than workers" may sound interesting, but, unless "peasants", "workers" and, above all, "prejudiced" have been given operational definitions, the hypothesis is not testable. "Prejudiced" as such, with-

out specifying that the prejudice is directed toward other racial groups, nationalities, or foreign foods, may be beyond measurement. Moreover, a specific hypothesis makes mention not only of the independent and dependent variables but also of the moderator and all control variables. As mentioned above, the effect of a certain fertilizer on maize production can only be reliably proven if all other factors which could also influence production, such as quality of soil, period of fertilizer application and meteorological conditions, have been taken into account. Thus, the conditions under which relationships between variables are tested must be stated explicitly.

4. *A hypothesis must be testable with available techniques.* Although some investigations may be relevant, value-free and specific, it may not be possible to carry them out because of lack of instrument or method to measure one or other of the variables. One can easily measure the temperature of a sick child, but how does one measure a lack of affection which affects the child's health? Thus, when formulating a hypothesis, it is very important to ensure that adequate techniques of observation and measurement are available. One way to go about this is to study carefully the operational definitions which should indicate clearly the methods of measurement.

The criteria for formulating a usable hypothesis emphasize strongly the importance of adequate operational definitions of all variables. These, added to the correct identification of all variables, constitute the fundamentals of a good research project.

A final word is included about the way a hypothesis can be formulated. When a causal relationship between two variables is suspected, it is possible in some cases to determine precisely the direction (positive or negative) of this relationship.

Hypotheses concerning the cause of marriage instability could be variably formulated as follows:

1. The young age of the partners at the time of marriage (under 23 years) has an effect on the stability of their marriage.
2. The young age of the partners at the time of marriage (under 23 years) has adverse influences on the stability of the marriage.
3. The young age of the partners at the time of marriage (under 23 years) has positive influences on the stability of the marriage.

The first formulation is **non-directional** since it does not indicate the direction in which the dependent variable will be influenced by the independent one. The second and third formulations indicate a negative and positive influence respectively and they are thus called **directional hypotheses**. Whether a hypothesis is presented in a non-directional or in a directional form depends on the extent to which the researcher is able to predict the type of relationship between variables. Of course, because a directional hypothesis is more precise and gives more information, it is preferred. More information about hypotheses is contained in the other book in this series.

Variables and Hypothesis Formulation | Chapter 4

EXERCISES

1. In the following statements identify the independent (IV), dependent (DV), control (CV) and moderator variables (MV).
   (a) The less first-year male students are supervised in their tutorial work the more they develop initiative and self-reliance as far as their reading is concerned. Female students, given the same conditions, develop less initiative.
   (b) In the food industry and for indigenous raw materials, the price of the end-product is influenced by the level of technology used and the cost of living of the workers. When imported raw materials are used, the influence of the previous factors is overshadowed by the foreign exchange rate.
   (c) The frequency of attendance at discos for young people between 16 and 20 years of age varies with the days of the week. The fluctuations are particularly strong for young men.
2. Referring to the statements presented in the previous exercise, formulate an operational definition for each variable.
3. Why do researchers use operational definitions?
4. Formulate at least one directional and the non-directional hypothesis for each of the following problems:
   (a) Is there a relationship between the involvement of women in cash-crop agriculture and the health conditions of their children?
   (b) Does the introduction of appropriate-technology devices in a village have a positive impact on the diet of inhabitants?
   (c) Is there a relationship between the marital status of women (married or single) and their participation in decision-making?
5. Criticize and improve upon the following hypotheses.
   (a) Urban life conditions are better than rural ones.
   (b) A religious person is more understanding than other persons.

CHAPTER 5

The Types of Research

In this chapter the different types of research are presented. Distinctions are drawn between quantitative and qualitative research, applied and basic research, and between exploratory, descriptive, correlational and explanatory research. Emphasis is placed on the relationship between the research problem and the type of research selected to investigate it. The characteristics of the problem, the initial level of knowledge, the properties of the variables, as well as the purpose of the investigation all influence the type of research to be used.

CHAPTER OBJECTIVES

The learner who has successfully completed this chapter will be able to:
- Compare and contrast the most commonly used types of research.
- Identify the type of research used in any study.
- Select the most appropriate type of research for a particular research problem.

WAYS OF CLASSIFYING RESEARCH

There are several ways of classifying research studies. One of the most important focuses on the methodology used. **Quantitative research** relies on measurement to compare and analyse different variables. In contrast, **qualitative research** uses qualifying words or descriptions to record aspects of the world. This difference is discussed in greater detail and illustrated below.

A second method of classifying research arises from the reasons for the research being conducted. Studies that aim primarily to increase human understanding of a particular aspect of society are often referred to as **basic social research**. In contrast, studies that aim primarily to solve a particular problem confronting a group of people are often referred to as **applied social research**. Participatory research and action-research tend to be more applied in nature, as do community needs assessments, evaluation research and monitoring. All of these are discussed in some detail in the next chapter.

A third and more traditional method for classifying research is based on the demands of the research question. In cases where very little is known about the research topic one speaks of **exploratory research**. Where the researcher is merely interested in describing a phenomenon the research is called **descriptive research**. When the research question requires an understanding of the relationship between variables, the research is called **correlational research**. Finally, when the research question demands that the researcher explains the relationship between variables and demonstrates that change in one variable causes change in another variable, the research is called **explanatory research**.

© Juta & Co Ltd

QUANTITATIVE AND QUALITATIVE RESEARCH

As mentioned above quantitative research methodology relies upon measurement and uses various scales. These are discussed further in Chapter 9. Numbers form a coding system by which different cases and different variables may be compared. Systematic changes in "scores" are interpreted or given meaning in terms of the actual world that they represent. Numbers have the advantage of being exact. "Three" means exactly the same thing to every human being who knows the concept, and will mean exactly the same thing in different social, cultural and linguistic contexts. Another important advantage of numbers is that they can be analysed using descriptive and inferential statistics. (For more information, the reader is referred to the other book in this series).

However, there are some kinds of information that cannot be adequately recorded using quantitative data. In many cases language provides a far more sensitive and meaningful way of recording human experience. In these cases, words and sentences are used to qualify and record information about the world. The research is qualitative in nature.

e.g.

When a researcher studies the education of a community she might do so in terms of the number of years of schooling that the majority of people living in that community have completed. In other words, "education" is defined as the "*number* of years of schooling". This study is quantitative.

However, the researcher might prefer to ask people what they know, and how they learned what they know. In this case members of the community might describe different educational techniques including experiential learning, learning by observing and copying other people in the community, learning by rote and so forth. They might speak about their practical knowledge and their understanding of their world. Here language is the tool by which social reality is recorded and the research is qualitative.

There are advantages and disadvantages to both quantitative and qualitative research methods. The skilled social researcher carefully chooses the most appropriate approach to a particular problem. In nearly all cases the line between quantitative and qualitative methods is somewhat blurred. In fact a comprehensive study will use both methods and thus cannot strictly be called either quantitative or qualitative.

It is sometimes the case that poorly thought out and non-systematic research is referred to as "qualitative research", merely because the scientific method has not been adequately adhered to. True qualitative research is a special area of study and beyond the scope of this volume. The interested reader is referred for instance to Denzin and Lincoln's *Handbook of Qualitative Research*.

BASIC AND APPLIED RESEARCH

Sometimes the researcher's primary motivation is to contribute to human knowledge and understanding relating to a particular phenomenon. This is usually achieved by gathering more facts and information which enables existing theories to be challenged and new ones to be developed. The actual utility or application of this newly acquired knowledge is of little concern to the researcher. This kind of research is called basic research.

At other times the researcher's primary motivation is to assist in solving a particular problem facing a particular community. This is referred to as applied research and is often achieved by applying basic research findings to particular communities challenges. In this way applied research may assist the community to overcome the problem or design interventions which will help to solve it.

e.g.

A researcher who studies the critical factors leading to the pollution of ground water in highly industrialized regions would be doing basic research since the study aims to increase human understanding of water pollution. A different researcher who is concerned with protecting the drinking water of a particular community that is located near a water polluting factory would be doing applied research, since the purpose of this study is to solve a particular problem facing this particular community, probably using the knowledge built up using basic research.

Whether the aim of the research is primarily basic or applied does affect the way in which the research is conducted. However, to some extent this way of classifying research projects is not very useful. It is not true that any particular study is only purely basic or purely applied. The researcher who finds a good way of protecting the water supply of a particular community will be able to share that same plan with other people working in similarly threatened communities. In this way that solution becomes part of more general understanding of water pollution. Similarly, the general study of water pollution should yield some new ideas on how local water supplies might be protected. As such the basic study finds application in the life of a particular community.

It often seems that the problems facing the developing world at the beginning of the 21st century are overwhelming. Ongoing wars, extreme poverty, global economic trends and diseases such as AIDS present regular emergencies and chronic threat to the majority of people on the continent. A great deal of Africa's scarce resources are spent on the struggle for basic health and safety for all the continent's citizens. It is becoming more and more clear that the most effective strategies for surmounting these challenges are based on concerted effort by whole communities of empowered people. Individual curative type interventions are enormously expensive and do not address the underlying social causes of many of these problems. Community-based projects with a preventative or resilience-building strategy appear to offer far more viable solutions.

The various ways in which research methodologies are applied to community projects are the topic of the following chapter.

DIFFERENT OBJECTIVES OF SOCIAL RESEARCH

A third and most important way of classifying the various types of social research is in terms of its objectives. Suppose that a research topic has been identified. In some cases the difficulty is simply that too little is known about a certain area to formulate a definite research question. Social anthropologists, for instance, are sometimes confronted with a situation where a certain group of people living in a remote area is virtually unknown to the world. Thus, before being in a position to search for an explanation related to the modes of living of these people, or some other characteristic, a certain amount of background information must be gathered. In such a case the most appropriate type of research is **exploratory research**.

In other cases enough background knowledge is available to permit quite a precise area of investigation. For instance, a researcher may be interested in finding out the opinion of a group of people towards a particular issue at a particular time. It may even be the case that, under other circumstances, the same type of investigation has taken place and only a *description* of the new situation is required.

> **e.g.**
>
> Pre-election surveys are regularly carried out before parliamentary elections to assess the attitudes of voters towards parliamentary candidates.

When a researcher is able to state a hypothesis, expressing the relationship between at least two variables, the results obtained will provide more than just a description of reality. In some cases the relationship between variables cannot be determined precisely, so that it is only expected that co-variation takes place. In other words, the researcher wishes to show that two variables change simultaneously, either in the same or opposite directions. This is called **correlational research**. Correlational research does not give an explanation of how variables are related, merely that they are, and the direction of that relationship.

> **e.g.**
>
> The size of children's feet and their language ability both increase between the ages of 0 and 6 years, but neither determines the development of the other. To give a less extreme example, one can suspect a relationship between students' performance in mathematics and in English at primary school without being able to explain the kind of relationship existing between the two variables.

On the contrary, as soon as a causal relationship between variables can be stated, an explanation can be found for the variation of at least one variable, the dependent one. When an explanation is sought for the relationship between variables, one is dealing with **explanatory research**.

When using an explanatory research method one acquires a deeper understanding of the relationships between variables than one does when using either correlational or descriptive methods. But, it should be clear that the choice of the type of research, whether descriptive, correlational or explanatory, cannot be arbitrary. It depends on the following factors:

1. *The object of research*

Does the researcher have enough information to establish a relationship between variables? Can the different variables be manipulated or controlled in order to permit a study of the effect of one variable on another? For example, a researcher working with people whose culture has not been studied in detail before, cannot begin to start making specific hypotheses until a comprehensive exploratory study has been undertaken.

2. *The aim of the research*

Does it benefit the researcher to establish a causal relationship, or is correlational or descriptive research more appropriate? For example, in pre-election times one might merely be interested in the proportions of the population that will vote for the different candidates, or one could want to know the factors which influence voting behaviour in order to improve the chances of a particular candidate.

3. *The nature of the data to be collected*

How sophisticated are the available techniques that will be used for data collection? Do they require further development before they can be used in more sophisticated research? How many subjects does the researcher have access to? For example, the impact of cerebral lesions on emotional states, or the effect of strikes on some aspects of the economy can only be observed in a few cases since a researcher cannot damage a

The Types of Research   Chapter 5

person's brain nor provoke a strike for the purposes of research.

A more detailed examination of the various types of research, highlighting their differences, strengths and weaknesses, as well as their underlying methods of investigation, follows.

Exploratory and descriptive research

The purpose of exploratory research is to gain a broad understanding of a situation, phenomenon, community or person. The need for such a study could arise from a lack of basic information in a new area of interest. Most frequently, though, one must become more familiar with a situation in order to formulate a problem or develop a hypothesis.

Essentially there are two alternatives for the design of exploratory and descriptive research. These are the case study and the survey. The case study is the detailed and thorough investigation of a few cases, whereas the survey is the collection of information on a wide range of cases, each case being investigated only on the particular aspect under consideration. These designs are discussed in greater detail in the Chapter 7.

e.g.

A researcher wants to investigate the causes of famine. A survey is conducted of all (or at least a range) of famine-stricken countries. The survey investigates general aspects of the phenomenon which one expects to be find in all cases. This may allow the identification of the main features of famine in the world. But by undertaking a case study in one or two countries only, the researcher would be able to examine in a much deeper way the roots of famine and to describe how particular characteristics within the environment contribute to this problem. It would, however, be difficult to show that the conclusions drawn from two countries were equally relevant to the experience of famine in other countries.

Similarly, using the survey method one can determine the proportion of a given population that holds racist attitudes, while by using case studies one can describe the manner in which such attitudes change.

The case study is a way of organizing social data and looking at the object of study as a whole. All aspects are considered, which means that the development over time of the event or person constitutes an important dimension. For instance, one may ask: How did the conditions deteriorate within a village, leading to famine? How did the feelings of a person towards other races gradually change? What were the incidents and thought processes that led to these changes?

Various types of information are collected in many different ways. For social issues, interviews allowing the interviewee to confide freely, as well as diaries, personal documents and participant observation are useful. The greater part of the data collected in these ways will be qualitative and more or less reliable, depending on the source of the data and the objectivity of the researcher. A case study of a particular village suffering from famine will also include quantitative data such as the number, age and occupation of inhabitants. The more diverse and relevant the questions asked, the greater the quality of the case study is likely to be.

The choice of one or the other technique is rarely arbitrary and depends on the aim of the research and on the type of data available. In particular, if an event occurs only rarely, conducting a survey would have to be excluded due to lack of sufficient data. In other situations, a case study may be inadvisable because it is very time-consuming and the data cannot be easily compared to other results.

© Juta & Co Ltd

Finally, the descriptive method is also used to test factual hypotheses, or statements that do not relate two or more variables but express facts about the world. "The sun is shining now" and "Lake Kariba is an artificial lake" are examples of factual hypotheses. In these cases, the researcher has only to observe directly whether the sun is shining, or consult some historical or geographical documents about the formation of Lake Kariba.

Correlational and explanatory research

When a hypothesis, relating two or more variables or expressing a causal relationship can be stated, the study becomes an hypothesis testing one. A short theoretical analysis is necessary to understand the differences between correlational and explanatory research and to determine which one to choose in a particular case.

Suppose that two variables, A and B, have been identified and that a relationship is observed between them. In other words, the researcher has noted some form of regularity in the way that the two variables vary in relation to each other. To use a concrete example, let A be malnutrition and B, illiteracy. Their simultaneous existence can be interpreted in three possible ways.

(i) Variable A is the cause of variable B or, in this case, malnutrition is the cause of illiteracy, as for instance, malnutrition affects the intellectual development of children.

(ii) Variable B is the cause of variable A or, in this case, illiteracy is the cause of malnutrition, since illiterate parents have no means to adequately feed their children.

(iii) Both variables A and B depend upon a third variable, or in this case, both illiteracy and malnutrition depend on socio-economic factors in the system, such as unequal distribution of wealth and services within the country.

The problem here is to find some criteria to determine which one of the three alternatives is correct. Firstly, what does a causal relationship between two variables imply? If A is the cause of B, then the occurrence of A, the cause, is a necessary and sufficient condition for B, the effect, to occur. By necessary condition is meant that B can never occur unless A occurs first. By sufficient condition is meant that wherever A occurs, B will occur. The occurrence of A can be either necessary or sufficient for B to occur; but A is the cause of B if, and only if, the occurrence of A is a necessary and sufficient condition for B to occur. Then B is the effect of A and there is a causal relationship between B and A.

e.g.

Malnutrition is a necessary condition for illiteracy if, whenever illiteracy is encountered, malnutrition is also present (although malnutrition can be found without illiteracy). Malnutrition is a sufficient condition for illiteracy if, whenever malnutrition occurs, illiteracy always follows (although illiteracy can be found without malnutrition). Finally, malnutrition is the cause of illiteracy if the latter occurs only when the former exists and does so as a prior or concommital condition. Neither can illiteracy be found among normally fed people, nor can malnourished people be literate.

Hence, to decide which one of the three previous interpretations of the relationship between variables is correct, three checks must be performed. Only if all three conditions are satisfied is a causal relationship between A and B assured. These conditions are the following.

1. Proof of the co-variance of A and B

In other words, the researcher must demonstrate that a relationship exists between the

The Types of Research Chapter 5

variation of A and B. Using the above example, the researcher must show some regularity in the presence (or absence) of both malnutrition and illiteracy.

2. *Proof of the non-spuriousness of the co-variance*

In other words, the researcher must exclude a third variable which alone can determine the variations of both A and B. Using the above example, the researcher must exclude all other factors which might influence the presence (or absence) of both malnutrition and illiteracy.

3. *Proof of a stable time-order*

In other words, the researcher must demonstrate that the cause always precedes the effect or, in terms of the example, that malnutrition always comes before illiteracy.

If points 1 and 2 above are proved, interpretations (i) and (ii) above may be correct. If A always precedes B (that is, there is a stable time-order) and point 3 is correct, interpretations (i) and (iii) could be correct. Taken together, it is clear that only interpretation (i) is possible, in other words, A is the cause of B.

From this short analysis it becomes obvious that the task of determining the existence of a causal relationship is a very complex and difficult one. It is based on systematic comparison, manipulation and control of variables. The plan of how to proceed in determining the nature of the relationship between variables is called a **research design**. This constitutes the backbone of explanatory research and the quality of the research strongly depends on the correct choice of design. Some research designs are presented in Chapter 7 together with a discussion of their relative weaknesses and strengths.

The purpose of correlational research is often only to detect the existence of a relationship between variables (co-variance) which suggests a possible base for causality. In this case, correlational research is useful as a first step to explanatory research. Correlation does not necessarily imply causation, but causation necessarily implies correlation, since if A causes B, both A and B vary together. Note that correlational research is at times the only possible research method. Often explanatory research is not feasible. This is the case when it is not possible to manipulate the suspected independent variable or to assess the time-order among variables.

Furthermore, in the case of a non-causal relationship, a correlational study can assess the type and the strength of the relationship between two variables. For example, one can correlate the productivity of a shoe factory with respectively the type of technology used, the state of repair of the machinery, the number of workers, their skills, their wages and conditions of service, the availability of raw materials, of spare parts, and so on. Each of these factors should, to a different extent, contribute to the variation of the productivity of the shoe factory. A correlational study will allow for an evaluation of the importance (or strength) of each relationship, or the contribution of each factor to productivity. This is of great practical relevance. It will also indicate whether each of these factors promotes productivity (positive correlation) or inhibits productivity (negative correlation).

Therefore, a correlational study is not only useful when no clear causal relationship exists but it also allows for an estimation of the strength of the relationship between two variables even when one variable is influenced by many others. Moreover, this type of research does not involve elaborate research designs. This discussion is elaborated in the other book in this series.

In conclusion, the three types of research (descriptive, correlational and explanatory)

© Juta & Co Ltd

Fundamentals of Social Research Methods

are applied to different aspects of the same research topic. For instance, concentrating on the results of an election, one can either *describe* the political trends, expressed by the number of seats won in parliament by each political party; one can *correlate* the level of education of the voters and their level of involvement in the election process; or one can analyse the cause-effect relationship between voting preferences of parents and that of their children, thereby attempting to *explain* voting behaviour.

EXERCISES

1. Describe the difference between applied and basic social research. What are the relative advantages and disadvantages of each?
2. Choose a research topic and formulate a descriptive, correlational and explanatory research problem related to aspects of your topic. Possible examples are:
   (*a*) the conditions of industrial workers in your country,
   (*b*) the economic development of a particular region,
   (*c*) recent educational reforms in the primary school curriculum,
   (*d*) the effectiveness of an AIDS education campaign, or
   (*e*) the impact of xenophobia on tourism.
3. What extra demands on research design are made by explanatory research, as compared with correlational research?

CHAPTER 6

Community-centred Research

There are many ways in which research methodologies can be employed by communities to access accurate information and to facilitate effective community development projects. Needs assessments, feasibility studies, and the evaluation and monitoring of community projects are all applied social research activities. Participatory and action-research are discussed as powerful approaches to carrying out these research tasks.

CHAPTER OBJECTIVES

The learner who has successfully completed this chapter will be able to:
- Discuss issues relating to participatory and action-research.
- Plan and conduct a needs assessment and feasibility study.
- Plan and conduct project monitoring as well as diagnostic, formative, and summative evaluation

RESEARCH AND COMMUNITY PROJECTS

Applied social research has an important role to play in the planning, management, implementation and evaluation of community projects. This role includes helping communities to assess their own needs and resources in a systematic manner, to determine whether particular plans of actions are feasible given the available resources and whether or not they are likely to attain the envisaged objectives. Properly designed monitoring systems allow project managers to keep constant watch over the progress of a project. Finally, summative evaluations allow all stakeholders including project managers, community-members, and funding agencies to measure the effectiveness of particular interventions on community life, and formative evaluations provide for the development of even more effective strategies for the future. Each of these functions is looked at in more detail below.

NEEDS ASSESSMENT

An important first step of any community intervention is a detailed analysis of the particular challenges facing that community, and the available resources with which those challenges may be met.

Usually community-based organisations, local leaders and other representative structures believe that they have a fairly good idea of the challenges facing the community. It is important to assess the extent to which these role players do actually understand the concerns and needs of all people within the community, and to what extent they have analysed the underlying causes of the problems. It is essential that scarce resources are

© Juta & Co Ltd

put to the best possible uses so that the community derives maximum long-term benefit.

Of course different community members have different needs. When resources are scarce these needs might exist in competition with each other. Difficult decisions must often be made about the best way to use limited resources. Good choices will only be made when decision-makers are in possession of all the relevant facts. With the correct information it is possible to prioritize the various needs and to tackle first, those which affect the community most profoundly. Very often these decisions have far reaching consequences for the community and many different factors must be weighed. In many cases a natural sequence starts to emerge.

e.g.

Money that is spent on building a new crèche to assist working mothers with small children, cannot also be used to start a brick-making project for unemployed adults. It might be best to first start the brick-making project which would reduce the cost of building a crèche. However, if the participants on the brick-making project include many mothers of young children, building the crèche first would increase participation in the project.

That a problem has been identified, does not imply that its causes are understood or that solutions are immediately apparent. Most community problems have multiple underlying causes. Unless the deep causes of a problem are addressed, the problem will only be solved in a superficial manner. It is likely that a similar problem will emerge in the same community in time. In the same way that it is necessary to treat the cause of an illness rather than the symptom, it is important to address the source of a problem, rather than its effects.

A range of research techniques might be used to gather the information needed to understand the root causes of community problems. This allows one to prioritize the problems with the aim that any community-based project creates the maximum good for the most people. Most important among these is the needs assessment survey.

The **needs assessment survey** is a survey of all facets of the community in order to define the various concerns of all the community's members. It is vital that all groups are included, especially those groups whose voices are unlikely to be heard at community meetings and through structures that claim to represent all the people of the community. Groups that are not sufficiently represented often include women, children, the elderly and the disabled. In some communities people from particular ethnic backgrounds or who follow particular religious beliefs find themselves without a voice in the usual structures. These people should also have a chance to discuss the problems facing their community. Exactly how a survey of this kind should be conducted is discussed in more detail in later chapters. Whatever the methods used it is imperative that all results are compiled into a report and made available to the community in either written or verbal format, depending upon what is most appropriate.

e.g.

In the years of 1984 and 1985 West Sudan suffered a two year drought which resulted in widespread famine since rural communities in that area depend wholly upon rainfed subsistence farming (Strachan et al., 1997). The immediate concern of providing sufficient food to prevent immediate and widespread starvation was partly met by international relief agencies. However, when the rains did start again in 1986, rural communities did not return to their original way of life and many people continued to starve.

The results of a needs assessment revealed that two factors prevented the region from regaining its self-sufficiency. There were no seeds to plant crops, and there was no workforce to farm the land. A closer investigation of the community and its history revealed the underlying causes of these problems.

When the famine struck, many men had moved to urban areas to find other sources of income (and thus food for themselves and their families). Those farmers that stayed had survived by eating their seed supplies. Younger women who were no longer employed in farming had taken over the upbringing of their children, a role usually performed by grandparents. With the food shortages and the loss of their role in the community, the old people had become a burden and many had moved away to the cities and were begging on the streets. When the rains returned, the seeds had been eaten, many men had moved away, and the women were caring for children where before they had been free to farm the land.

Thus a problem of not enough food has its roots in problems of urbanisation and migration, as well as family and community structure. Supplying food will never solve this community's problems. However, the establishment of a "seed bank", the development of more effective irrigation systems, and a range of other projects including the introduction of new farming techniques and literacy classes, enabled the community to adapt to its changed circumstances.

As in the previous example, the information emerging from the needs assessment should place community leaders and decision-makers in a better position to make the right choices for the future well-being of the community. Very often those choices involve some kind of community-based project which must be carefully planned and implemented.

FEASIBILITY STUDIES

Although planning community projects is not strictly within the realm of research methodology, it is often closely tied in with needs assessments, feasibility studies, as well as the monitoring and evaluation processes. In fact it is very important to the long term success of the project that the planning and research processes are completely integrated. It is very difficult to know at the beginning of a project what its final outcome might be. Every community project contains some degree of uncertainty. However, before large amounts of money, materials, time and energy are poured into a project, one should be as certain as possible that the project will work. This can be achieved through a feasibility study.

e.g.

Can one be sure that even with a "seed-bank" farmers will actually return to their land and start the process of food production again? Will women stay in literacy classes for long enough to actually learn to read and write, or will they lose interest and stay away? Even if women do learn to read and write, will this put them in a position to find alternate ways of earning income?

A feasibility study must do two things:

1. It must help project planners to identify each of the assumptions underlying the project plan. In other words, what have the planners *assumed* will happen as a result of the project?

2. It must estimate the likelihood of each of those assumptions being met. Where the assumptions have a good chance of being met, the project can go ahead as planned. But, where the planners have made risky assumptions, it may be better to rethink the project or at least develop contingency plans.

Fundamentals of Social Research Methods

The process of identifying the underlying assumptions is a difficult one. It is most effectively achieved by looking critically at each step of the planned problem and asking how things might turn out in an unexpected way. Questions that begin with the words "what if" are very useful.

e.g.

The project planners in the example from Sudan might assume that women want to learn to read and write. What if this were not true? Or, what if the men in the community do not want the women to learn to read or write? Since Sudanese society has strict social structures particularly with respect to the social roles of men and women, this is not an unlikely state of affairs, and might jeopardise the success of the whole project.

Once the underlying assumptions have been identified, it is necessary to determine how likely such unexpected results are. Very often these can be answered using social research methods. In the last example, the probable success of literacy classes with women can be estimated by talking to men and women in the community about how they feel about the women learning to read and write.

Once again, the value of valid information should not be over-estimated. A clear minded analysis of the plan for a community-based project might lead to substantial savings in the long run. Many projects are weakened by inadequate planning and failure to systematically consider other possible outcomes of the intervention. However, assuming that the project planning has been done properly and the feasibility study shows that it has a reasonable chance of attaining its stated objectives, implementation of the project can begin.

PROJECT MONITORING

Typically community-based projects require careful management of resources and people, as well as regular reporting. This is most effectively achieved through a systematic monitoring system.

The terms "monitoring" and "evaluation" are often confused. They are actually entirely different enterprises, rely on different methods and have different objectives. **Project monitoring** is a tool for managing the ongoing implementation of a project. It is important that the monitoring framework is established during the planning phase of a project. To be effective, this framework must be in place before the implementation phase begins. The following steps outline a method for establishing a monitoring frame.

1. Establish indicators for each activity, as well as short-term and long-term outcomes involved in the project. Indicators are variables which can be systematically measured and which will inform the project managers of the extent to which a particular aspect of the project has been achieved. Table 6.1 gives some possible indicators for the project in the example from Sudan.

    It is advisable to find more than one indicator for each of the components of the project. This is because some indicators may work better than others. It is very helpful when indicators support each other. For the same reason it is also helpful to use indicators that are both quantitative and qualitative in nature.

2. Design an instrument to measure each indicator on a regular basis. Such instruments should not be overly complex or unwieldy. This is important because many community projects have many indicators. Unless each one can be relatively easily measured, the monitoring process becomes more work than the actual implementation process. This

Table 6.1
Outcome indicators: an example

Activity	Indicators
• Providing seeds to farmers	• Number of farmers receiving seeds per year
• Running literacy classes	• Number of people attending classes

Short-term goal	Indicators
• Increased farming	• Amount of land being farmed
• People learn to read and write	• Number of people completing course

Long-term goal	Indicators
• Self-reliance in food production	• Levels of malnutrition

must be avoided since it uses up valuable community resources and often results in the monitoring being poorly attended to. Guidelines for the development of measuring instruments are contained within Chapter 10 of this volume.
3. Set clear targets for each indicator to show when an activity has been completed, or outcome reached. For example it might be the project's aim to teach 2000 people in a particular community to read and write.
4. During implementation, measure each outcome regularly so as to be constantly aware of which aspects of the project have been successfully completed, which aspects are progressing smoothly, and where any problems lie.
5. Produce regular brief reports to keep all participants up to date on the progress of the project.

Monitoring becomes an important management tool since it allows for the setting of suitable goals and deadlines, provides targets for everyone involved in the project and gives early warning when things are not going as planned. In this way problems can be quickly solved and the chances of the project achieving its stated objectives are greatly enhanced.

The final aspects of community projects to be considered here are to do with evaluation.

PROJECT EVALUATION

The methods of social science can be used to assess the design, implementation and usefulness of social interventions. This type of research is called **evaluation research**. Social interventions are most often thought of as sophisticated programmes (such as drug rehabilitation programmes, campaigns against malnutrition, skills training courses, or the introduction of appropriate technologies to promote small-scale industry). Actually, any attempt to change the conditions under which people live (no matter how simple, or who is responsible for them) can be thought of as a social intervention. As has already been shown, one of the central concerns of social research is action. Evaluation research aims to test interventions to see how effective they are and therefore represents an important means of linking action and research in a constructive manner. Social interventions may benefit from evaluation research in a number of ways. Three of the most important are listed below.
1. Evaluation research may be used to identify neglected areas of need, neglected target groups, and problems within organizations and programmes. This is referred to as **diagnostic evaluation**.
2. A comparison of a programme's progress with its original aims is another of the functions of evaluation research. This may serve to adjust the programme to the particular needs and resources of the community within which it is situated.

Evaluation designed to promote the effectiveness of a programme is called **formative evaluation**.
3. Finally, evaluation research can furnish evidence of the usefulness of a programme. In this way a programme may gain credibility with funding organizations, as well as the community within which it is operating. This is known as **summative evaluation**.

Although different, these three types of evaluation are complementary and most evaluators are expected to think about all of them simultaneously.

Diagnostic evaluation

Diagnostic evaluations are designed to inform researchers and project managers about the present situations within communities, highlighting current problems, trends, forces and resources, as well as the possible consequences of various types of intervention. Thus, diagnostic evaluation is a technique for gathering data which is crucial in the planning of a new project. As such it is important that this research is carried out before a project is designed. The different ways in which diagnostic evaluations assist organizations and communities are elaborated upon below.

Firstly, it often happens that an organization or community is aware that something is going wrong, but is unable to identify exactly what the problem is. In other words, organizations and communities often find it difficult to define their problems in a precise manner.

e.g.

A community suffers from a high incidence of youth crime. Community members may well be aware of the problem, but have not managed to determine whether the majority of youths are committing crimes or whether there is only a small group of delinquents. They do not know whether the crimes are all of a particular type or very general in nature.

A second instance of where diagnostic evaluation can help communities and organizations is particularly appropriate for societies undergoing rapid social change. Such organizations or communities might desire change but do not fully conceptualize how these changes will affect them. Diagnostic evaluations can serve to map out the full range of probable outcomes of any project.

e.g.

An organization wishes to change its management structures through affirmative action procedures. Although the goal of this action is clear, the project managers are convinced that affirmative action may lead to fears and hostility among current managers. This might result in little support for new managerial staff. It is clearly important that the full implications of this type of programme are thought out well in advance.

Thirdly, during the initial planning stages of a project, it is useful for the project manager to specify the project's broad aims in a couple of points. These broad aims may be usefully broken down into several more manageable objectives which should be stated explicitly and in detail. This would allow them to be evaluated (using other evaluative research techniques) at a later date. The specification of both the broad aim and the various objectives must be guided by carefully conducted diagnostic research.

Finally, the researcher and the project manager should investigate problems which may arise during the course of the project. Where such problems cannot be avoided, contingency plans should be established to overcome them, so that the project may achieve its objectives.

e.g.

The question of appropriate methods to generate community policing in developing countries provides a clear illustration of the role of diagnostic research in social intervention.

It is important, firstly, to understand that the pressure to adopt community policing principles and strategies comes primarily from government. Such methods entail quite drastic changes in the values, attitudes and perceptions of all parties (replacing authoritarianism with democratic participation).

In order to plan an effective community policing programme, it is important to understand the current attitudes and values of people in both the target community and the existing police service. Members of the target community may be distrustful of members of the police service, due to their experiences of policing in the past. Members of the police force face a loss of status and power and, as a result, may be resistant to change. On the other hand, the community can expect to be better protected and enjoy more security, whereas the police will experience fewer threats and more acceptance from the community. Also, it is important to consider the ways in which people from both groups may react when the new policing strategy is put into effect. Community members may refuse to support the police in their work and members of the police may resist or even undermine the action, hoping thereby to restore the old methods of policing.

Plans to change the current approach to policing which are based upon an understanding of peoples' attitudes, values and expected responses, are far more likely to be successful than those which are not.

Formative evaluation

Formative evaluation relates to the development and implementation of a programme. Its aim is to shape the programme so that it will have the greatest beneficial impact upon the target community. Formative evaluation is an evaluation of the programme in order to improve it. Longer term interventions use formative evaluations at regular intervals during the life of the programme to ensure that it adapts to changes in social reality and thus continues to produce the greatest possible benefit. The questions which the social scientist must consider are of both a theoretical and a practical nature. On a theoretical level, the social scientist must consider whether the content of the programme has been adequately adapted to the social reality and whether conceptual definitions have been adequately operationalized. This is especially important when the particular body of social theory has its roots in either the United States of America, Europe or parts of the world where the social reality is very different to that of Africa. All too often social scientists wrongly assume that conditions and people are the same all around the world and that theories developed in far-off places are just as valid locally. On a more practical level, the social scientist must think about problems such as the availability of resources for the project, the most effective ways of using the available resources, potential areas of difficulty in the programme, and so on.

There are many different ways of carrying out formative evaluations and the method depends largely upon the project being assessed. Very often, however, the evaluation relies heavily upon the social scientist's experience of similar programmes, understanding of social reality and theoretical knowledge. In some cases, social scientists may not have all the available information needed for a satisfactory formative evaluation.

One very useful method which does not depend on the social scientist's expertise in the area of the programme is the **reputability study**. This technique involves the researcher identifying experts from within the community, from academic institutions, from government and non-government organizations, and elsewhere. Note that "experts" are not only people with academic qualifications or important positions. People from the community in which the programme is to be run (who may have no qualifications or titles) are experts on conditions prevailing in the community, the nature and extent of community problems, the community's likely reaction and many other aspects of a programme. The choice of experts is a sensitive issue and one should be careful to ensure that a wide range of people are represented so as not to bias the final results. The researcher interviews the experts (either individually or as a group) and presents an overview of the programme. The experts are asked for their opinions on the way the programme has been planned and the method of implementation. These comments and criticisms form the base of the formative evaluation.

A second technique used to evaluate and improve the methods and materials of a programme is the **pilot study**. A pilot study involves testing the actual programme on a small sample taken from the community for whom the programme is planned. This allows the evaluator to identify any difficulty with the method or materials and to investigate the accuracy and appropriateness of any instruments (such as screening tests, biographical questionnaires, and so on) that have been developed. It also allows the researcher to determine the community's likely response to the actual programme when it is implemented. In cases where a pilot study uncovers many difficulties in the design of a programme, it is necessary for the planning to be revised and further pilot testing of the new design may be necessary.

The reputability study, the pilot study and many other techniques aim to provide information to the designers of social interventions so as to assist them in the planning and implementation of their programmes. This includes information regarding the chosen aims and objectives of a project, the structures set up to achieve those objectives, as well as the methods chosen to implement them.

Summative evaluation

Another broad aim of evaluation research is summative. Summative evaluations set out to determine the extent to which programmes meet their specified aims and objectives. This information is used to gain credibility with various groups of people, particularly potential funders and target communities. Moreover, successful programmes may be replicated in other communities. If the designers of a programme can demonstrate scientifically that their programme has had certain positive effects, then people are likely to be much more enthusiastic about the programme being implemented in their community. They are also more likely to receive funding for similar programmes. Although summative evaluations ought always to happen at the end of a programme, they are often carried out at regular intervals during the life of long programmes as well. The process of summative evaluation research generally occurs according to the following five steps.

1. *The identification of the programme's aims and objectives*

The programme is thought of as the "treatment", that is, it is one level of the independent variable (the other being "no treatment"). Summative evaluation compares the "treatment" group with a "no treatment" group to see whether the "treatment" has caused any positive change in the former. To assess the change, the researcher must know what the "treatment" is designed to achieve. The identification of the programme's aims and objectives requires close co-operation between the programme developers and the social scientist carrying out the evaluation. Unless the social scientist knows exactly what the programme aims to achieve, the evaluation cannot proceed to the next step. The question of whether or not the aims and objectives were adequately chosen falls in the domain of formative evaluation and is not considered here.

2. *The formulation of the aims and objectives in measurable terms*

At this point it is important for the researcher to translate the aims and objectives into observable changes which can be measured in the target community. The variable which is expected to change will become the dependent variable of the evaluation research. In other words, the conceptual definitions of the programme designers must be translated into operational definitions so that they can be studied through the methods of social science. (Refer to Chapter 4 for a discussion of conceptual and operational definitions.) Typical questions that the evaluator may need to consider are: How should people from the target community behave if the programme is successful? What should they be able to do? What type of action is expected from them? What statements on the behaviour of these people can be used to assess whether or not the aims and objectives have been fulfilled? Note that all these questions relate to observable behaviours, rather than self reports. Almost all programmes aim to induce observable changes of behaviour which can be most accurately measured and studied. However, some programmes also produce effects which are less easily observed in peoples' actions, such as emotional and psychological changes. These may be measured by asking people for subjective reports of their own experiences, or by creating situations where these are likely to be translated into observable behaviour.

No matter what kind of measure is chosen, it must be directly relevant to the aims and objectives of the particular programme.

3. *The construction of the instrument of measurement*

An instrument must be found or designed which is capable of accurately measuring the dependent variable chosen in the previous step. A wide variety of such instruments is available to social scientists, including carefully designed psychometric and sociometric tests, interviews, questionnaires and observation techniques. The most common of these are discussed in detail in Chapter 10.

4. *Designing the evaluation study and data collection*

Designs used for summative evaluation are discussed in detail in the next chapter. Note that in order to carry out a summative evaluation it is necessary for the researcher to compare the group that received the "treatment" with a similar group that did not receive the "treatment". These two groups represent the two levels of the independent variable discussed at step one. The groups are similar to start off with. Thus, if the group receiving the "treatment" changes positively, the researcher can conclude that the "treatment" has been successful.

5. *Reporting back*

Once the evaluation has been completed, the researcher should present the findings to those responsible for the intervention, the participants and any other interested groups. This must be done in such a way that the methods, results and conclusions of the evaluation can be easily understood, even by people with little experience of social research.

Evaluation research: An example

A development organization in KwaZulu-Natal, South Africa in the period 1990–1992, aims to help unskilled people to find employment and to become productive members of the community. It is hoped that these people will be able to bring resources into the community and thus improve their own, their families' and their community's living conditions. The organization is situated in a large urban community and sets out to provide training in practical skills such as carpentry, metal work and brick laying. At the end of the first year of operation, the organization asks an outside researcher to carry out both formative and summative evaluations on the programme.

The *summative evaluation* will be considered first. Step one of the research is to determine the exact aims and objectives of the project. The overall aim of the project is community development, but, in order to achieve this aim, several objectives have been specified. These are to help unemployed people to find work by providing them with skills required by the market-place. In a more complex real world situation the researcher should also look at exactly what group of people the project aims to benefit, how these people are selected, and so on. In this simplified example, the aims and objectives as specified above are sufficient.

In the second step of the summative evaluation conceptual goals must be translated into observable measures. Such measures may be operationalized as whether or not a person finds a job within six months after completing a training course, or whether they have mastered a particular skill or set of skills. Moderator variables such as the amount of effort put into the job search might also need to be considered.

The third step requires the researcher to find or construct an instrument to measure the concepts operationalized in step two. Whether or not a person finds a job within six months can be easily and accurately determined through observation and ongoing communication with the trainees. Whether or not a person has mastered a skill would most appropriately be measured with some kind of practical test of ability. Such a test would have to be carefully designed in order to discriminate between trainees who have and have not mastered their chosen skills.

Next the researcher must choose a research design. (Refer to Chapter 7 for more details). Unless prior notice of the need for evaluation was given to the evaluator by the project managers, it will be impossible at that stage to carry out a pre-test/post-test design. In fact, this more complex design requires that the trainees be assessed prior to the training. If the training has already begun when the evaluation is commissioned, the possibility of using the pre-test/post-test design does not exist. This is just one of the reasons why it is important that managers give evaluators ample warning of their evaluation requirements. For this example it is assumed that the researcher is using a post-test only design. An important part of the design is to find an appropriate comparison group. In this case, a comparison group would be a similar group of people from a neighbouring community perhaps, who are similarly unemployed and unskilled.

A comparison of the different skills of people from the two groups will allow the researcher to evaluate the effect of the skills training programme and these results must be presented to the project managers in a way that is easily accessible to them.

The *formative evaluation* requires a different approach to the problem. In this case the researcher is trying to find out how the training programme may be improved to better achieve its aims in future. With this in mind, the researcher may choose to interview the participants in the programme. This would include trainees, trainers, potential employers, as well as programme managers. Questions should cover a broad range of topics relating to the functioning of the programme. Some areas of interest may be the content of the training courses, the methods of training employed, the teaching skills of the trainers, the structure of the organization, the setting of the training, and so on. These interviews are likely to uncover a variety of problem areas within the programme and these can then be presented to those responsible for the project so that adjustment and "fine-tuning" can be performed and the whole project improved.

Some concluding comments on evaluation

Firstly, although presented separately in this chapter, diagnostic, formative and summative evaluation are all interrelated and occur side by side in the course of ongoing interventions. During diagnostic evaluation, background circumstances highlighting the need for an intervention, as well as the forces which are expected to influence the intervention, are identified. The aims and methods are assessed using formative evaluation and recommendations for improving the project are discussed. Finally, the summative evaluation determines whether the aims have been met. If not, those responsible for the programme must consider further diagnostic and formative research in order to isolate and resolve problem areas. Comprehensive and integrated programme evaluation, which uses all three forms, maintains ongoing effectiveness, facilitates flexibility in response to changing circumstances and ensures credibility and the ongoing existence of programmes.

Secondly, very few interventions have only one aim. In most cases, programmes have several related goals and it must be decided whether the evaluator is to investigate all or only one of the intervention's goals.

Thirdly, the evaluation process demands a very close working relationship between those responsible for the planning and implementation of an intervention and the evaluators. In some cases this relationship may be difficult to maintain, particularly where the results demonstrate that the intervention is not meeting its stated aims. In these circumstances it is the responsibility of both parties to work together to resolve the problems in the intervention in order to ensure maximum benefit to the target community.

Fourthly, the question of who should evaluate interventions is often a difficult one. Researchers should remember that it is impossible for one person to be both "a player" and "the referee". Insiders (people who have helped to plan and implement a project) are the most knowledgeable about the area, but also the most subjective. Outsiders may not understand the aims and objectives of the project as well as an insider, but are likely to be far more objective. The question of who should evaluate interventions must be decided by those responsible for the intervention and depends upon a number of questions: Are there insiders available who have the skills to conduct an evaluation? Are the funds available to employ outside evaluators who are often more expensive? And how important is an external reviewer to the evaluation?

Finally, some evaluators consider it their task to carry out a cost benefit analysis comparing the input and output of an intervention. In virtually all cases, the cost of an intervention must be taken into account when measuring its effectiveness. Although for sophisticated programmes cost benefit analyses require the additional skills of an accountant, the costs of most interventions can be investigated by a social researcher using the methods discussed above.

PARTICIPATORY RESEARCH

In contrast to the other kinds of research previously discussed, participatory research is distinguished by two characteristics: the relationship between the people involved in the research, and the use of research as a tool for social change, as well as for increasing human knowledge. Thus, the conventional roles of researcher (the expert) and subjects (naive objects unaware of the research hypotheses) are changed. **Participatory research** encourages the active participation of the people whom the research is intended to assist. In this way, it empowers the people to be involved in all aspects of a project, including the planning and implementation of the research and any solutions that emerge from the research. Everybody involved in the research project works together as a team.

Participatory research techniques focus on particular problems facing communities and attempt to use research (and the resulting action) as a tool to bring about social change. As such participatory research tends of be more applied in nature. Such social change is achieved through the democratic collaboration of social researcher, community members and various other parties. Together and as equal players, the participants investigate the problem and its underlying causes (including socio-economic, political and cultural factors) and then take collective action in order to bring about long-term solutions to problems.

Participatory research uses all the conventional tools of social research. However, tools which acknowledge the value of the opinions and thoughts of all people, such as focus groups, depth interviews and participant observation, tend to be more popular than structured interviews, questionnaires and simple observation. As a result, there is no one way of doing participatory research. A form of participatory research that is growing in popularity is action-research, an approach which suggests a particular complementary relationship between action and research.

ACTION-RESEARCH

Participatory research is not necessarily action-research, although action research is always participatory. Beyond the characteristics of participatory research introduced above, **action-research** demands that social scientist and community work as equal partners in the planning and implementation of a project. Each brings valuable resources to the project. Furthermore, action and research take place alternatively in an ongoing learning process for everyone involved. Because of this dynamic processes between researcher and community, and between research and action, there is no general formula for doing action-research. One can, however, sketch a very broad framework that describes how action-research projects often proceed.

1. Request for assistance

Ideally the initiative for an action-research project comes from members of a community who find themselves in difficulty. The idea should never come from social researchers who believe (rightly or wrongly) that they know what is best for a particular community and set out to demonstrate to the community the best way to proceed. Very often requests for assistance come to social scientists via social workers and others in the front line of service delivery. This is because community members themselves are often not aware that the services of social scientists are available to them. They are, however, familiar with people who work within the community and it is to these people that problems are first referred. In this way, social workers play a very important role in bringing the challenges facing communities to the attention of social scientists. They can also help social scientists achieve a better understanding of what is happening on the ground.

e.g.

Parents and teachers of a secondary school are concerned about the high drop-out rate at the school. As a result they call a meeting to discuss this problem. At the meeting various possible reasons for the drop-out rate are discussed, but it soon becomes clear that the problem is complex and that no easy solution is likely to emerge. As a result, the group decides to ask the school counsellor for assistance. The counsellor, being unequipped to solve this problem, puts the community representatives in touch with a social scientist who then facilitates an action-research process in order to help find a solution.

There are, however, times when the social scientist (who usually enjoys a high level of education) has information which is not available to some communities. A community may be in difficulty without knowing it.

e.g.

A good example can be found in the AIDS pandemic. Social scientists became aware of the spread of HIV and the effects of AIDS long before people in rural areas who had little access to media and other sources of information. Such communities could be unaware of the danger. In these cases, the social researcher is obliged, where possible, to make information available and to formulate the problem so that communities may respond effectively to it.

At all times, however, the social scientist must be wary of patronizing a community by dictating what problems that community is facing and how such problems ought to be solved.

2. Negotiation

Negotiation most often occurs between the social scientist and representatives of the community. This raises an important ethical issue for the social scientist. In some cases, community representatives may not be truly representative of the community. It may be necessary for the social scientist to check out whether the situation, as presented by the community representatives, accurately reflects the will of the majority of people within that community. This is called an "accountability gap". Also, the social scientist and the community representatives should make sure that every person or organization who may have something important to contribute to the project is present to discuss the problem. This list may include religious, labour, political, youth and other kinds of groups, as well as government, non-government and funding organizations.

At this point all the participants should establish a broad ethical framework based on mutual trust, within which they can work together. In other words, if the representatives from any group feel that they will not be able to work usefully with people from another group (for whatever reason), this should be discussed during this phase. In a community where rival gangs exist in violent conflict, one gang may refuse to participate in the project if the other gang is present. In this case a process of mediation is needed before the project can begin. Opposing religious groups and political parties may experience similar problems.

Once a comfortable working relationship has been established, it is time to consider the goals of all the groups that will be involved in the project. In most cases these goals will be different. Consider an action-research project involving only two parties or co-researchers: the community and a team of social scientists. The community desires a solution to its particular problem. The social scientists hope to identify a more general solution adaptable to a range of similar problems that may be experienced by other communities. For the social scientists' goal to be met, the community may have to participate in a far more complex project than its original one. Similarly, if the community's goal is to be achieved, the social scientists cannot stray too far from the specific details of the problem at hand. Thus both the social scientists and the community must reach a compromise on the goals of the project. The complexity and importance of negotiation increase when more than two parties are involved in the project.

Some writers suggest that the best way to resolve these difficulties is to construct a formal action-research contract. Such a contract would outline exactly what each party is expected to contribute to the project and what each party can expect to gain from the project. Table 6.2 contains an illustration of such a contract for the simple example discussed above.

As soon as such a contract has been agreed upon, the participants are ready to enter the next phase.

3. Planning

In the third phase of the action-research project, all the groups involved must work together to find a way of solving the community's problem and of meeting all the goals set out in the action-research contract. Essentially, this phase involves three distinct tasks. Firstly, the co-researchers must find a way of defining the problem that is clear and acceptable to everyone. Very often this is not as straightforward as it sounds. The co-researchers may have different ways of explaining the world. Reaching a point of *shared understanding* might require long and patient discussion. Secondly, the co-researchers must determine exactly what information is needed in order to find a solution to the problem and how that information is to be collected. This is the essence of the action-research project because at this point the co-researchers decide what their specific aims are and how these aims are to be achieved. Also at this point it is necessary for the participants to decide how the data will be collected. Finally, the co-researchers must break the action-research project down into manageable tasks and distribute responsibility for each of these tasks among the participants.

It is during the negotiation and planning phases that the participants build up a rapport, or sense of co-operation. A good relationship between everyone involved is essential for the success of the action and research involved in the final stages.

Table 6.2
A simple action-research contract

Community	Social researcher
To provide: • active participation • first-hand, practical knowledge of the problem on the ground • material resources • skills	*To provide:* • active participation • academic knowledge and theory • academic and research skills • access to material resources • skills training
To receive: • a solution to their particular problem • a solution for future similar problems • skills to solve future problems • skills training and access to resources	*To receive:* • a general solution to similar problems applicable to a range of similar communities • increased understanding of the problems faced by some communities • development of theory • publication

4. Implementation

Once the co-researchers have made a plan about how to proceed with the project, implementation can begin. It is during this phase that action and research take place. Very often implementation begins with a period of research where the resources and needs of the community are systematically assessed and the necessary information to guide appropriate action is gathered. This process then informs some kind of action which the action-research partners undertake together. Thereafter, the results of the action are assessed and a further period of research (although this time of an evaluative nature) is initiated. Depending upon the results of this research it may be necessary to develop or completely redesign the original action undertaken. In this way, action and research continue as alternate processes in the search for solutions to the community's problems. The relationship between action and research is illustrated in figure 6.1.

This repeated cycle of research and action, with neither possible without the other, produces a process of ongoing learning and empowerment for all the participants in the study.

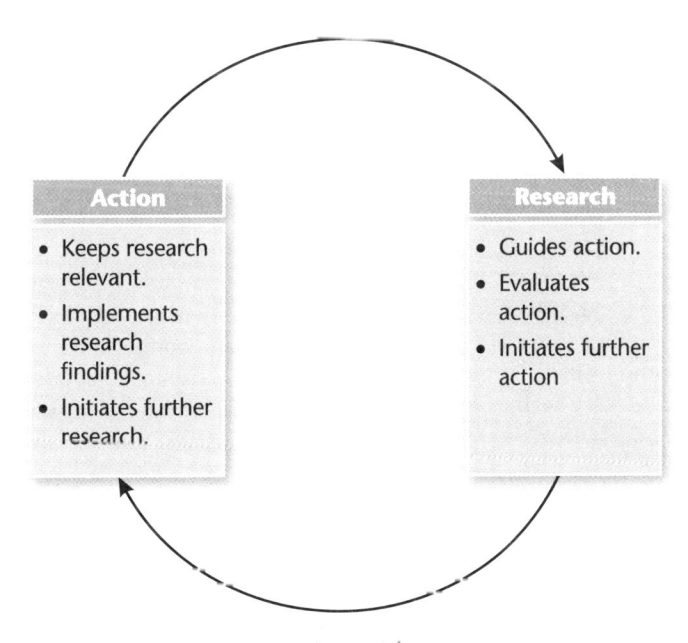

Action
- Keeps research relevant.
- Implements research findings.
- Initiates further research.

Research
- Guides action.
- Evaluates action.
- Initiates further action.

Figure 6.1
Relating action and research

Action-research: an example

Consider a small, peri-urban community facing problems of unemployment. A social scientist agrees to facilitate an action-research project in order to address this community's needs. The first step would be to identify and meet with community representatives in order to determine the extent of the problem and the resources that the community is prepared to commit to the project. At this point, other role players will also be called in. These might include investors, funding agencies, small business support agencies, training institutions and the like.

After discussion, the co-researchers may decide that before any action can be undertaken it is necessary to collect some background information. What skills are currently available in the community? What sort of self-employment schemes are available and which are the previous sources of employment of community members? Moreover, a wide range of social and cultural variables may influence the income generating possibilities within the community. On the basis of this information, the committee may choose to develop a farming co-operative in order to provide work for some community members, as well as to provide sustenance for the rest of the community. Simultaneously, the community may wish to embark on an extensive programme of skills training in management and accounting to run the co-operative better. This could involve development agencies and outside funders.

After a few months it will be necessary to evaluate the progress made. This will entail investigating the functioning of the newly formed co-operative. Here it may be discovered that the co-operative is experiencing problems due to the diffusion of responsibility for tasks, lack of commitment to or belief in the project, or the lack of specific skills, such as marketing the agricultural products. Further action will have to be taken in order to address these new concerns. Also, it may be discovered that even with new skills, community members are still unable to find employment. At this stage the co-researchers may wish to discuss and implement self-employment initiatives based within the community. Again, these will have to be developed and evaluated in the future, thereby initiating further action and research.

Throughout this process both the social scientist and the community are gaining valuable knowledge, experience and skills. The social scientist is gaining firsthand experience of the problems encountered by particular communities and the effectiveness of different solutions. This experience will be extremely valuable in dealings with other communities. Apart from the obvious advantages to the community of removing a particular obstacle to its well-being, its members are also learning more about their own problems and resources, as well as problem-solving strategies which will serve the community well for a variety of other difficulties which may arise in future.

Using action-research in developing countries

Action-researchers are often criticized by social scientists who are accustomed to conventional research methods.

In an action-research project extraneous variables are difficult, often impossible, to control. It is therefore very difficult to be sure that positive results are due to the action taken by the co-researchers.

e.g.

A community sets up a transport system for taking pregnant women and mothers with young children to hospital in an attempt to lower the infant mortality rate. At the same time, the government installs a freshwater supply to the community. If a decrease in infant mortality is measured, it is not possible to determine the respective contributions of either of these two life improvements.

The close relationship between "researcher" and "subjects" makes it quite difficult for the "researcher" to be objective and the research is, therefore, vulnerable to all kinds of bias.

e.g.

In the failing co-operative of a previous example, a social scientist who has developed a strong rapport with the people responsible for the co-operative, may be reluctant to admit that the source of the co-operative's problems

Community-centred Research

is the lack of commitment by the members to the project.

The necessary narrow focus of research (to a particular community with a particular difficulty) prevents the social scientist from generalizing research findings to other communities.

e.g.

Imagine two communities afflicted by civil violence. Whereas in one instance the people have a good relationship with the police, in the other the police are not trusted at all. In this case, solutions generated in one community are unlikely to be applicable in the other and vice versa.

Action-researchers usually respond to these criticisms by acknowledging that action-research is not the only form of research available and that for some kinds of problems action-research is not appropriate. However, in developing countries where communities are in great need of immediate solutions to vital survival problems, where social researchers are few and far between and often quite ignorant of the reality to be addressed, and where financial resources are scarce, action-research is a particularly valuable tool because:

1. it is concerned with solving particular problems facing communities;
2. it helps individuals, organizations and communities to learn skills and access resources so that they can function more effectively in future;
3. it provides a way of spreading the understanding gained through research to people and communities who can benefit from those findings;
4. it attempts to understand the person and the community within a broader social context;
5. it aids communication between social researchers and communities in need of assistance;
6. it shakes the "ivory tower" of many social scientists and makes their work directly beneficial to society.

EXERCISES

1. Find a report or description of a community project being run in your area. Work out some questions that an evaluation of this project should answer. Plan a diagnostic, formative and summative evaluation of the project.
2. Look through a recent newspaper and see what problems communities in your area are facing. Assuming that you were approached by representatives from a community, how would you go about facilitating an action-research project? What steps would you take? What problems might arise? How will you deal with them?
3. What strategies might one employ to prevent an accountability gap from developing within a particular community?
4. Discuss the differences between monitoring and evaluation.

CHAPTER 7

Research Design

In the previous chapters different types of research were presented, amongst them research types that are based on hypotheses to be tested. Whether in correlational or explanatory research, the testing of hypotheses is a delicate task. Although this testing is usually based on probabilistic reasoning, it must leave as little doubt as possible. In order to achieve this, the researcher must logically exclude all reasonable explanations, other than the one that she wishes to demonstrate. The testing procedure must therefore satisfy some criteria of logic rigour. These are expressed, for different situations and problems, in procedures to be followed, namely the research designs. The present chapter aims to introduce the most common research designs used in social science.

CHAPTER OBJECTIVES

Learners who have completed this chapter will be able to:
- Explain the fundamental principles of research design.
- Develop appropriate research designs for particular research questions.
- Identify and avoid a broad range of biases that affect research design.
- Evaluate the internal and external validity of any research project.

WHAT IS RESEARCH DESIGN?

Research design relates directly to the testing of hypotheses. It is a specification of the most adequate operations to be performed in order to test a specific hypothesis under given conditions. It is not, however, to be confused with research management which is a plan to guide the researcher through the research process. The important question facing the scientist is: What steps should be taken in order to demonstrate that a particular hypothesis is true and that all other possible hypotheses must be rejected?

e.g.

A researcher observes a high incidence of depression in a poor community. She suspects that the cases of depression are caused by long-term unemployment. In order to lobby for a job-creation programme in the area, she has to demonstrate the correctness of her hypothesis. She has, therefore, to plan a study which shows that in this community, depression is largely due to unemployment and not due, for instance, to the past history of the people, their age or gender, or the poor living conditions in the community.

In order to achieve the objectives of social research, the scientist requires a carefully thought out strategy. The first steps in constructing a good research design require the researcher to answer several fundamental questions about the research. These relate to the focus, the unit of analysis and the time

© Juta & Co Ltd

THE FOCUS OF RESEARCH

Social research can be used to explore almost any topic of the social world, although with differing degrees of success. However, it is useful to try to classify the most common of these, since they sometimes require different types of research design. The focus of research may be understood in terms of three different categories: conditions, orientations and actions.

- *Conditions* are studied when the researcher wishes to explore the current state of the subjects of the research. For example, a researcher who measures the unemployment rate in twenty West African cities is interested in the current condition of the labour market in those cities. Similarly, a researcher interested in the health of elderly rural people might measure their heart-rate after light exercise.
- *Orientations* are concerned with subjects' attitudes and beliefs. Researchers interested in religious and political views would, for example, be interested in orientations.
- *Actions* are also very often the focus of research. These actions may be observed directly or may be reported by the actor or others who observed the actor. For example, a study of how people travel to work in urban areas might involve extensive observations of road, taxi and bus routes as well as trains (direct observation), or might rely on interviews with workers or employers (an indirect method).

In most cases these three are not mutually exclusive and the social researcher must be sensitive to all simultaneously. The relationship between unemployment and depression involves all three. Experiences of being without work are likely to depend upon the length of time subjects have been unemployed and their current savings (conditions), their beliefs about themselves, their futures, and their families (orientations), as well as the amount of energy they spend each day looking for, or trying to create, work (actions).

THE UNIT OF ANALYSIS

The second important factor that the researcher must consider when planning an appropriate research design is that of the **unit of analysis**. This becomes particularly important when the researcher begins to draw a sample with which to work. Sampling is discussed in Chapter 8. The unit of analysis is the person or object from whom the social researcher collects data. The data from such a unit can only describe that unit, but when combined with similar data collected from a group of similar units, provides an accurate picture of the group to which that unit belongs.

> **e.g.**
> A researcher is interested in the physical health of people in a rural community. Using a medical screening procedure, this researcher collects medical data from 100 carefully sampled people (the units of analysis of this study) living in that community. By analysing the data from these 100 different people, a general estimate of the health conditions in this particular community is constructed.

Although many people believe that social scientists always focus upon the experiences of the individual person, this is not always the case. There are several different possible units of analysis. These also fall into broad categories.

- *Individuals* are the most common unit of analysis. In this case, the researcher investigates the conditions, orientations or actions of a group of individual people. When the individual is used as the unit of analysis, the people that actually take part in the study are often chosen because they belong to particular groups, such as police officers, women, people with cancer, and so forth.
- *Groups of people* are also sometimes studied. Some examples of research where the unit of analysis is more than one person are studies of siblings and identical twins, marital relationships, family functioning, and small group functioning. In this case an entire group (and not each of its members) constitutes one unit and can be compared to another group (another unit).
- *Organizations* with formal structures are a particular kind of group that is often used as the unit of analysis of social research. In this case, questions of interest might relate to proportions of employees from different social groups, organizational structure, profit, and communication channels.
- Occasionally, the unit of analysis is a *period of time*. For example, a researcher may wish to determine whether there is a systematic change in infant mortality in a given community over a twenty-year period (each unit is one year), or how much rain falls each month over a year (each unit is one month).
- Finally, a common unit of analysis is a particular *social artifact*. Social artifacts are the products of social beings and can be anything from poems and letters to automobiles and farming implements. A systematic analysis of such artifacts may provide valuable information about the individuals and groups that created or used them.

It is very important that the researcher keeps the units clearly in mind throughout the research process. It is often very tempting to draw conclusions about one unit of analysis when in actual fact the research focused on a different one. This is called the **ecological fallacy**.

e.g.

A comparison of rural communities which have relatively few young men and peri-urban communities with their large numbers of young men, reveals that the peri-urban communities tend to have a higher incidence of alcoholism than the rural ones. The researcher uses this to demonstrate that young men are more likely than other groups within the community to abuse alcohol.

The data does not, however, show this. The possibility exists that men and women of all ages consume more alcohol when living in a peri-urban area due to the greater stresses of living near a city and the easy availability of drink. The researcher has made the error of drawing conclusions about individuals when the research examined groups of people (different communities).

The tendency of researchers to focus on particular units of analysis, is another potential flaw in social science research. This is a form of *reductionism* and was mentioned in Chapter 1. Psychologists tend to focus on the individual, sociologists investigate groups of people, as do economists. Anthropologists and historians often consider only social artifacts. Most social phenomena can only be explained if one understands the dynamics operating at a number of different levels.

e.g.

In recent years large numbers of people have immigrated to South Africa from various other African countries. Some rapidly become integrated into South African society, while others remain isolated and may experience physical, emotional and social problems. To understand why some people adjust quickly and others do not, the social scientist must consider the political and economic realities of the country from which people have come, as well as their personal ability to form friendships in a new place and adapt to different social norms. In other words, it is necessary to investigate some aspects of the individuals, as well as the social context from which they came.

It cannot be denied that social scientists with backgrounds in different disciplines are often trained to operate with particular units of analysis only. It should be remembered that virtually nothing in the world is dependent only upon one of those levels and that in order to be effective in one's work one needs to consider social reality at many levels simultaneously.

THE TIME DIMENSION

A third fundamental aspect of any research is the manner in which it deals with time. Observations may all take place at a particular time or may be deliberately stretched over a long period.

When all data is collected at the same time the research design is **cross-sectional**. The discussion of correlational research in Chapter 5 is relevant here. The researcher using this design attempts to understand a topic by collecting a *cross-section* of information relevant to that topic. For example, a survey of nutrition patterns and infant mortality across a variety of living conditions may reveal differences between people's nutrition and the conditions under which they are living, as well as a relationship between these factors and infant mortality. The inherent difficulty with cross-sectional designs is that because they do not allow the researcher to measure change over time, (since all the data is collected at once), it is very difficult to demonstrate causality. In the above example, the researcher may be able to demonstrate that infant mortality and nutrition are related, but will not be able to show that poor nutrition is a cause of infant mortality. (Refer to the requirements of causality discussed in Chapter 5.)

Nevertheless, the immediate nature of cross-sectional designs as well as the relative ease of data collection make these designs the most common choice for social scientists.

Longitudinal designs spread data collection out over time. For example, a researcher interested in unemployment in Cape Town between 1990 and 1999 conducts a broad yearly survey in the city in order to find out what proportion of the population is employed at any one time. Data collection occurs several times, in 1990, 1991, and so on. (Note that the survey must take place during the same period of each year in order for the results to be comparable.) Once all the data has been collected, the researcher may be able to demonstrate that there is a predictable trend in the level of unemployment in Cape Town, data which may be useful to job-creation programmes, town planners and many other people.

Evaluation research (discussed in the previous chapter) is most often longitudinal in nature. Some particular longitudinal designs are introduced below.

■ *Reputability studies* are longitudinal because the same group of people is interviewed on several occasions over a period of time. The previous chapter contained some details about this kind of design.

■ *Cohort studies* use a particular type of longitudinal design which tracks particular groups over time. For example, the "Birth to Ten" project running in South Africa (Richter et al., 1995) is recording the development of hundreds of South African children over the first ten years of their lives. These researchers record a wide range of physical, emotional, social and educational variables relating to children's development.

- *Tracer studies* are used to "trace" people, or to follow their lives over a period of time. In most cases, the data is collected at only one point (perhaps ten years after graduation or release from prison). As such, the tracer study is not strictly longitudinal, but produces data which simulates longitudinal design.

TYPES OF RESEARCH DESIGN

Every project requires a research design that is carefully tailored to the exact needs of the problem. Of the many different designs that have been developed by social scientists over the years, only the few that are most frequently used are presented here. More complex designs can be studied in specialized books.

Research designs have two essential components. The first is *observation*. At some point in every research project the researcher must observe and measure variation in the different variables involved in the research. Some research designs require that the researcher observe more than one group, at more than one time. The second essential component of research design is *an analysis of the relationships between the variables*. This may be done by manipulating certain variables in order to observe the effect on other variables, or by observing corresponding changes in more than one variable.

Three categories of research design can be distinguished, classified according to the level of scientific rigour involved in proving the causal relationship.

- **Pre-experimental** designs are the least adequate in terms of scientific rigour and thus are least likely to establish a clear causal relationship between the independent and dependent variables. In cases where quasi-experimental or experimental designs are not possible, the researcher is forced to use a pre-experimental design, as these have far fewer requirements than the other designs. Three pre-experimental designs, the one-shot case study, the pre-test/post-test design and the intact groups design are presented below.

- **Quasi-experimental designs** are designs which do not meet the exacting criteria of experimental designs, but which manage to approximate experimental conditions. Although these designs have fewer requirements than experimental designs, they can achieve a similar level of scientific rigour. Two quasi-experimental designs, the contrasted groups design and the time-series design are presented below.

- **Experimental designs** are the most rigorous of all the designs and have strict requirements. Three experimental designs, the pre-test/post-test control group design, the post-test only control group design, and factorial designs are presented below.

Although the designs are presented here in order of increasing scientific rigour, it should be noted that experimental designs were developed before quasi-experimental designs. The latter were developed to accommodate the constraints of social reality that would not be accounted for using the former. Thus quasi-experimental designs appear as amendments to stricter experimental designs.

PRE-EXPERIMENTAL DESIGNS
One-shot case study

The one-shot case study is most often used to determine whether an event (or intervention) has any effect upon a group of subjects.

Fundamentals of Social Research Methods

The dependent variable is measured after the event (post-test) and conclusions are drawn. The one-shot case study is presented diagrammatically in figure 7.1.

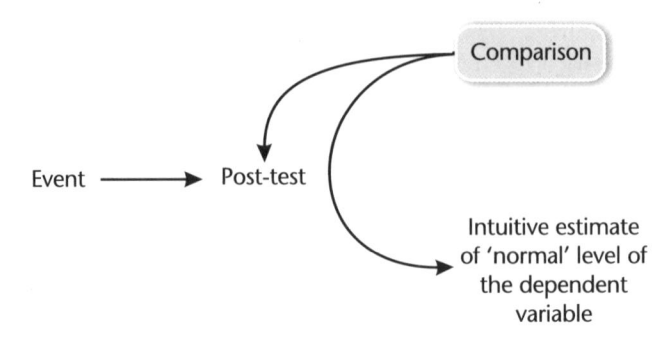

Figure 7.1
One-shot case study

e.g.
A factory manager is concerned about the daily number of absentees. A system of monitoring attendance is introduced (the event) and thereafter the number of absentees (the dependent variable) is recorded every day. Finding that the number of absentees is low, the manager concludes that the new monitoring system is a success.

Unfortunately, this conclusion is not really justified. The central objection is that, without some measure of what the absentee rate was like before the monitoring device was installed, it is very difficult for the manager to argue convincingly that absentee rates after the installation are any lower than they were to start with.

The lack of an initial measure of functioning, often referred to as the "baseline", makes it very difficult to convincingly demonstrate change resulting from the event. The following design is used to overcome this problem.

Pre-test/post-test design

In the pre-test/post-test design the researcher measures the dependent variable before (pre-test or baseline) and after (post-test) the event that is expected to bring about some change. As a result, the scores on the dependent measure can be compared over two points of time and the difference between the before and after scores may be due to the event that occurred between them. The design is presented diagrammatically in figure 7.2.

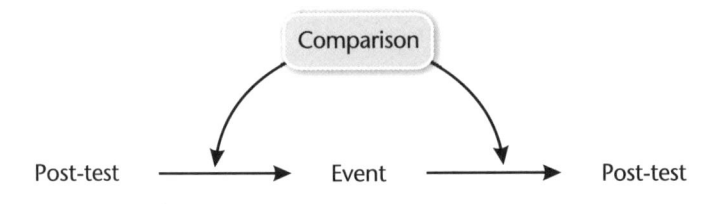

Figure 7.2
Pre-test/post-test design

> **e.g.**
> Using this design, the manager of the factory is required to measure the daily absentee rate before installing the new monitoring system. The new system is then put into operation and, shortly thereafter, the absentee rate is measured again. A finding that the absentee rate has dropped from 10 workers per day (pre-test) to 4 workers per day (post-test) represents a difference of 6. Since this change occurred when the new system came into operation, the manager has far more convincingly demonstrated that the monitoring system is effective in reducing absenteeism.

However, even this approach raises some concerns. It is not impossible that other changes occurred at the same time as the event and that these (and not the event) were responsible for the change in the dependent variable. This is particularly true when a long period of time has elapsed between the pre- and post-tests. These other changes that might be confounding the study are of two different types: those which occur within the environment and those which occur within the subjects.

Events that arise within the environment are referred to as **history**. Using the same example, it might have been the case that the workers' attendance was influenced by fear of losing jobs due to increasing unemployment, changes in weather conditions which make it easier to get to work, or an end to a flu outbreak in the area. Any of these can be used to explain the change in the absentee rate and the manager still has not demonstrated conclusively that the device works.

Events that arise within the subjects are referred to as **maturation**. It is also possible that the workers' attitude to their job has changed and, as a result, they are staying away from work less often. Again, this confounds any change which might have occurred due to the installation of the new monitoring device and the manager cannot show that it actually works.

In cases where subjects must be tested (such as tests of memory or driving skill) a bias called **test effect** may arise. Subjects may become bored with the test procedure, or they may become practiced and thus improve, or they may become fatigued. In other words, this bias results from a change in subjects' response to the test instrument with repeated usage.

A final source of error in the pre-test/post-test design is that of **regression towards the mean**. All variables fluctuate somewhat due to chance. It is possible that the initial measurement (pre-test) was not an accurate reflection of the dependent variable. As a result, the second measurement (post-test) is likely to be different and closer to the actual level of the dependent variable, regardless of the effect of the event. Using the previous example, it may have happened that on the day that the initial measurement was taken an unusually high number of people were absent from work. As a result, it is likely that the second measurement will be lower, even if the new monitoring device has no effect.

The pre-test/post-test design is the most common design for impact studies or summative evaluations (discussed in the previous chapter). In this case the event is the intervention that is being evaluated.

Some of the errors of the pre-test/post-test design can be avoided if the following design is used.

Intact group comparison design

Instead of using only a single group, the intact group comparison design uses two groups, one of which is effected by the event or treatment, the other of which is not. Instead of comparing the performances of one group before and after the event or treatment, this design compares the scores of two groups, only one of which was effected by the event or treatment. Since both performances are measured at the same time, the intact group comparison design overcomes the difficulties of history, maturation and regression towards the mean. This design is presented diagrammatically in figure 7.3.

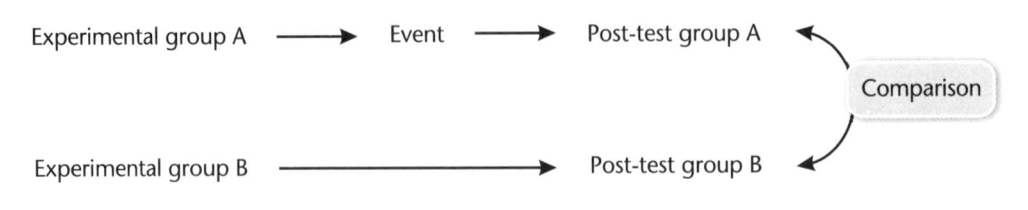

Figure 7.3
Intact group comparison design

e.g.
This design requires that the factory owner or researcher has access to two factories. The workers of factory A are to be the experimental group. The workers of factory B are to be the comparison group. The new monitoring device is installed in factory A in order to deal with the problems of absenteeism. Shortly thereafter, the daily absentee rate is measured for both factories (post-test). If the absentee rate is lower for factory A than for factory B, the manager can argue that the monitoring device works.

Unfortunately, while this design does overcome problems of history, maturation, test effect and regression towards the mean, it introduces new problems of its own. The difficulty with this design is knowing for sure that the two groups are similar to begin with. In the previous example it may be that working conditions in factory B are a lot poorer than in factory A and that the absentee rate is higher for factory B anyway. The possibility that the groups were originally different or may react differently to the same event or treatment is the crucial weakness of this type of design.

Any group that exists prior to a research study is called an intact group. It is not possible to be sure that two such groups are equivalent. This is a problem for many studies which try to examine the differences between pre-existing groups. Examples of such groups are men and women, people of different cultural and ethnic backgrounds, people of different incomes, people of different religious beliefs and many others.

QUASI-EXPERIMENTAL DESIGNS

Quasi-experimental designs allow the researcher to maintain a higher level of control and rigour than is possible in pre-experimental designs, even when the demands of experimental designs cannot be met (See below).

Contrasted group design

One solution (but not the best) to the problems of the intact groups design is to use groups that are clearly in contrast. In other words, the researcher's goal has changed from finding similar groups to finding groups that are essentially dissimilar, or contrasting in the main characteristic. If the

Research Design

researcher knows that groups are different in terms of one aspect (the independent variable) and records a difference between the groups in terms of another aspect (the dependent variable), then she can conclude that the differences in the dependent variable are due to the differences between the two groups. Note that the important difference between this design and the others discussed thus far is that this design does not allow for an independent event or treatment but is based on differences that already exist between the two groups. This design is illustrated in figure 7.4.

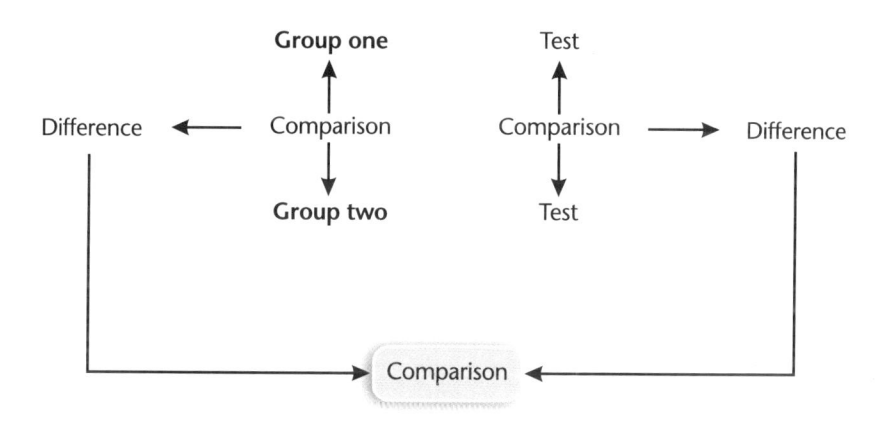

Figure 7.4
Contrasted group design

e.g.

One may wish to assess the influence of the education of parents on the performance of children in mathematics. To carry out this research design the researcher forms two groups of children, those whose parents have a university degree and those whose parents did not complete high school. The researcher matches the children in terms of sex and age. These are contrasting groups of children since the education of their parents is clearly different. By comparing the differences in mathematics scores for these two groups of children, one can infer that parental education has an effect upon performance. Clearly, if the maths performance of the two groups of children is not different, then one would infer that the education background of parents has little influence on their children's maths performance.

Time-series design

Time-series designs represent an improvement over the one group pretest/post-test design of the pre-experimental group. Rather than relying on a single measurement before and after the event or treatment, several measurements both before (pre1, pre2 and pre3) and after (post1, post2 and post3) the event or treatment are made. This allows one to observe the effects of history and of maturation, test effects and regression towards the mean. This is achieved by comparing each measurement with the measurements that were taken before and after it. Differences between those measurements taken before the event (for example, pre3 – pre2) and between those taken after the event (for example, post2 – post1), but not between the before and after measurements, must be due to such variables as regression towards the

© Juta & Co Ltd

Fundamentals of Social Research Methods

mean, history, maturation and test effect. The biases can be taken into account when differences due to the treatment are examined and interpreted. The most important difference is thus the one between the before and after measurements (that is, post1 – pre3) since this must be due to the event or treatment. Putting all this information together allows the researcher to draw conclusions about the effect of the event or treatment taking into account the effect of the various confounding variables.

The limitation of this design lies in the difficulty of obtaining a series of repeated measures. It is often difficult to test the same group of people six to eight times. Further, over time some group members may no longer be available which changes the composition of the group. This bias is called **experimental mortality** and is discussed in greater detail in Chapter 11. Time series design is illustrated in figure 7.5.

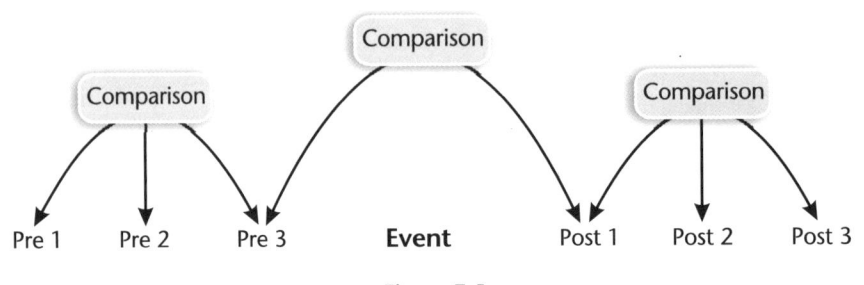

Figure 7.5
Time series design

e.g.

Return to the example of the factory manager and the problems of absenteeism. Using a time-series design, the level of absenteeism would be measured several times before the new monitoring device was installed. Differences between these initial scores are due to secondary factors such as regression towards the mean, history, maturation and test effect. A similar set of records from after the monitoring device had been installed would provide complementary information. By comparing the level of the scores before and after the installation, the manager would be able to tell whether or not the new device made a significant difference. Typically the data of such a study could be graphed as shown in figure 7.6

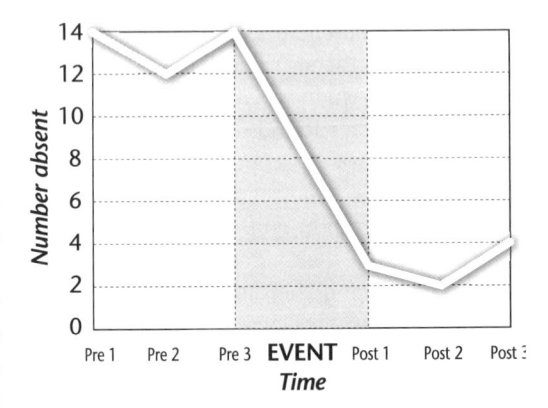

Figure 7.6
Charting time series data

Research Design

Chapter 7

e.g.

A further example illustrates the usefulness of time series design. Maganu and Rumish (1994) present the following analysis of the incidence of tuberculosis in Botswana. During the period 1975–1985, the number of new cases of tuberculosis reported each year dropped by between 2 and 8%. From 1985–1990, the incidence of tuberculosis did not change significantly. However, in the period 1990–1994 the number of reported tuberculosis cases has increased by 200% per year. Clearly something important has changed, but what? The answer is found in the fact that nearly all of the new cases reported in the last four year period also tested positive for HIV.

Many other quasi-experimental designs intended for coping with different problems of social reality exist and are discussed in more advanced texts. A researcher confronted with a particular problem should consult specialized literature on the subject.

EXPERIMENTAL DESIGNS

Most experimental designs are characterized by their use of **randomization** to create two or more equivalent groups. The use of randomization negates the difficulties of ensuring that the groups are identical. (The symbol "R" is used in the following diagrams to identify groups which have been generated using random procedures.)

Randomization requires that every subject involved in the study has an equal chance of landing up in any of the groups. This can be achieved by first identifying the entire group of subjects, then randomly dividing this group into two or more subgroups (depending on the chosen design) through the use of random number tables, coin flipping or various other randomization techniques. It is important that some systematic random technique of determining which subject falls into which group is required. *Arbitrary* assignment to groups is not necessarily *random*. (Techniques for generating random numbers are discussed in more detail in Chapter 8.)

When two groups are created using randomization they are most likely to be equivalent. This is particularly true when the researcher is working with large groups. The smaller the groups, the less sure the researcher can be that they are actually equivalent. The advantage of randomly generated groups is that the researcher starts the experiment with two (or more) equivalent groups. If only one group is subjected to the treatment, the researcher can be reasonably sure that any difference between the groups thereafter is due to the effects of the treatment and nothing else. The group which does not receive the treatment is called the **control group**, while the group that receives the treatment is called the **experimental group**.

Of course, it is impossible to randomly assign subjects to groups when the independent variable cannot be manipulated. An obvious example of a variable that cannot be manipulated is sex. Virtually all people are either male or female and the researcher can do nothing about it. The same is true of religious affiliation, cultural background, income, age, place of residence and many others. When one of these is the independent variable, the researcher must use other techniques to establish equivalent groups.

Another procedure is **matching** the elements of the group. In this case, the control for the equivalence of the two groups is based on the knowledge of the main characteristics of the elements, persons, events or objects to be investigated. The researcher forms pairs of members having identical characteristics considered as relevant for the research. The members of each pair must differ in terms of the independent variable. For the example of absenteeism, the workers

© Juta & Co Ltd

could be matched on such properties as age, sex, skill, health, family situation and work experience. Each member of each pair is then randomly assigned to a different group. In this way the two groups so constituted will have equivalent properties.

Another method of matching, which has the advantage of being more efficient especially in the case of large groups, is aimed at forming groups which have the same global characteristics. For instance, the two groups must have the same number of males and females, the same average height, and the same number of skilled workers. Of course the matching is not as precise as in the first case. It is essential that the matching is done for *all* relevant factors. Where important factors are neglected in the matching process, the groups are no longer equivalent for the purposes of the research, and the results are compromised.

The choice between randomization and matching often does not exist. Matching procedures can only be used if enough variables relevant to the research are known. If, for instance, age is an important factor but the experimenter is not provided with the ages of participants, no matching can be done on the basis of age. Moreover, if the number of variables to control is large, it will become difficult to find enough individuals with the same combination of characteristics. Furthermore, if the groups are very large, the matching procedure will become very time-consuming, tedious and costly.

It is only though the creation of equivalent groups by randomization or matching that the following experimental designs are possible.

Pre-test/post-test control group design

The pre-test/post-test control group design requires that subjects are randomly assigned to two groups, one of which becomes the experimental group and the other the control group. Note that a control group is similar to the comparison group of the intact group's design, except that it is arrived at through random assignment. Both groups are measured at the beginning of the study. Thereafter, the experimental group is subjected to the event or treatment. Following the treatment both groups are again measured. Now the researcher can compare the pre-test and post-test scores of the experimental group, as well as the post-test scores of the experimental and control groups, in order to assess whether the event or treatment made any difference to the scores of the experimental group. This is illustrated in figure 7.7.

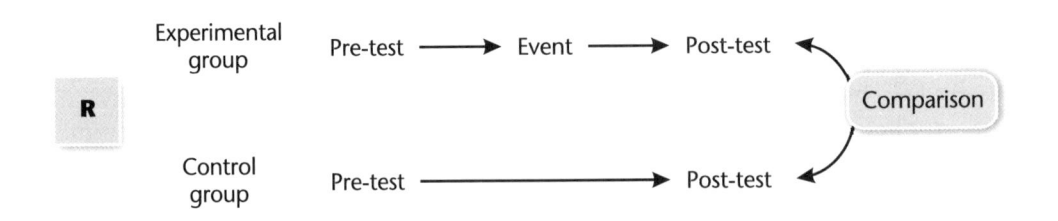

Figure 7.7
Pre-test/post-test control group design

Research Design

Chapter 7

e.g.

The factory manager of the earlier examples would first have to assign the factory workers randomly to two different groups. Random assignment means that one can assume that these groups are equivalent. In other words, it is expected that the proportion of absentees in both groups is about the same. The next step is to collect absentee data from both groups (pre-test). Thereafter, the new device is put into operation on the one group only. This becomes the experimental group. The other group continues as before and is the control group. Shortly thereafter, the manager must again record the absentee rates of each group. By comparing the pre-and post-test scores for the experimental group, as well as the post-test scores for the experimental and control groups, the manager can tell how much difference the new device has made and how much change was due to the other variables which confound the pre-test/post-test design of the pre-experimental group.

Because of randomization it is expected that the two groups will be equivalent at pre-test. However, it is possible that they will differ, in which case, the difference in the pre-tests is taken into account when comparing the post-test results. Note that this design also allows the researcher to measure the effects of history, maturation and regression towards the mean.

This design provides a powerful method for impact studies or summative evaluations. It is the design of choice where the possibility of random assignment exists.

Post-test only control group design

An experimental design which has virtually all the experimental rigour of the pre-test/post-test control group design is the post-test only control group design. Randomization aims at ensuring that the experimental and control groups are identical except for the fact that only the experimental group receives the treatment or event. Therefore the pre-test/post-test comparison incorporated into the previous design may be superfluous. The simpler design represented by figure 7.8 does away with the pre-testing.

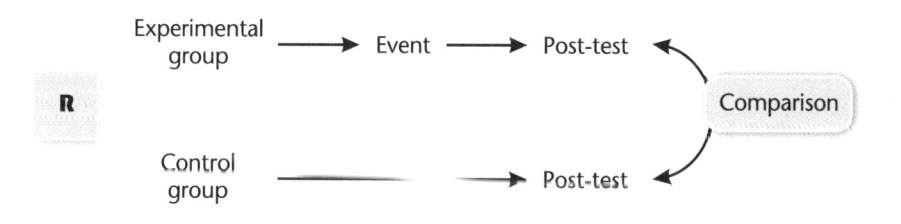

Figure 7.8
Post-test only control group design

e.g.

Using this design, the researcher would again divide the workforce randomly into two equal groups and install the new monitoring device in the work area of one group. Note that this is done without pre-testing. Shortly thereafter, the post-test measurement is taken of the two groups and the results compared.

e.g.

A second example is taken from education. This design is very useful for assessing the efficiency of a new teaching method. A class of pupils is randomly divided into two groups. One group, the experimental one, is subjected to the new method, while the control group continues to be taught using the old method. After a certain period, both groups are given a competency test to assess their progress on the taught subject. Note that if the pre-test/post-test control group design had been used it would have meant constructing two equivalent competency tests, one to be given before the treatment and the other after the treatment. Not only is it technically difficult to construct two tests to assess the same knowledge content and skills, but also, the pupils' results in the second test would be influenced in various degrees by their experience of the first test. This would make an assessment of the effects of the new teaching method very difficult to gauge.

Since all the data is collected at one time, the problems of maturation, history, test effects and regression towards the mean do not arise. However, it is impossible for the researcher to be sure that the two groups are indeed equivalent to start with. When a random assignment technique is used and there are enough subjects in the study (at least thirty in each group), the researcher can safely use the post-test only control group study.

Factorial designs

Factorial designs can be thought of as generalizations of either the pre-test/post-test control group design or the post-test only control group design. The important difference, however, is that factorial designs can incorporate two or more independent variables, whereas the previous designs only allow for a single independent variable. A factorial design with two independent variables, each having two levels will be studied here. Call the variables x and y, and their levels x_1, x_2, y_1, and y_2. The following table illustrates how an analysis of the relationship between these two independent variables demands four experimental groups in the design.

Table 7.1
Factorial design with two variables

	x_1	x_2
y_1	x_1y_1	x_2y_1
y_2	x_1y_2	x_2y_2

Thus this design requires four groups (x_1y_1, x_2y_1, x_1y_2 and x_2y_2) and in an experimental design it is required that these groups are constructed using randomization. Depending upon the size of the sample and the particular needs of the researcher, the groups may be pre-tested. As for designs with only one independent variable, the pre-test is not essential but can provide extra information. Shortly thereafter, the groups are exposed to different combinations of the two (or more) independent variables and then post-tested. The researcher then searches for differences between the levels of the independent variables, that is between x_1 and x_2 and between y_1 and y_2. Such differences are called **main effects**. Further, the analysis may reveal that there is an **interaction** between the two variables. This means that both variables in conjunction are producing a particular pattern of results which cannot be explained in terms of only one variable. Figure 7.9 illustrates a post-test only factorial design with two variables, each with two levels.

Research Design

Group 1 $x_1 y_1$ → Post-test
Group 2 $x_1 y_2$ → Post-test
R
Group 3 $x_2 y_1$ → Post-test
Group 4 $x_2 y_2$ → Post-test

Comparisons:
2 main effects
and interaction

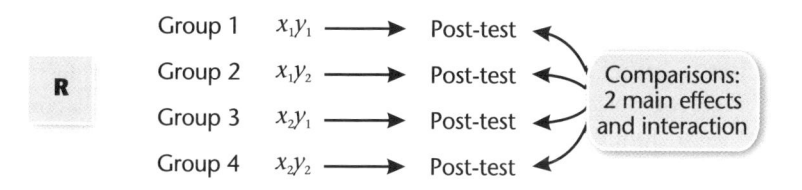

Figure 7.9
Factorial designs

e.g.

Imagine that the factory manager of the previous examples wished to examine the effects of different work hours or shifts, as well as the use of the monitoring device upon absenteeism. There are therefore two independent variables each with two levels: work hours with day (x_1) and night (x_2) shifts, and the monitoring system without (y_1) or with the device installed (y_2). To put the design into effect the manager randomly assigns each person in the work-force to one of four groups. Random assignment implies that these groups are equivalent for all other variables. Each group then gets a different combination of the independent variables as follows. Group 1 works the day shift (x_1) without the new monitoring device (y_1). Group 2 works the day shift (x_1) but with the new monitoring device (y_2). Group 3 works the night shift (x_2) but without the new monitoring device (y_1) and group 4 works the night shift (x_2) with the new monitoring device (y_2). Once the four groups have been working under these conditions for a short period, the manager measures the rate of absenteeism of each group. A comparison of groups 1 and 2 with groups 3 and 4 reveals whether the shift made any difference. A comparison of groups 1 and 3 with groups 2 and 4 reveals whether the new monitoring device made any difference. By examining the scores of all four groups, the manager is able to discover whether the new monitoring device and the shift interact. A possible interaction is presented in the chart shown in figure 7.10.

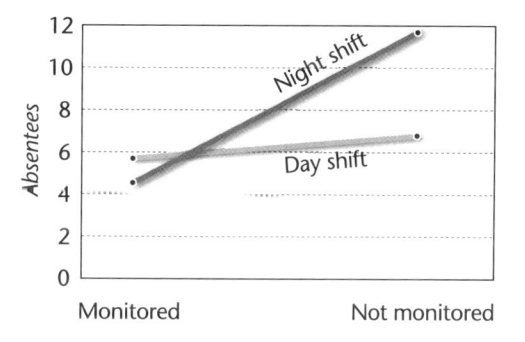

Figure 7.10
Charting an interaction effect

Note that the lowest level of absenteeism was recorded for the group that was monitored and worked the night shift. The group that was monitored and worked the day shirt produced the next lowest score of absenteeism. The third lowest absenteeism score came from the group that was not monitored, but which worked the day shift. The highest level of absenteeism was recorded for the group that was not monitored and which worked the night shift. From these results the manager can conclude that when workers are monitored the levels of absenteeism for the day and night shift are quite similar whereas, when not monitored, workers resort to absenteeism much more often during the night than the day shift.

DEVELOPING A RESEARCH DESIGN

Very often research is hampered by constraints of resources, subjects and time.

© Juta & Co Ltd

Rarely can any of the designs discussed in this chapter be imposed directly on to actual research projects. Rather, these designs explain the logic of social research and should serve as a foundation for good research design. The researcher's work is complicated by many sources of bias and error which must each be dealt with as effectively as possible to ensure the high quality of the research.

In developing a design for a particular research problem there are several questions to be considered.

1. Is a cross-sectional or longitudinal design more appropriate? Studies involving change over time virtually always use longitudinal designs. Cross-sectional designs are most useful for describing populations, and differences between populations, at a particular moment in time.
2. If a longitudinal design is used, how many repeated observations will be made? How will the problems of history, maturation, test effect and regression to the mean be addressed? Is there are danger of experimental mortality affecting the usefulness of the design?
3. Is it possible to create equivalent groups either through randomization or matching? If this is possible then experimental designs are the most appropriate. If not, the researcher is forced to use a quasi-experimental design.

It is important for social scientists to be very critical of their own and their colleagues' research designs. The following sections explore the critical evaluation of research designs by discussing the common sources of bias in designs, as well as criteria against which designs should be evaluated.

SOURCES OF BIAS IN RESEARCH DESIGN

Because every research project has its own particular set of problems, a complete list of the possible sources of bias in research does not exist. However, Campbell and Stanley (1966) list a set of common problems which affect many different designs and these are discussed below. There are many other sources of bias which relate to methods of data collection, subject selection and data presentation. These are discussed in other chapters and only those relating to research design are dealt with here.

History and maturation

History refers to changes which occur in the world, other than those intended by the researcher, and which might effect the results. Maturation refers to changes that occur within subjects and thus confound the researcher's design. These effects are particularly problematic to designs which require that data be collected at more than one time. One common solution is to collect data at a single point in time. The post-test only designs are advantageous in this respect. A second solution is adopted by the pre-test/post-test control group and times-series designs, where repeated measurements allow the researcher to estimate the effects of history and maturation. These effects are then taken into account in the interpretation of the results.

Regression towards the mean

Regression towards the mean arises when researchers base their conclusions upon single measurements. If a pre-test score is unusually high due to chance factors, the post-test score is likely to be lower, regardless of any changes due to the experimental variables. The most effective solution to this problem is the repeated testing adopted by times-series designs.

Test effect

Prior exposure to a test or measurement technique can bias a person's responses. This is particularly problematic when subjects are tested and retested, as in all pre-test/post-test and time-series designs. Particular test effects are boredom (when exactly the same test is repeated), practice (as subjects learn how to respond to the test) and fatigue (particularly when the test procedure is lengthy). To counter these effects the researcher should reduce the number of times that subjects are tested, vary the test slightly so as to reduce boredom and practice effects and use shorter tests to reduce fatigue. Alternate instruments are technically very difficult to construct and are also draining on resources.

Instrumentation

Some of the many difficulties of developing appropriate instruments are discussed in a later chapter. However, instruments present a problem for design as well, particularly when different instruments are used to test the same concept. The researcher must be sure that the instruments are equally sensitive and accurate otherwise changes between the two measurements might be due to differences in the instruments and not due to any differences within the subjects. Also, instruments constructed for use in developing countries should be sensitive to peoples' lack of experience with high technology, as well as differences in culture. Where possible, instruments should be pre-tested on a pilot group in order to check their appropriateness, accuracy and, where more than one instrument is used, their equivalence.

Sometimes when measurement instruments are used in inappropriate ways very powerful reactive effects are produced. For example, it is not uncommon for potential employees undergoing a selection procedure, to be subjected to instruments that were designed for the measurement of mental illness. In this case, potential employees will be extremely sensitive to being turned down for reasons of mental health, and are unlikely to respond truthfully to the instrument. This defeats the purpose of the selection assessment.

Experimental mortality

Often subjects drop out of a research project during the data collection procedures. This is particularly true of research which takes place over an extended period of time. Longitudinal time-series designs, in particular, are vulnerable to this source of error. Although experimental mortality produces enormous difficulties for data analysis, the most important problem relates to the design of the research. It is possible, if not likely, that the people who drop out of a study are systematically different to those who remain with the study until the end. This may result in biased findings. The researcher should design the research so that it is convenient for the subjects to participate until the end, and should impress upon the participants the importance of their continuing co-operation.

Reactive effects

When subjects are aware of being observed they behave in unnatural ways, that is, they "react" to being observed. One example of a reactive effect is test anxiety. The measuring instrument may increase the arousal levels of some participants and thus influence their scores. Similarly, some subjects try to please the experimenter and provide those results that they believe are desired. Others will do just the opposite and try to confound the study in order to find out how the researcher will react.

A well-known reactive effect is called the Hawthorne effect. The Hawthorne effect occurs when subjects of a study feel that their selection makes them a privileged group and, as a result, they perform differently than they would otherwise.

The most effective way of countering this source of bias is to use unobtrusive techniques of data collection. In other words, if the subjects are not aware that they are being observed, there is no reason to expect them to act unusually. Of course, this is not always possible. In other cases the researcher should collect data in a way that causes the least disturbance to the participants' lives. Practically, this may mean collecting data in subjects' usual environments, using techniques which do not require special skills or unusual apparatus.

Selection bias

Since most studies incorporate more than one group of participants, it is important that the researcher be sure that these groups are equivalent to each other in all respects except for the independent variable of the study. When the independent variable is beyond the researcher's control and a quasi-experimental design has to be chosen, there is little that can be done. When the researcher is in control of which subjects fall into which group, there are two techniques which can be used to ensure that the groups are similar. The best technique for a large group of participants is random assignment, which was discussed earlier in the chapter. This entails assigning the subjects to different groups on the basis of a randomization procedure. When the researcher has only a few participants and has reason to believe that randomization might not result in equivalent groups, the option of matching is available.

VALIDITY OF RESEARCH DESIGN

The central aim of research design is to establish a relationship between the independent and dependent variables with a high degree of certainty. The potential of a design to achieve this aim is referred to as the validity of the design. Validity is measured in terms of two separate but related dimensions: **internal** and **external validity**.

Internal validity

Internal validity is concerned with the question, "Do the observed changes in the dependent variable *actually* relate to changes in the independent variable?" In other words, internal validity examines the extent to which a particular research design has excluded all other possible hypotheses which could explain the variation of the dependent variable. In order to achieve high internal validity a research design should control as many extraneous variables as possible, and should deal with problems such as history, maturation, regression to the mean, test effects, instrumentation effects, experimental mortality and selection bias.

External validity

External validity is concerned with the question, "Do the results obtained from this particular sample of participants apply to all subjects in the population being studied?" In other words, external validity examines the extent to which the results of the study can be *generalized*. The researcher must consider two factors in order to achieve high external validity.

Firstly, the sample must be representative of the population in question. How one goes about selecting representative samples is the topic of the next chapter and will not be addressed further here. However, unless a sample is representative of a population, the researcher's conclusions cannot be applied

Research Design

to that population and may thus be of little value.

Secondly, the researcher must ensure that the study simulates reality as closely as possible. The conditions and situation must be seen as normal, depicting the usual reality of the participants. This means that the tests and tasks that are required of the subjects must be planned so as to minimize the whole range of reactive effects. When people behave differently due to their participation in a research project, the findings are immediately less valid than they would have been had the subjects behaved as they would on every other day of their lives. Techniques for ensuring less reactivity include making data collection as unobtrusive as possible and testing people within their usual surroundings.

Relationship between internal and external validity

Unfortunately, internal and external validity tend to be inversely related. That is, studies with high internal validity often have low external validity and vice versa. Studies that take place in a particular social context have high external validity but cannot control the wide variety of real world variables which could interfere with the effect of the independent variable on the dependent variable. Thus these studies have low internal validity. Similarly, studies which take place within more controlled environments have high internal validity, but they may be so far removed from everyday reality that their external validity is low. Very seldom does a design achieve high levels of both internal and external validity. In most cases social scientists tend to design studies which have either high internal or external validity and then compare with other studies in the same area which have high validity on the other dimension.

EXERCISES

1. What is the weakness of using a comparison group instead of a control group and what is the role of random assignment?
2. Take any of the research problems or hypotheses mentioned in earlier chapters and develop a couple of different research designs that could be used. Compare and contrast the advantages and disadvantages of the different designs you have chosen.
3. Explain the role of history, maturation, and test effect in a pre-test/post-test design, and how these biases do not affect a time-series design.
4. Develop an example similar to the ones presenting in this chapter. Apply the pre-test/post-test and time series designs. Which are the relative advantages and disadvantages of the two designs?
5. Complete the following table:

Design	Advantages	Disadvantages
One-shot case study		
Pre-test/Post-test design		
Intact group comparison design		
Contrasted group design		
Time-series design		
Pre-test/post-test control group design		
Post-test only control group design		
Factorial designs		

CHAPTER 8

Sampling

The purpose of this chapter is to introduce the concept of sampling. Why is it advantageous in research to restrict the investigation to a small but well chosen group of subjects (the sample) that represent a much wider group (the population)? How is it possible to sample in such a way as to be able to generalize the results obtained from a sample to the whole population? What are the different methods of sampling, their strengths and weaknesses? What could be the biases or other errors introduced at the sampling stage of the research process? These are some of the questions discussed in this chapter.

CHAPTER OBJECTIVES

Learners who have completed this chapter will be able to:
- Discuss the rationale for and difficulties associated with sampling.
- Compare probability and non probability sampling.
- Identify and evaluate the sampling method used in any study.
- Select the most appropriate sampling method for a particular research problem.
- Carry out the sampling procedures required by a selected method.

THE PURPOSE OF SAMPLING AND TYPES OF SAMPLING

How does one judge that the customer service of Bank A is better than that of Bank B, that Shop C is better equipped than its competitor D, or that a shirt of Make X is of higher quality than a shirt of Make Y? Judgement is usually based on experience, either personal or reported by others. One may observe how many times and how long customers have to wait in a bank before being attended to; how often an item was found in Shop D when it was not available in Shop C, and so on. On the basis of few observations one generalizes, or infers, properties of the whole. One draws conclusions.

Sampling theory is the scientific foundation of this everyday practice. It is a technical accounting device to rationalize the collection of information, to choose in an appropriate way the restricted set of objects, persons, events and so forth from which the actual information will be drawn.

Without doubt, if one wants to collect accurate information about a group of persons or objects, the best strategy is to examine every single member or element of the group. But it is also possible to reach accurate conclusions by examining only a portion of the total group. This assessment of only a portion of the group is commonly used in both the social and natural sciences. Medical assessments of blood characteristics of a patient are done after analysis of just a few drops of blood. Similarly, the interviewing of just a few students can allow an inference about the attitudes of the whole class towards a particular lecturer. Admittedly, many factors might reduce the accuracy of the results based on a small section of the whole group, but these are not of immediate concern and will be dealt with later.

The entire set of objects or people which is the focus of the research and about which the researcher wants to determine some characteristics is called the **population** (or the universe). It could be a population of all cars assembled at a factory during 1995, all houses in a town, or all primary school teachers in a country at a specific time. The subset of the whole population which is actually investigated by a researcher and whose characteristics will be generalized to the entire population is called the **sample**. A sample could consist of every tenth car produced in a factory, every fiftieth house in a town, or 100 primary school teachers selected from a list of trade-union members. In these samples, a car, a house or one primary school teacher constitutes an element or **unit of analysis**. Specific values or quantities that relate to the population, such as the average age of all primary school teachers, are called **population parameters**. The corresponding values or quantities that relate to the sample, such as the average age of the 100 teachers constituting the sample, are called **sample statistics** or simply **statistics**. Statistics are estimates of population parameters.

Sampling theory is in fact the study of the relationship between a population and the samples drawn from it. Since the aim of research is to determine some characteristics of a certain population, one of the objectives of sampling is to draw inferences about the unknown population parameters from the known sample statistics. These are obtained by collecting data from the sample. The process of generalizing from findings based on the sample to the population is called **statistical inference**. (The study of techniques of statistical inference constitutes the main objective of the other book in this series.)

Sampling means abandoning *certainty* in favour of *probability*. Because a large part of the population has not been investigated, statements made about the population on the basis of what has been found to be true for the sample are, of necessity, probability statements. One is aware of introducing possible error by asserting that the units which had not actually been studied would produce the same results as those studied. Here probability is understood as the likelihood of an event happening, an element being found, or a statement being true. An example of a probability statement is: If the average age of a sample of primary school teachers is 34 years, the average age of the whole population of teachers probably lies between 32 and 36 years. If the sampling, or selection of a sample, is correctly and carefully carried out, the margin of error can be accurately calculated in many instances.

The main *advantages of sampling*, as compared to the collection of data on the whole population, are the following:

1. Gathering data on a sample is less time-consuming. If a student population numbers 4 000 it would take a researcher at least 4 000 hours to conduct a one-hour interview with each student. It would take only 200 hours, or 5% of the time, to interview a sample of 200 students.

2. Gathering data on a sample is less costly since the costs of research are proportional to the number of hours spent on data collection. Moreover, a large population may be spread over a large geographical area, involving high travel expenses. Such expenses are likely to be reduced by reducing the number of respondents to be studied. Other expenses such as the cost of reproducing data collection instruments like questionnaires are also reduced.

3. Sampling may be the only practical method of data collection. This is the case in studies where the property under investigation necessitates the destruction of the object. When testing the resistance of an object to wear and tear, such as testing the lifespan of an electric light bulb, one must wait till the bulb is "dead". It would be inadvisable to test an entire population, for example, the annual output of a light bulb plant, as the plant would have no bulbs left to sell. This is called destructive sampling. Therefore testing can only be conducted on a sample population.
4. Sampling is a practical way of collecting data when the population is infinite or extremely large, thus making a study of all its elements impossible.

The limitations and weaknesses of sampling will be discussed separately for each type of sampling, and again in the discussion of sampling errors at the end of this chapter.

MAIN SAMPLING CONCEPTS

Good sampling implies:

1. a well-defined population;
2. an adequately chosen sample, and
3. an estimate of how representative of the whole population the sample is, that is, how well in terms of probability the sample statistics conform to the unknown population parameters.

This last topic will be introduced here but not elaborated upon. (For more detail refer to the second book in this series.)

A well-defined population

As mentioned above, a population, sometimes referred to as a "target population", is the set of elements that the research focuses upon and to which the results obtained by testing the sample should be generalized. It is absolutely essential to describe accurately the target population. This can effectively be done by clearly defining the properties to be analysed, using an operational definition. Once this is done it should be possible to compile a list of all elements of this population or, at least, to determine whether or not an element belongs to the population under investigation. In this sense the population will be well-defined.

e.g.

In defining the student population of a university, it would not be adequate to draw a list of students living on campus. Such a list would exclude students residing off campus and part-time students. An attendance list of students at lectures will not constitute a population either, as it excludes correspondence students and absentees. The population will only be clearly determined when the term "student" is given an operational definition, for example, "a person who is registered at a university for the purposes of studying", or more narrowly, "a person who studies full-time on the premises of a university". It is important to note that the results obtained on a sample drawn on the basis of the narrow definition of a student cannot be generalized to the broader student population which includes part-time and correspondence students. This is an error often made and overlooked.

Once an operational definition is given, boundary conditions are established which make it easy to ascertain whether or not an element belongs to a population. A sample can then be easily selected from the population.

Although social scientists are often involved in constructing samples from populations of human beings, there are many other possibilities as well. Consider the economist who is interested in economic indicators over an extended period of time. She will sample from a population of dates. A historian interested in a particular person's life story might use a sample drawn from the population of all the person's written correspondence. A geographer might work with a sample of water catchment areas while a theologian might look at the attendance at a sample of different churches. Whatever the unit that comprises a particular population, the same basic sampling methods apply.

The sample

Although a subset of the population, the sample must have properties which make it representative of the whole. To follow up the example of the students, selecting a sample of very dull, brilliant or mature students would be wrong because they would not represent the whole of the student body. Thus one of the major issues in sampling is to determine samples that best represent a population so as to allow for an accurate generalization of results. Such a group is called a **representative sample**.

The first means of ensuring a representative sample is the use of a complete and correct **sampling frame**. This is the list of all units from which the sample is to be drawn. To use a telephone directory for selecting a sample would be wrong as it would include only people owning a phone. Such a sample could never be representative of an urban population in a developing country. It might at best represent high-income urbanites, but usually not even that. An inadequate sampling frame that discards parts of the target population has been the cause of many poor research results. Particular care must be taken to avoid this pitfall.

It must therefore be stressed that an adequate sampling frame should exclude no element of the population under investigation. An even stricter requirement would be that all elements of the population have the same chance of being drawn into the sample or, at least, that this probability can be specified. In consequence, sampling theory distinguishes between probability or random sampling and non-probability sampling.

Probability or **random sampling** occurs when the probability of including each element of the population can be determined. It is thus possible to estimate the extent to which the findings based on the sample are likely to differ from what would have been found by studying the whole population. In other words, the researcher can estimate the accuracy of the generalization from sample to population.

Non-probability sampling refers to the case where the probability of including each element of the population in a sample is unknown. It is not possible to determine the likelihood of the inclusion of all representative elements of the population into the sample. Some elements might even have no chance of being included in the sample. It is thus difficult to estimate how well the sample represents the population and this makes generalization highly questionable.

Probability samples are of a much higher quality because, when properly constructed, they are representative of the population. Although it is difficult to determine the extent to which non-probability samples are representative of the population, they have some practical advantages. When the necessary population lists are not available non-probability sampling remains a possibility for the researcher. Also, non-probability sampling is almost always cheaper, faster and quite adequate for homogenous populations. Finally, it should be noted that to some extent, the disadvantages of non-probability sampling can be reduced by enlarging the sample. Non-probability sampling is thus frequently used in the social sciences.

Sampling

In the following section, the most common sampling procedures will be examined. These are:

1. Probability sampling, which includes:
   (a) simple random sampling,
   (b) interval or systematic sampling,
   (c) stratified sampling, and
   (d) cluster or multi-stage sampling.
2. Non-probability sampling, which includes:
   (a) accidental or availability sampling,
   (b) purposive or judgemental sampling, and
   (c) quota sampling.

TYPES OF PROBABILITY SAMPLING

Simple random sampling

Firstly, it is important to clarify what is meant by "random" since, in everyday language, it is often used to mean "accidental". It is not random to choose the first ten students who enter a lecture theatre, or students sitting in the front row. Neither is it random to choose ten students with average test results. In all these cases, some underlying criteria were used to select the samples which might have properties peculiar to them. For example, the first students arriving for the lecture may be the most dedicated ones. The ones sitting in the front row may have poor sight or may want to attract the attention of the lecturer. Even the sample of "average" students does not represent the heterogeneity of the student population. Random expresses the idea of chance being the only criterion for selection. Thus, the selection of an element from a population is called random when the chance, likelihood or probability of being chosen for the sample, can be calculated for each element of the population.

Accordingly, simple random sampling is a sampling procedure which provides equal opportunity of selection for each element in a population.

There are various techniques for selecting randomly. The most common are the lottery techniques, where a symbol for each unit of the population is placed in a container, mixed well and then the "lucky numbers" drawn that constitute the sample. The symbol for each unit of the population can be names of participants, written on identical pieces of paper, or a number assigned to each participant. Of course, sample size must be established beforehand, otherwise one would not know how many "symbols" to draw.

A more sophisticated method, particularly useful for large populations, is the use of **random number tables** or electronic number generators. Random number tables are found in many books on research methodology and most spreadsheet programmes and even some calculators have random number generators, all of which are based on mathematical processes.

A section of a random number table is included below:

98	08	62	48	26		45	24	02	84	04
33	81	51	62	32		41	94	15	09	49
80	95	10	04	06		96	38	37	07	74
79	75	24	91	40		71	96	12	82	96
18	63	33	25	37		98	14	50	65	71

(Excerpt from Blalock, 1972, p 555)

Suppose that from a population of 500 units a sample of 50 units is to be randomly drawn. The first task is to number all 500 units consecutively, from 001 to 500. These being 3-digit numbers, one should select any three adjacent digits and, reading row or column-wise, write down 50 numbers under the value of 500. To use the random figures given above in the table, one would start with the first three digits in the first row — 9,

8, 0 — and continue down the column. The result would be:

980, 338, 809, 797, 186, followed by, 862, 151, 510, etc.

Underlined numbers represent selected units of the population. Numbers higher than 500 are ignored because the population consists of only 500 units.

Instead of starting with the first column in the first set of figures one could begin, for example, with the third column of the second set of figures and arrive at:

028, 150, 370, 128, 506, thereafter 404, 949, 774, etc.

This would result in a different, but equally randomly selected sample, and the end result would be similar. Alternatively, one could proceed across instead of down, with the result:

980, 862, 482, 645, 240, 284, 043, 381, 516, etc.

or,

980, 862, 482, 633, 815, 162, 328, 095, 100, etc.,

all achieving a sample selected totally at random. Note that if a number occurs twice it is ignored, as a unit can only be selected once.

Assuming, as a further example, a population size of 25 217 from which a sample of 300 must be selected, one proceeds in the same manner. This time 5-digit (instead of 3-digit numbers) are used and figures greater than 25 217 are excluded.

98 086, 24 826, 45 240, 28 404, 33 815, 16 232, 41 941

The use of electronic random number generators is equally effective and more commonly used today. In the same way as for tables, the units of the population are numbered. The random number generator is set to produce random numbers smaller than or equal to the total number of units in the population. As many numbers as are required in the sample can be generated in this way. A researcher who constructs a sample in this manner is using simple random sampling, where all the units of the analysis have the *same* probability of inclusion in the sample.

The use of random numbers is very reliable and the techniques are simple. However, they are limited by their reliance on the existence of a complete list of all the elements of the population. This condition is often not met in actual life situations. Population censuses in less industrialized countries are seldom up to date. The same is true for lists of traditional midwives, small scale enterprises, groundnut growers, and so on. The danger of incomplete or biased lists must be emphasized. Moreover, if the population is very large, the randomization process may be very time consuming.

Interval or Systematic Sampling

This type of sampling is very similar to the previous one. This technique, instead of relying on random numbers, is based on the selection of elements at equal intervals, starting with a randomly selected element on the population list.

In the example of selecting 50 units out of a population of 500, the length k of the intervals is determined by the following ratio.

$$k = \frac{500}{50} = 10$$

i.e. $k = \dfrac{N}{n}$

$$= \frac{\text{Size of population}}{\text{Size of sample}}$$

(Note that the symbol N represents the number of units of analysis in the population, while the symbol n represents the number of units in the sample).

Sampling

In this example every tenth unit should be selected for the sample. The starting element should be any number between 1 and 10, or in the general case between 1 and k. Thus, if the starting element selected is 4, the 50 sample elements will be 4, 14, 24, 34, 44, . . . , 484, 494. This sampling procedure is simpler and quicker than the use of random numbers. It would be most convenient, say, when undertaking research that involves sampling houses in a town. Following a pre-chosen street, and having determined the size k of the interval, one can select every k-th house for the sample.

Unfortunately, this method also has constraints. Like simple random sampling it relies on the availability of a complete, unbiased population list. Moreover, this list must not have any cyclical or periodic characteristics. This can be clarified using the previous example. If, at regular intervals along the predetermined street, there are houses with peculiarities such as corner houses containing shops, one should compare the length of this interval with k. If the two intervals coincide, the consequence may be that too many corner-houses with shops, or none at all, are selected for the sample. In both cases the sample will not accurately represent the population, but give a distorted image of it. An even more trivial mistake would be to adopt a 6-day observation cycle when comparing the volume of sales in different supermarkets: Mondays in shop A, Tuesdays in shop B . . . Saturdays in shop F. Surely, the large difference in sales between shops A and F can be attributed more to the Saturday shopping habits of people than to intrinsic properties of the shops.

Thus, when a peculiar regularity is detected in a list and the peculiarity coincides with the size of the interval k, the list should either be rewritten to avoid this regularity or another method of sampling should be adopted.

Stratified random sampling

As mentioned previously, simple random sampling, and even systematic sampling in its purest form, are seldom used in social sciences research because they are cumbersome for large populations. But they become useful tools when used as part of other random sampling techniques, such as stratified and cluster sampling. More about cluster sampling later.

The principle of stratified random sampling is to divide a population into different groups, called strata, so that each element of the population belongs to one and only one stratum. Then, within each stratum, random sampling is performed using either the simple or the interval sampling method. Although many samplings are performed, each is done for a relatively small population only. This increases the availability of adequate lists and facilitates selection of a simple random sample without decreasing the quality of the sample in any way.

e.g.

Assume that research on the attitudes of a rural population towards co-operative production is to be conducted. The size of the rural adult population is 8 000. It is expected that attitudes will vary with sex and age of participants. The composition of the population regarding these two variables (sex and age) is:

Table 8.1
Stratified sample

Age	Females	Males
20–40	2 000	1 500
Over 40	2 500	2 000
Total	4 500	3 500

A random sample of 500 people is to be drawn, taking into account the differences in age and sex. Since the proportions of the different strata within the sample must be the same as for the population, the size of each stratum must be calculated in proportion to the total population. The ratio of sample to population is given by:

$$f = \frac{n}{N} = \frac{\text{size of the sample}}{\text{size of the population}}$$

In the present example:

$$f = \frac{500}{8\,000} = \frac{1}{16}$$

Each category of the population must be multiplied by this fraction to obtain the corresponding category of the sample. The results are as follows:

	Population		Sample	
Age	Females	Males	Females	Males
20–40	25%	18.75%	125	93,75
> 40	31.25%	25%	156,25	125

Rounding off 156,25 to 156 and 93,75 to 94, one checks that the total size of the sample is 281 + 219 which equals 500.

The next step of the procedure is to use a simple random or systematic sampling method to draw the different samples: a sample of 94 males out of the stratum of 1 500 males between 20 and 40 years, and a sample of 125 males out of the 2 000 men of 40 years and older, and so on. The last step is to combine all individuals of the four subsamples to form the desired sample of 500 persons who are to represent the total population of adult rural dwellers in the attitudinal study.

To clarify the advantage of stratifying a population, an extreme case is given. Suppose that, using the previous example, it is suspected that men are strongly opposed to co-operatives while women vigorously support them. Suppose also that the population is very heterogenous and that due to urbanization, men constitute only 10% of the population. In other words, out of the population of 8 000 people, 800 are men and 7 200 are women. When selecting a sample of, say, 100 out of this population, using simple random sampling, chance factors may strongly distort the proportions of men and women. For such a small sample it is possible that only four men (4%) are selected out of the 800 men, and 96 women out of the 7 200 women. This gross under representation of men will heavily distort overall research results and the finding will be that the total adult population of region X is strongly in favour of co-operatives, which does not reflect reality. The distortion is caused by the sampling method, in this instance simple random sampling. (Note that only for very large samples can one be assured that the composition of the population will be reflected in the sample when simple random sampling is used).

Stratified sampling, on the other hand, by preserving proportions even of very small samples, will allow for any small minority to be properly represented. Of course, if the population is very homogenous, with no marked opinion difference between sexes, or if both sexes are fairly equally represented (48% vs 52%, for instance), simple random and stratified sampling will lead to about the same results.

Because even stratified random sampling presupposes a definite population with a known composition, the correct choice of the criteria for stratification is crucial. However, it permits great accuracy even for small samples, which reduces the cost of sampling considerably.

Cluster or multi-stage sampling

One of the major constraints common to simple random, systematic and stratified sampling is the availability of complete lists of elements or units. Often such complete lists do not exist. Possibly a list has been compiled or could easily be compiled at district or village level. For example, each

Sampling

school may have an up-to-date list of pupils, but no national list may be available. A village headman can help in compiling a list of all widows or orphans in the village, but such information is very seldom found in a birth-and-death register at national level. At grass roots level, many small income-generating groups may have been formed, more or less structured, more or less temporary, but few may be registered as co-operatives or members of a union. The great majority of such groups remain informal and are known only within their direct environment. For these cases another type of sampling must be used.

The principle underlying multi-stage sampling is to start by sampling a population which is much more general than the final one. In a second stage, on the basis of the first sample, a new population is considered, one which is less general than the first one, and a new sample is subsequently determined. The procedure is continued until the population to be investigated is reached and a final sample is drawn. At each stage, sampling is done in a random way, using one of the three previously mentioned sampling techniques.

e.g.

Suppose that a researcher would like to investigate the health conditions of orphans aged below 10 years in the whole country, using a sample of 500 orphans. It is unlikely that a list of all these orphans in the country exists and so cluster sampling must be used. The researcher should follow the following steps:

1. Obtain a list of all the districts in the country (level one). Use simple random sampling to select five districts.
2. For each of the five districts selected get a list of party wards (level two). Use simple random sampling to identify five party wards in each district. This will produce a total list of 25 party wards.
3. For each of the 25 party wards get a list of party branches (level three). Use simple random sampling to identify ten branches in each ward. This will produce a total list of 250 party branches.
4. At branch level it should be possible with the help of branch authorities to compile a list of all the orphans under ten years of age (level four) living in each branch's area. Use simple random sampling to select two orphans from each branch, thereby producing a final list of 500 orphans as required.

In summary, the clusters considered in this example were districts, party wards, party branches and then orphans. The elements of each population are qualitatively different (geographical areas, administrative units and human beings) but decreasing in their generality. Preceding units contain subsequent units. The specification of each unit and its corresponding sample constitutes a stage and each stage is characterized by a random sample. In this case there are four stages.

The advantage of multi-stage sampling goes beyond its application when other sampling methods fail due to a lack of complete lists of elements of a population under investigation. Even if a complete list of populations can be compiled directly, multi-stage sampling can cut down expenses firstly by reducing the cost of compiling long lists and, secondly, by reducing the travel expenditure necessary when respondents are spread over a large area. In fact, if a complete list of orphans were available and a simple random sample of 500 was selected, these 500 orphans would be spread all over the country. This would mean high travel costs and great loss of time. A cluster sampling, by selecting only a few geographical areas (five districts), reduces travel costs and time and permits careful planning of the data-collection process.

TYPES OF NON-PROBABILITY SAMPLING

Accidental or availability sampling

This sampling method, the most rudimentary one, consists of taking all cases on hand until the sample reaches the desired size. The interviewer will choose, for instance, a convenient place where he is assured of finding many people: a supermarket, a bus-stop, or a bar. Obviously, this can introduce serious biases, as men will be over-represented in bars, and old and wealthy people will be under-represented at bus-stops. Taxi drivers, waiting at a stand for customers, would welcome a chat with the interviewer but might not be representative of a population. Students are the usual "guinea-pigs" of social scientists though still not representative of the whole population. This makes generalization based on such samples extremely risky, although the samples so chosen are convenient for researchers in terms of time and money.

Purposive or judgemental sampling

This sampling method is based on the judgement of a researcher regarding the characteristics of a representative sample. A sample is chosen on the basis of what the researcher considers to be typical units. The strategy is to select units that are judged to be the most common in the population under investigation. For instance, a typical school pupil may be thought of as being: "12 years old, male, Catholic and having parents in a clerical profession". Only students meeting these criteria will be chosen for the sample.

The great danger in this type of sampling is that it relies more heavily on the subjective considerations of the researcher than on objective criteria. Although it has some value, especially if used by an expert who knows the population under study, this technique often leads to non-representative samples.

Quota sampling

This sampling method could be considered as being the non-probability equivalent of stratified sampling. The purpose here is to draw a sample that has the same proportions of characteristics as the population. However, the sampling procedure, instead of relying on random selection, relies on accidental choice.

Suppose that the population under study is estimated to consist of 40% men, 25% of whom are above 40 years and 15% of whom are between 20 and 40 years, and, of the 60% female population, 30% are in each of the above age groups. If one intends to draw a sample of 200, one will interview people in each category as they come (that is, by using accidental sampling) until one has gathered a group of 80 men (40% of 200) of whom 50 are above 40 years and 30 between 20 and 40 years. The female subsample consists of 120 women, 60 in each age category. This sample will also be drawn by interviewing any available woman in each of the desired categories, stopping the interviewing process when the desired number of women in a particular age category has been reached.

	Population		Sample	
Age	Male	Female	Male	Female
20–40	15%	30%	30	60
> 40	25%	30%	50	60
	40%	60%		

If, for some reason, one group is incomplete, for instance if one could find only 30 women above 40 years instead of 60, the researcher would weight the result of this group by multiplying it by two. In other words, the inadequacy of the sample can be corrected in the analysis by *weighting* the results of different strata in terms of their proportions of the population. Although much less accurate than stratified sampling, which is a random sample, this method is often more convenient and economical. No lists must be compiled and all data can be collected at an arbitrary location.

OTHER TYPES OF SAMPLING
Sampling with or without replacement

This refers mainly to simple random sampling techniques where selected elements can, or cannot, appear twice in a sample. In the former, one speaks of **sampling with replacement**, that is, the drawn element is replaced among the other elements of the population and can thus be drawn a second time. The latter refers to **sampling without replacement**.

A finite population sampled with replacement can theoretically be considered as infinite, since any number of samples can be drawn without exhausting the population. If the size of the sample is small (less than 5% of a population) the chance of including the same element more than once in a sample is also quite small. Thus, in this case, the characteristics of sampling without replacement closely approximate those with replacement. Finally, if the population is infinite, sampling with or without replacement will produce identical results.

Independent versus related/dependent samples

As already mentioned in Chapter 7 when dealing with randomization of groups, two or more groups or samples might have been selected in such a way as to make them independent. Each unit is drawn randomly from the population and is also randomly assigned to one or the other group. Groups formed in this way constitute **independent samples**. Alternatively, groups or samples can be related, usually when their elements have been matched on specific properties. In such cases they are called **related** or **dependent samples**.

e.g.
A researcher wishes to draw two samples of men and women from a large corporation's workforce. However, in her study she wishes to control for age and seniority within the company. Therefore, she must find pairs of men and women who have similar ages and seniority within the company. In other words, they are the same for the variables she wishes to control (age and seniority) but differ in terms of the variable that she is studying (sex). Two senior managers both aged 43, one being male and the other female would be such a pair. Similarly two 20 year old entry level people would also be a pair if one was male and the other female.

When researchers draw up samples in this way, every member of the sample has a partner somewhere else in the study and so the samples can no longer be thought of as independent of each other. They are related or dependent.

SAMPLE SIZE

A very important issue in sampling is to determine the most adequate size of the sample. A large sample is more representative but very costly. A small sample, on the other hand, is much less accurate but more convenient. A census, which is a survey of the whole population, will be more accurate than a survey using a restricted sample, but it will be very expensive and its results may take so long to analyse that they become outdated.

The major criterion to use when deciding on sample size is the extent to which the sample is representative of the population. This can be expressed in terms of probability. One usually expects to have a 95% chance that the sample is distributed in the same way as the population. Formulae exist for determining a sample size which satisfies such a given level of probability, but fall beyond the scope of this book. One can, at least, note that the more heterogeneous a population is, the larger the sample must be to cover correctly the characteristics of the population. Thus, the "rule of thumb" for choosing a sample size that is five per cent of the population remains quite an inaccurate guide-line, though certainly usable when precise formulae are lacking.

SAMPLING ERRORS AND RELATED PROBLEMS

As has been repeatedly mentioned, the purpose of sampling theory is to select samples which reproduce as closely as possible the characteristics of a population. This aim is never completely achieved due to two types of error. The sampling errors of the first type are those due to **chance factors**. It may happen that, in a particular sample, one element and not another has been included. These sampling errors can be calculated statistically and are studied in detail in the other book in this series. Note that this type of error is an inevitable result of sampling and can never be completely eliminated.

Among the sampling errors of the second type are those due to **bias in selection**, arising primarily from faulty technique. These biases are frequently avoidable. They may or may not be deliberate. For example, an interviewer may fail to take into account one criterion, such as the age of respondents, or the respondents themselves may give incorrect information about their age. Some strata of a population may be over- or under-represented in a sample. For example, a sample that contains 50% rural and 50% urban respondents would under-represent the rural population and over-represent the urban population of virtually all less industrialized countries today.

Even when a representative sample has been drawn, a very important source of bias is due to **non-response error**. This type of error comes about when an element of the sample does not respond to a measurement instrument for some unknown reason. As a consequence such elements are excluded from the group, a move which changes the constitution, and thus the representativeness, of the sample. There are many reasons for non-response. Firstly, it may not be possible to interview or test a person because of illness, language difficulty, or other factors. Secondly, it may be that the chosen respondents cannot be found because of changes in residence or name, or because of death. Thirdly, the selected person may be absent whenever the interviewer calls, purely by chance. Lastly, the person can refuse to collaborate and not answer questions or give information.

The issue of biases related to the sample will be discussed again in Chapter 12 when all possible sources of bias in research are dealt with.

Sampling

EXERCISES

1. What is the rationale for using samples? Do you agree that samples should be used only when it is impossible to obtain a complete list of a population?
2. Explain the difference between probability and non-probability sampling, and in particular, between:
   (a) simple random sampling and accidental sampling, and
   (b) stratified sampling and quota sampling.
3. In conducting a survey, interviewers are instructed to single out 400 respondents, 160 of them urban and 240 rural, because the population of 12 000 is split 40/60% between urban and rural areas. It is indicated that the rural population is stratified by sex in the proportion of 3 200 men and 4 000 women; in the urban population there are 2 000 women and 2 800 men.
   (a) Which sampling procedure(s) would give the best results? Explain why.
   (b) Calculate the strata required for a sample of 400 people, where stratified random sampling is to be used.
4. Using the table of random numbers on page 87, draw a sample of 5 units from a population of 270.
5. How would you conduct a multi-stage sampling in the capital city of your country in order to obtain a sample of 100 unemployed young men aged 14–18 years? How would you proceed using accidental sampling? Analyse the biases introduced by using this last method.
6. In order to find out about commonly bought food and household items in a town, a researcher stands at the check-out counter of the town's largest supermarket for two days (Mondays and Tuesdays), for one month. All items bought by every fourth customer are recorded. Identify the type of sampling used and discuss the adequacy or biases inherent in this method.
7. A representative sample of 1 000 people in a town must be obtained for an investigation into reading habits. Which of the following methods of obtaining the sample is most appropriate, and why? Why are the others less appropriate?
   (a) Choosing 1000 names from the telephone directory.
   (b) Stopping people at random outside a mainline bus station.
   (c) Asking 10 libraries to supply 100 names.
   (d) Asking 1000 university students to participate in the study.
   (e) Standing outside libraries and asking 1 000 people to be involved in the study.
   (f) Since none of the above would give rise to a representative sample, what sampling procedure would you develop to take into account all the different groups within the total population?

CHAPTER 9

Data Collection: Basic Concepts

A research project stands or falls on the quality of the facts on which it is based. An excellent research design and a very representative sample are not sufficient to ensure good results if the analysis rests on incorrect data. The importance of constructing an appropriate and accurate instrument for measuring and collecting data is an absolute necessity. But, before dealing with different techniques of data collection, some basic concepts must be discussed: in particular, the different scales of measurement. These depend on the type of research and the type of data being collected. Finally, social scientists should never forget their obligations to research participants from whom information is sought and obtained. Since, through data collection, the researcher comes into direct contact with other human beings, it is of prime importance that attention is drawn to some ethical considerations concerning the rights of the participants.

CHAPTER OBJECTIVES

The learner who has successfully completed this chapter will be able to:
- Identify and use in an appropriate way the various scales of measurement.
- Apply the appropriate ethical standards to the process of data collection.

FACTS, DATA AND MEASUREMENT

Facts are empirically verifiable observations. Data consists of measurements collected as a result of scientific observations. In other words, data are facts expressed in the language of measurement. Here the word measurement is used in its general sense and need not necessarily be expressed numerically. For example, one can measure the intensity of an attitude or feeling. A person's views on an educational reform could be positive, neutral or negative. The fact that this person takes a definite position towards an issue becomes data once it is expressed as a measurement.

Data can be classified according to the way in which it was collected or in terms of its intrinsic properties.

When researchers collect their own data for the purpose of a particular study, the data is called **primary** data. Data collected in this way is most appropriate to the aims of the research, since the data gathering is directed towards answering precisely the questions raised by the researcher. Very often, however, researchers must use data collected by other investigators in connection with other research problems, or as part of the usual gathering of social data as in the case of a population census. Such data constitutes **secondary data**. The adequacy of such data for a particular research problem may not be very good, since the purpose of its collection might have been slightly different to that of the present research. The data might also have been based on different operational definitions and little may be known of other possible biases in the data collection, such as sampling biases. Thus, when research is based on the analysis of secondary data, great care must be taken in its interpretation. (See the record method in Chapter 10.)

As mentioned earlier, data consists of facts expressed in the language of measurement. The type of measurement used is closely related to the type of facts. The size of a table can be expressed in number of centimetres, resulting in **quantitative data**. The colour of a table can be described by its quality of being red-brown, dark-brown or white, which constitutes an example of **qualitative data**. Some properties of objects, persons or events cannot be quantified. This may be due to their nature, or the present nonavailability of adequate measuring instruments. In some cases quantitative measurements would be meaningless to the research, for example, describing the colour of a table by its wavelength. Whether data is quantitative or qualitative is very important since it determines how data can be utilized. The tendency exists to consider numerical (quantitative) data as more reliable and easier to utilize, in particular by statistical techniques, than qualitative data. However, science is inconceivable without non-numerical data to assist in interpreting numerical data. The disregard of qualitative information would lead to an incomplete description of social reality. Moreover, in specific areas of social reality, purely qualitative research is often the most adequate method of investigation, and involves sophisticated techniques which are beyond the scope of this book.

SCALES OF MEASUREMENT

Quantitative measurements can be compared in terms of magnitude (for example, comparing the size of two buildings, measured in metres). A broader aspect of measurement is expressed by the type of scales used to measure things: the sets of rules utilized for quantifying (assigning numerical scores), or for classifying a particular variable. The type of scale is determined by the presence or absence of three properties.

1. The existence of *magnitude*, which is the possibility of comparing different amounts or intensities so as to assess whether two values or levels of a variable are the same, or one is lesser or greater than the other.
2. The existence of *equal intervals*, which allows magnitude to be expressed by a certain number of units on a scale, all units on the scale being equal by definition.
3. The existence of an *absolute zero*, which is a value indicating that the measurement of a variable is meaningless in circumstances in which the variable is non-existent.

On the basis of these three properties, four different measurement scales exist: nominal, ordinal, interval and ratio scales.

Nominal scales are the most rudimentary. They name rather than measure. They simply classify information into categories or groups. These categories cannot be compared to one another as they are qualitatively different. Thus, nominal scales do not satisfy any of the three properties outlined above. When classifying the variable "sex" into the two categories of "male" and "female", one uses a nominal scale. The same is true when measuring the marital status of respondents (single, married, divorced, widowed) or the tribe, region or country of origin of respondents. Even feelings can be classified using nominal scales: a person is happy, sad, angry, and so on.

Ordinal scales are more complex and informative than nominal scales. They allow comparison and establish rank-order

Data Collection: Basic Concepts

between different values of a variable. It is thus possible to state that one value is greater or less than another. The feelings of a respondent are not just classified into happy or unhappy, but into very happy, happy, indifferent, unhappy, and very unhappy, thus enabling the comparison between degrees of happiness of different persons. Of course, this type of measurement still does not allow one to assess that person A is twice as happy as person B, because, even though a relative magnitude can be given to the feelings of persons A and B, there exists no unit to measure them. Thus, only one property of scales is present, that of magnitude. Other examples of variables measured on the ordinal scale are the grade a student gets on an essay, or the tax bracket into which a person falls.

Interval scales are an improvement over both nominal and ordinal scales in the sense that a comparison between different values of a variable is made more accurate by the introduction of equal intervals or units of measurement. For example, after the concept of "employment" has been operationalized, a person is classified as employed or unemployed on a nominal scale; employed full-time, employed part-time or unemployed on an ordinal scale; employed for a certain number of hours per week on a scale possessing equal intervals (one hour). In the last case, a person employed for forty hours a week is employed twice as long as a person working only twenty hours a week. Here the unit underlying the scale is the hour. Typical examples of interval scales are all the scales based on the set of real numbers. For example, the money owned by somebody could be US $3 000 (or Rands, Kwacha, Shillings), another person could be US$1 500 in debt, which is expressed by a negative number (US –$1 500). Note that this scale has magnitude as well as equal units of measurement, values of 0 as well as negative amounts are all meaningful. In other words, this scale has no absolute zero.

Ratio scales possess the three properties of magnitude, equal intervals and an absolute zero. A person can be 22 years old but nobody is minus 5 years old. Before birth, which in this case is the absolute zero, age does not exist and therefore cannot be measured. The unit or equal interval is the year, so that a comparison between a 40-year-old father and his 20-year-old daughter can be made. The father is twice as old as the daughter. As a further illustration, consider the performance of students, as measured during their period of schooling. The performance as shown in writing an essay is measured with an ordinal scale by letters like A – excellent, to E = failure. But suppose that the students are asked to write a multiple-choice test. In this case, a point is attributed to each correct answer and the performance of a student is expressed by the number of points achieved (with one per cent as the unit). In this case a number below zero is meaningless as zero denotes total failure. The scale used is thus a ratio scale.

Note that when using a nominal or ordinal scale the researcher is classifying subjects by placing them into different categories. Interval or ratio scales on the other hand, demand that a score is taken from each subject. This difference is crucial when the researcher begins to analyze quantitative data using statistical methods (Refer to the other book in this series.)

RELATIONSHIP BETWEEN TYPE OF RESEARCH AND METHOD OF DATA COLLECTION

In Chapter 5, different types of research were discussed. Some methods of data collection were mentioned, among them observation, use of questionnaires or interviews, and the use of more sophisticated instruments. It was noted that the same method of collecting data can be used for different types of research. Observation is at the core of case studies, but also of field experiments. Questionnaires can be used to explore or describe a situation, but also to assess a correlation between two variables. In other words, the same method of data gathering can be adapted to different types of research, provided that the research design and the way the collected data will be analysed are directly related to the chosen type of research.

It is important to note that many variables can be measured using more than one type of scale. For example, while it is possible to categorize each family in a village as living above or below a set "poverty line" (that is, an ordinal scale), it is also possible to measure the exact income of each family (thereby using a ratio scale). In fact, if the researcher allows for the fact that families might be in debt, the scale would be an interval one. The choice of scale depends upon the nature of the research question as well as what is possible in a particular research situation.

ETHICAL CONSIDERATIONS RELATED TO DATA COLLECTION: THE RIGHTS OF RESEARCH PARTICIPANTS

Throughout the process of data collection the problem of persuading participants to co-operate with the researcher is ever present. Lack of co-operation leads to non-response, to incompletely filled-out questionnaires, and to unreliable results. While lack of co-operation can be disastrous in a research project, participants have the *right* to refuse to participate. This is a right that researchers must respect. Generally accepted ethical rights of participants which a social scientist should respect are discussed below.

Right to privacy and voluntary participation

Social research often invades a person's privacy. An interviewer may want information of a private nature or a scientist may need to observe people in situations that are harmful, or at least uncomfortable, to participants. People should not be subjected to research of such a nature unless they agree to it. Participation in research must be voluntary and people can refuse to divulge certain information about themselves. This right to privacy demands that direct consent for participation must be obtained from adults and, in the case of children, from their parents or guardians. Moreover, this consent must be informed, in the sense that the participant must be aware of the positive or negative aspects or consequences of participation. The research may involve stress, discomfort or even harm to the participants which they may not be prepared to tolerate. On the other hand, their "suffering" may lead to positive and more general social benefits. Thus, by explaining positive and negative aspects, co-operation can be negotiated.

Anonymity

Many people, for the sake of scientific progress, are prepared to divulge information of a very private nature on condition that their name is not mentioned. For instance, anonymity may be of great importance in studies where employees are asked to make statements about their employer, their working conditions, or where someone reveals personal addiction to drugs.

Generally, anonymity does not constitute a serious constraint in research, as social scientists usually are more interested in grouped data than in individual results. Thus, either the names of participants can be omitted altogether or respondents can be identified by number instead of by name. Since anonymity is regarded as essential by many respondents, they must be convinced that it will be respected. In this way researchers can avoid biased responses from participants.

Confidentiality

In many studies anonymity cannot be maintained. This is the case when data is collected using interviews. The interviewer has direct contact with all participants and is able to recognize each one of them. In this case, respondents must be assured that the information given will be treated with confidentiality. That is, they must be assured that data will only be used for the stated purpose of the research and that no other person will have access to interview data. Assured of these conditions, a respondent will feel free to give honest and complete information. Moreover, one should be aware of the particular importance of anonymity and confidentiality in certain types of research such as the case study.

In general, social scientists should accept responsibility for protecting their participants. Many researchers have been strongly criticized for having reached very interesting findings at psychological or physical cost to participants.

EXERCISES

1. Using actual examples, distinguish between facts and data. Explain what you understand by primary and secondary data. What are the shortcomings of the latter types of data?
2. Indicate what scales of measurement are used in the following examples:
    (a) opinion on the quality of a film expressed freely by a group of teenagers;
    (b) degree classification of graduating students;
    (c) brands of toothpaste;
    (d) income of workers at a car-assembly plant;
    (e) amount of calcium deposit (in milligrammes) in the organs of rats that have been subjected to different experimental treatments.
3. A drug was tested on a group of prisoners to observe its effects on human beings. What are the ethical issues raised by this study?

CHAPTER 10

Techniques of Data Collection

The purpose of this chapter is to demonstrate the construction of tools necessary to collect data and the way the information should be recorded. Social scientists rely mostly on reactive research methods, as opposed to unobtrusive measurements. In other words, in much social science research, the researched person is aware of being studied and reacts to stimuli, such as questions presented by the researcher. The most frequently used method of gathering information is by directly asking respondents to express their views. Therefore, the emphasis of this chapter is placed on interviews and questionnaires. It is hoped that the reader will not only find guidance on choosing the most appropriate method of data collection but also some practical instruction on how to proceed with particular regard to the preparation of useful questionnaires and interview schedules.

CHAPTER OBJECTIVES

Learners who have completed this chapter will be able to:
- Collect data through simple and participant observation.
- Develop structured and unstructured interview and questionnaire schedules.
- Edit data sets and check them for completeness, accuracy and uniformity.
- Contrast laboratory and field experiments. Select the most appropriate data collection techniques.

OBSERVATION

Although a seemingly straightforward technique, observation must be pursued in a systematic way, following scientific rules, if usable and quantifiable data are to be obtained.

Simple observation, also called **non-participant observation**, is the recording of events as observed by an outsider. For example, an observer placed at a road junction can observe traffic and record the number of cars passing or pedestrians crossing the road, the speed of the cars, the number and causes of accidents, and so on. A researcher can observe the social behaviour of people interacting in bars, shops, pleasure resorts or at political rallies, by recording the number of times people who do not know each other exchange words, the topic and length of conversation, the way the interaction starts and ends, and so on. But this method has some weaknesses. People who feel that they are being observed may change their behaviour, become uneasy or stop activities altogether. Thus, although simple (or non-participant) observation is based on the assumption that the observer merely records facts without interaction with the observed, in fact, the observation itself introduces biases as people become aware of being observed.

To avoid this indirect interference with the observed person, a more complex form of observation, called **participant observation**, can be used. In this case, the observers hide the real purpose of their presence by themselves becoming participants. They join the community or group under investigation as one of its members, sharing in all activities. Becoming an insider allows a deeper insight into the research problem, since the researcher enjoys the confidence of participants and shares their experiences without disturbing their behaviour. This method has been found particularly useful for anthropological research and studies of minority groups, such as prisoners or homeless people. The weakness of this method is that researchers risk losing their objectivity. Being directly involved with people and their daily concerns for an extended period of time may predispose one to be emotionally engaged with them, and thus to lose detachment from people and events. Also, because notes may have to be taken down secretly or from memory, inaccurate information may be recorded.

Participant observation is a very demanding way of gathering data and may involve extended periods of residence among respondents. For this reason, a **modified participant observation** method, which restricts the researcher to participation only in major events, such as village meetings or ceremonies, is often preferred.

The third type of observation is that done under **laboratory** conditions and is mainly used in psychology. It is a hidden observation of the behaviour of one or more persons in a room with one-way windows or false mirrors. In this case, although the negative aspects of laboratory experiments are present (see below), the distorting factors associated with simple or participant observation are removed.

In all three cases one should keep in mind the following rules.

1. Observations serve clearly formulated research purposes. Thus, observations must be planned systematically, specifying what and how to observe.
2. Observations should be recorded in a systematic, objective and standardized way.
3. Observations should be subjected to control in order to maintain a high level of objectivity. Thus, many observers should be able to record the same phenomena or events, in the same way, with the same results.

Observation as a method of data collection has some major limitations that must be noted. Not only is it costly and time-consuming, but it cannot be applied to many aspects of social life. One cannot directly observe attitudes or beliefs, for example. Neither can one easily observe phenomena related to the private spheres of life (such as aspects of family life) or phenomena spread over a long period of time (such as the career of a politician). Biases due to the subjectivity of the observer can be partly alleviated by the introduction of mechanical devices, such as tape or video recorders, as long as the participants are not aware of their presence. But, other limitations remain and these make it necessary to introduce alternative techniques.

INTERVIEWS AND QUESTIONNAIRES

There are many possible ways of gathering information directly from participants if such information cannot be obtained from observation. These methods also have advantages and disadvantages.

The first of these methods is the **interview**. An interview involves *direct* personal contact with the participant who is asked to answer questions relating to the research problem.

One method of getting people to express their views is the **non-scheduled interview**, which consists of asking respondents to comment on broadly defined issues. Those interviewed are free to expand on the topic as they see fit, to focus on particular aspects, to relate their own experiences, and so on. The interviewer will intervene to ask for clarification or further explanation, but not to give directives or to confront the interviewee with probing questions. Usually no time limit is fixed for completing an interview of this kind.

The non-scheduled interview is very useful in exploratory research where the research questions cannot be narrowly defined. It is also an excellent technique when no comparison is sought between the responses of different participants, but when each participant is considered as a specific case, such as in a case-study. The interviewer is present mainly to record the information. However, it is also essential to direct the flow of ideas and to intervene and ask questions. One can influence an interview in many ways. For example, the quality of personal contact can induce a respondent to speak with more or less confidence. The interviewer's presence may enhance comprehensiveness and objectivity in the recording of information, but it can also cause interviewed people to refrain from expressing their real opinions or true feelings.

Frequently there is a need for more specific and detailed information which can facilitate comparison of the reactions of different participants. In this case, the interviewer has a much more precise goal and the types of questions to be answered by all interviewees are fixed. A **non-scheduled structured interview** is conducted. It is structured in the sense that a list of issues for investigation is drawn up prior to the interview. The list will contain some precise questions and their alternatives or subquestions, depending on the answer to the main questions. But it is a non-scheduled interview in the sense that the interviewer is free to formulate other questions as judged appropriate for a given situation. Respondents are not confronted with already stated definitions or possible answers, but are free to choose their own definitions, to describe a situation or to express their particular views and answers to problems. Here again, the influence of the interviewer can be considerable. It is therefore important that one refrains from influencing the respondent by the way one asks questions. At the same time one should be alert, detect missing information and ask for it to be supplied. Improper recording of answers can also result in incomplete and biased information. This type of interview presupposes some prior information, an understanding of the problem under investigation, and a need for more specific information. A non-scheduled structured interview is very useful in pilot surveys, meant to aid the formulation of accurate and precise questions followed by a representative or even exhaustive, set of possible answers (see multiple-choice questions below).

The most structured way of getting information directly from respondents is by means of a **scheduled structured interview**. This method is based on an established set of questions with fixed wording and sequence of presentation, as well as more or less precise indications of how to answer each question. This questionnaire must be presented to each respondent in exactly the same way to minimize the role and influence of the interviewer and to enable a more objective comparison of the results. In order to be useful and reliable, a questionnaire must satisfy a range of criteria.

Lastly, questionnaires can be used without direct personal contact with respondents. These are **self-administered questionnaires**, and are completed by respondents themselves, without the assistance of an interviewer. This can be done either by distributing the questionnaire and collecting it once it has been filled out, or by mailing it and asking respondents to send it back. It is then called a **mail questionnaire**, which is definitely a *non-personal* method of gathering data.

In summary, the following techniques are available:

1. non-scheduled, unstructured interviews;
2. non-scheduled, structured interviews;
3. scheduled, structured interviews;
4. non-personal data collection — self-administered and mailed questionnaires.

e.g.

Suppose that a survey is to be conducted on the diet of an urban population. A *non-scheduled, non-structured interview* will consist of giving some general guidelines to the interviewer, such as: "investigate the eating habits of the participants and their families, how such habits vary with season and age of the family members, and how stable these habits are".

A *non-scheduled, structured interview* will indicate more information to be gathered by the interviewer, for instance: investigate the diet of the participants and their families with reference to:

1. the consumption of meat, milk and other sources of protein;
2. the consumption of vegetables and fruits; and,
3. the consumption of starchy foods.

Determine the regularity of these three broad food categories, taking into consideration the seasons and the age of consumers. Investigate the adaptation of the diet to the needs of children.

A *scheduled, structured interview* could be conducted by using a questionnaire, containing some of the following questions (where the appropriate answer must be ticked).

1. Do you eat meat?
   ☐ never
   ☐ less than once a week
   ☐ once a week
   ☐ twice a week
   ☐ once every second day
   ☐ once a day

2. Do you eat fish?
   ☐ never
   ☐ less than once a week
   ☐ once a week
   ☐ twice a week
   ☐ once every second day
   ☐ once a day

3. Do you drink milk?
   ☐ never
   ☐ in tea or coffee only
   ☐ in porridge only
   ☐ just pure milk
   ☐ other (explain) . . . .

A *self-administered questionnaire* may not be suitable in this case as many low-income, urban respondents do not have the necessary reading and writing skills. If their literacy level is high, respondents could be sent the kind of questionnaire illustrated above, accompanied by a covering letter with instructions.

Comparison of the different techniques

The aim of the four methods illustrated above is to convert into data information given directly by a person, as opposed to information gathered by the observation of a

Techniques of Data Collection

person. The type of information gathered directly is mainly:

- what a person knows: knowledge, factual information;
- what a person likes or dislikes: values, preferences, interests, tastes;
- what a person thinks: attitudes, beliefs;
- what a person has experienced or is experiencing.

Since this information is gathered by questioning people rather than by observing their behaviour, some basic conditions must be met to assure objectivity.

Firstly, the respondents must co-operate. They must be willing and motivated to share their knowledge.

Secondly, respondents must express what they perceive as their reality rather than what they wish reality to be, what they think it ought to be, or what they believe to be the best answer to satisfy the researcher.

e.g.

A member of a small village co-operative is asked to comment on the co-operative's work atmosphere and team relationships. This villager is expected to assess whether the contacts among members are cordial, friendly, neutral, ambivalent, or even tense and hostile. To deny the existence of tension because "we are all Christians", or to exaggerate poor relationships in order to make the story more interesting, will negatively affect the level of objectivity of the study.

Thirdly, respondents must be aware of what they feel and think and be able to express it in order to communicate the information. This may be a problem with young children who are unable to analyse their feelings or accurately describe their experiences. In this case, observation of their behaviour will yield more objective information than direct questioning. Inability to analyse feelings or to describe problems can also occur in adults, especially when asked questions foreign to their way of thinking.

In the light of the above difficulties, researchers should always keep the following in mind when using interviews.

1. To what extent are the respondents prepared to co-operate and what factors might influence co-operation? These factors might include lack of time, fatigue, other priorities, social norms and values, culturally diverse customs and personal beliefs. In many African cultures issues of sex and sexuality are not discussed publically or with people of the other sex.

2. To what extent might a question influence the respondents to show themselves in a good light, to answer so as to please the researcher, or to distort reality in other ways? For example, a woman with an abusive husband may wish to present herself and her family in a positive light, and thus be unwilling to discuss domestic violence honestly.

3. To what extent do the questions ask for information that the respondents do not have, do not understand properly, or are not sure of? In other words, to what extent do the questions force respondents to guess the answers? For example, asking a woman how much her husband earns will produce difficulties if she does not know how much he actually earns.

Advantages and disadvantages of unstructured or semi-structured interviews

As pointed out earlier, unstructured and semi-structured interviews are very helpful in exploratory research, as well as when considering a pilot survey before the formulation of a final questionnaire. These methods help to clarify concepts and problems and they allow for the establishment of a list of possible answers or solutions which, in turn, facilitates the construction of more highly structured interviews. In particular, they facilitate the elimination of superfluous questions and the reformulation of ambiguous ones. They allow also for the discovery of new aspects of the problem by exploring in detail the explanations supplied by respondents.

e.g.

Why are women more conservative in their farming practices than men, when at least in principle, both groups have access to the advice of agricultural extension workers and to training courses? How do social and family constraints act on women to discourage them from attending courses? Unstructured interviews can encourage each of these women to describe her own experiences. The resulting detailed and extensive list of reasons given should lead to a classification of all factors at stake. Among these may be such reasons as non-availability of other people to care for children, husbands' apprehension about their wives sleeping outside the village, negative attitudes of male agricultural trainers towards women, and so on.

The wealth and quality of the data gathered are strongly dependent on the skill of the interviewer and the confidence inspired in respondents. The type of questions asked and encouraging comments made at the correct moment are also very important.

The weakness of unstructured interviews lies partly in the fact that if the interviewers are not competent they may introduce many biases. In particular, recording the comments of participants is a delicate matter because of the great variety of answers and their complexity. Moreover, interviews are time-consuming and thus expensive. One way of reducing the costs associated with this technique is to conduct interviews over the telephone. However, such an approach excludes a considerable part of the general population, especially in African countries with poorly developed communications infrastructure.

Advantages and disadvantages of structured interviews

Structured interviews have a different aim to unstructured ones. Based on categories of answers already known, their aim is mainly to determine the frequency of various answers and to find relationships between answers to different questions. This is achieved by comparing the responses of large numbers of participants. The competence and influence of the interviewer are much less important and the recording of answers is usually quite straightforward.

Moreover, compared to self-administered questionnaires, questionnaires filled out by an interviewer have definite advantages. Firstly, they can be administered to respondents who cannot read or write. This is particularly applicable to a large section of the population in less industrialized countries, to poor sectors of the population and to young children.

Secondly, they help overcome misunderstandings and misinterpretations of words or questions. As a result, the answers given are clearer. This is possible because in case of doubt the interviewer can ensure that respondents correctly understand the questions. Interviewers can also ask respondents for explanations concerning some of the answers.

Thirdly, interviewers can ensure that all items on the questionnaire have been considered and that respondents did not omit difficult questions. The interviewer can reassure respondents and encourage them to persevere.

However, structured interviews have quite important disadvantages. To begin with, personal interviews are costly in time and money. Interviewers have to spend a certain number of hours interviewing each participant separately and they may also have to travel extensively to reach respondents. These constraints normally result in a small sample for study.

The employment of many interviewers in data collection enables researchers to deal with large samples more quickly than if only one interviewer collects all the data. But, unless interviewers have been carefully trained, there is a danger that they will subtly affect respondents' answers. This will lead to serious disparities in the results and reduce their comparability.

Lastly, the presence of an interviewer can be perceived as a handicap as far as anonymity and respect for the private life of the interviewees are concerned. The respondents may be embarrassed by questions which touch on confidential and private issues in front of an interviewer, whereas they would answer more freely and honestly if left alone to fill in the questionnaire. Moreover, such factors as the social status, sex and age of an interviewer can affect the respondents' answers. For instance, female interviewers may collect more and better results from female respondents than male interviewers on topics involving sexual practices, birth control, or wife-beating.

Advantages and disadvantages of mailed questionnaires

The most important advantage to using mailed questionnaires is that a large coverage of the population can be realized with little time or cost. It is relatively easy to select 2 000 or even 5 000 people in different areas of a country and send them questionnaires by mail.

Also, since respondents are asked to mail back the filled-out questionnaires without indicating their name, anonymity is assured and this will help them to be honest in their answers. At the same time, bias due to personal characteristics of interviewers is avoided, as no interviewers are used. Some types of questions, which might require reflection or consultation before answering, will be more appropriately dealt with when the respondent has more time for an answer and no waiting interviewer to cause a hasty response.

Although these advantages seem to be considerable, self-administered questionnaires in general, and mail questionnaires in particular, have many disadvantages, especially when used in developing countries.

The main prerequisites for the use of mail questionnaires are a sufficient level of literacy and familiarity with the language used. These are not usually satisfied by a large proportion of the population of a less industrialized country. In countries where a number of different languages are spoken, respondents may be obliged to participate using a language other than their home language. A related issue is that, when sending out questionnaires, it is usually not possible to assess in advance whether or not the respondent has this minimum level of literacy. For this reason, and because of social and cultural constraints, questionnaires may be filled out by people other than the chosen participant. In particular, many heads of household consider it their prerogative to answer for their wives, daughters or other dependents. Similarly, managers may ask their secretary or other subordinates to fill in the questionnaire for them.

Moreover, the response rate for mailed questionnaires tends to be very low. Very often out of the total number of questionnaires sent out, only 20 to 40% are returned. Many factors contribute to this poor return. The respondent may never have received the questionnaire due to poor mail service in rural areas, or, in the case of women, they may have married and changed their name and residence, or the questionnaire may have been confiscated by the husband. It could also be that the participant lacks interest and has misplaced the questionnaire or cannot be bothered to fill it in; or is too busy to fill it in. To these unreturned questionnaires must be added the high number of incorrectly or incompletely filled-out ones that must be discarded. It is very common for respondents of self-administered questionnaires to skip over difficult or embarrassing questions, thereby spoiling the whole questionnaire.

This low response rate has important negative consequences for the quality of the research. The representativeness of the sample may be undermined since non-respondents are usually quite different from respondents. They may have particular features such as being poorly educated, old people, women, people with no stable residence, or individuals who are suspicious of research. Their absence from the sample will constitute an important bias. It is possible to increase the response rate by using a covering letter convincing respondents of the relevance of research, by adding a self-addressed, stamped envelope to the questionnaire, and by keeping the questionnaire short and well-formulated. Nevertheless, low response rate remains a source of bias in the mail-questionnaire method.

Because of some of the problems mentioned above, questionnaires should have simple and straightforward questions. The type of answer expected and how the answer should be recorded must also be unambiguous. The need to avoid misunderstood questions in investigating complex research issues prevents researchers from using this technique of data collection in such cases.

Focus groups

A type of interview that is being used more and more commonly is the focus group. A focus group consists of between four and eight respondents who are interviewed together. It is important that the focus group participants are carefully selected according to explicitly stated criteria. The focus group is conducted in an unstructured or semi-structured way. In other words, the researcher or facilitator of the focus group draws up a list of broad questions, topics or themes. These are used to develop a discussion among the focus group participants. It is important that the researcher has a good understanding of the topic before drawing up the list of questions or themes. Depending on the nature of the research question and also on the participants, it may be necessary for the facilitator to work in a more or less structured manner.

The advantages of using focus groups are that participants are able to discuss the issues in question with each other. One person's ideas may set off a whole string of related thoughts and ideas in another person. Similarly one participant may disagree with and question the remarks of another. When this happens there is an opportunity for the whole group to explore the disagreement in detail, thereby producing a much deeper understanding of the problem. A careful record of the debate between participants can give the researcher much deeper insight into a topic than would have been gained from interviewing all the participants individually.

Another important advantage of this technique is that it provides an opportunity for participants to learn from each other, and perhaps to resolve important dilemmas with which they are confronted. This is very useful in action-research where part of the researcher's goal is to help address a particular problem facing a particular group of people.

e.g.

A researcher is interested in agricultural development in rural communities. She selects six women who are involved in setting up rural agricultural projects to participate in a focus group. It is likely that their discussion (facilitated by the researcher) will be very useful in identifying all the concerns that must be taken into account in this kind of project. However, the sharing of ideas and experience might also assist all those women (and the projects in which they are involved) to become even more effective.

Also, many African cultures make constant use of small groups to address concerns within the community. For this reason, the focus group method of data collection might turn out to be extremely comfortable for many people and may for this reason be the method of choice.

There are, however, many potential dangers in using focus groups and the success of this approach depends in large part upon the skill of the group facilitator. Group facilitation is aimed at ensuring that a safe environment for uncensored communication is created. In particular, the facilitator should ensure that everyone in the group has real opportunities to contribute, and that the group does not prevent some members from freely expressing their ideas. Some members of the group might tend to dominate and they would need to be restrained by the facilitators. Others might find it extremely difficult to express their thoughts and they would need encouraging. Some group members dominate others purposefully or without realizing it for a range of different reasons. People with more education, or more self-confidence, or better linguistic skills will tend to speak more than others. Thus the results of the focus group could be biased towards those people who contributed more to the discussion.

e.g.

A researcher wishes to identify the chief sources of workplace stress within a large corporation. He randomly selects eight people from the company and puts them together in a focus group. As it happens this group comprises a senior manager, three junior managers and five lower level employees. It will be very difficult for the less senior employees to speak openly in front of the other members of the focus group. Even if they are courageous enough to express their opinions, they may not have the skills to do so as effectively as their seniors. In this case, the researcher would be better advised to use individual interviews or to set up separate focus groups for people of different seniority within the company.

The problems of group dynamic are addressed through the skill of the facilitator and through the careful selection of group members. Wherever possible all groups members should be equally comfortable with the language of the group, have similar levels of education, social status, and so forth.

Another important danger relates to the composition of the group. Biases due to social desirability are extremely important in focus groups. It is difficult for people to speak honestly and openly about some issues to a single interviewer. It is very much harder to speak about those issues to a group of peers, especially when the group members know each other. Thus focus groups are not the best method of data collection when the research topic touches on sensitive subject material.

In summary, although there are many important advantages of using focus groups there are also potential pitfalls. The researcher must consider carefully the reasons for using the focus group technique and pay strict attention to the composition and facilitation of groups.

Fundamentals of Social Research Methods

Table 10.1
Data collection — advantages and disadvantages of various techniques

Technique	Advantages	Disadvantages
Questionnaire	• Easily standardized. • Low drain on time and finances. • Very little training of researchers.	• Difficult to interpret subjects' responses. • Difficult to check that subject understands the questions. • Low response rate and response bias.
Mailed Questionnaire	• Easily standardized. • Low drain on time and finances. • Very little training of researchers. • Reach a geographically spread sample.	• Difficult to interpret subjects' responses. • Difficult to check that subject understands the questions. • Very low response rate and response bias. • Questionnaire may not be fully completed.
Standardized Interview	• Relatively easily standardized. • Can ensure that subject understands questions. • Can clarify, interpret subjects' responses. • Better response rate.	• Very time-consuming and expensive. • Research assistants need training. • May introduce interviewer bias. • Bias due to social desirability.
Exploratory Interview	• Do not impose structure on to interview. • Can access what subject feels is important. • Useful for generating hypotheses.	• Very time-consuming and expensive. • Research assistants need training. • Very difficult to standardize and analyse. • Bias due to social desirability.
Focus Groups	• Participants share views and discuss ideas. • Participants gain insight into pressing concerns. • Many African cultures rely on small groups for decision-making.	• No individual responses since participants influence each other. • Without skilled facilitation some participants may be excluded. • Bias due to social desirability is extreme.
Telephone Interview	• Cheaper than other interviews. • Reach a geographically spread sample.	• Research assistants need training. • May introduce sampling bias. • Many kinds of people cannot be reached at all by telephone.

Techniques of Data Collection | Chapter 10

CONSTRUCTING A QUESTIONNAIRE

Whether conceived to be filled in by a respondent directly or by an interviewer, a questionnaire remains a complex instrument of data collection. In a previous chapter, sampling theory was studied as being a science in which very precise procedures can be determined and sampling errors can be estimated. In the case of the construction of a questionnaire, however, although general guidelines can be given, as well as some clues on how to avoid particular pitfalls, there exist few specific rules. There are many types of questions, question formats and interviewing techniques available to the researcher. There is usually little chance of assessing whether a questionnaire, constructed differently, would have led to better results.

Before going into the technicalities, here are some general guidelines.

1. *Do not begin to develop a questionnaire by drafting questions.*

Instead, use the following procedure:

(a) List the specific research issues to be investigated by the questionnaire.
(b) Decide what kind of data is needed to study those issues. Here the use of dummy tables (empty tables showing how the data will be presented) could help to anticipate how the data will actually be utilized in the analysis. Constructing such tables will lead to the identification of the variables to be considered.
(c) Formulate specific questions to measure those variables.

Consider again the study concerning the relationship between the involvement of co-operative members in terms of time available and regularity at work, on the one hand, and their family commitments on the other. Assuming that some of the issues to be investigated are:

- the different family and social constraints and how they affect the work of the co-operative;
- the average time spent on co-operative activities;
- the time-table of co-operative members and how often it is not followed;
- the reasons for not respecting the adopted time schedule.

A dummy table reflecting some of these points might look as follows:

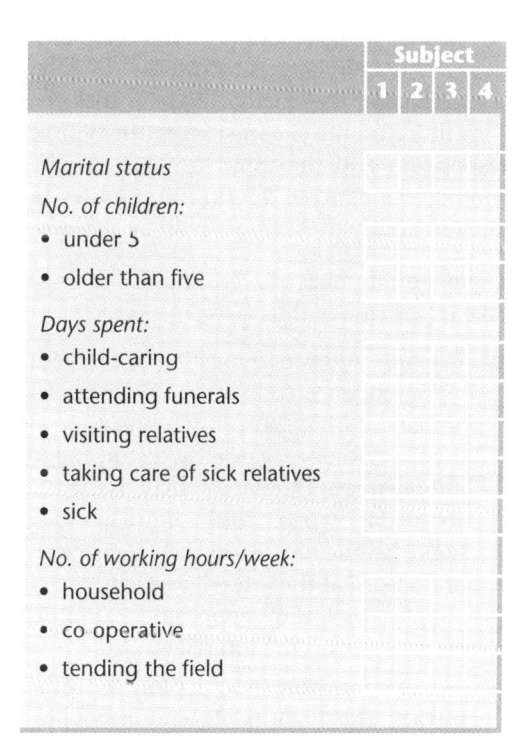

	Subject				
	1	2	3	4
Marital status				
No. of children:				
• under 5				
• older than five				
Days spent:				
• child-caring				
• attending funerals				
• visiting relatives				
• taking care of sick relatives				
• sick				
No. of working hours/week:				
• household				
• co-operative				
• tending the field				

Some suitable questions might be:
1. Are you single/married/divorced/widowed/separated?
2. How many dependent children live with you?
3. How many dependent children are below the age of 5 years?

© Juta & Co Ltd

4. How many days during the last 6 months did you stay at home to attend to a sick child.

_____

2. *Always take into account the needs, interests and problems of respondents.*

These are, in fact, more important than academic factors. In other words, design a respondent-centred questionnaire or interview.

An interview or self-administered questionnaire should never be of such a length that respondents become tired to the point of refusing to collaborate. If this happens, they will use any means to end the exercise, thus reducing the quality of their answers. Depending on the circumstances, the type of respondent and the topic, a questionnaire should take between 15 and 90 minutes to answer. Multiple sessions should be avoided.

There are a number of precautions one must take in the case of interviews.

- The time and venue must be convenient to respondents. Long interviews at places of work, during short lunch-breaks or in the street can be regarded as disturbing to interviewees. Interviews may be more acceptable when done after working hours at the home of the participant, provided that the interviewee is not very busy, accepts the venue, and can thus concentrate on the interview.

- The environment should allow for some privacy. The majority of respondents prefer that other people do not listen to their answers, in particular if some of the questions are quite personal. A further reason for preventing family members, neighbours or colleagues from listening to the interview is that if they are "contaminated" by hearing another person's answers, the researcher will not be able to include them in the sample. Thus, with the exception of focus groups, interviews in public should be avoided.

- Co-operation of respondents should be gained by using official permission and support, such as village authorities, and by explaining the aim of the research and the relevance of the study. One should stress that the respondents have been specially selected and one should dissipate suspicion by emphasizing the confidentiality of the interview.

- The language and vocabulary used should be adapted to the respondent (see also questionnaire wording below). When translation into a local language is needed, great care should be given to the choice of words. Double translation (for example, from English, into Tswana or Shona and back to English) done by different translators reduces the danger of inaccurate translation.

- Difficulties arising from interviewers' personalities should be reduced. Interviewers must avoid being impatient, hurried and aggressive. They should also not be too friendly and accommodating. They must be aware of their own influence on respondents in order to control it. Thus, they should try to adapt to the environment in which the research is conducted, even in their way of dressing and behaving. Interviewers should guard against the respondents' developing negative or biased attitudes towards the interview as a whole.

3. *The researcher should give great attention to the wording of questions.*

- Questions should be simple and short. Complex questions should be broken up into several simple ones.

- Questions should be unambiguous. Words which are too general, too vague, or which could give rise to different interpretations, should be replaced with more specific terms. For instance, words like "often", "many", "enough" should be replaced by "3 times a week", "ten", and "2 meals a day". Expressions like "dependent children" should read "children you are responsible for and who are living with you even if not necessarily your own". Words like "drugs" should be replaced by "medicine", or "aphrodisiac", according to the need.

- Questions should be understandable. Use vocabulary adapted to the level of education of the participants. Avoid technical expressions and sophisticated language.
- Questions should not be double-barrelled, that is, contain two questions in one. If one is asked to answer "yes" or "no" to the question "Do you like to go to the cinema and have a good laugh?" One excludes in a yes/no answer the possibility of going to the movies for reasons other than to laugh. Thus, a double-barrelled question should be divided into two.
- Leading questions should be avoided. These are questions that favour one type of answer over another, or associate a particular response with an important personality. Questions starting with "Don't you agree that ...", or ending with "... is it not so?", are leading questions. For instance, "Don't you agree that students are very irresponsible?", "Students are very irresponsible people, is it not so?", or "Do you support the statement of the Prime Minister that students lack a sense of responsibility?", induce biased answers and should therefore be avoided.

4. The researcher should structure the questionnaire carefully.

- A logical sequence of questions which exhausts one topic before shifting to the next is the most meaningful approach. Often an even more structured method called the **funnel questionnaire** is used. One starts with very general questions and proceeds, by successively narrowing the scope, to the focus of the problem under study. Before asking for the opinion of respondents on a particular event involving, for example, a politician, one could investigate the general interests and hobbies of the respondents, their political views and affiliations, and their sources of information.
- The inverted funnel sequence, also called a **filter questionnaire**, is based on the same principle, except that one reverses the process and starts with very specific issues that later lead to more general ones. Both methods can be used to instil confidence in respondents and to permit discovery of inconsistencies.
- The repetition of the content of a question, formulated in different ways and placed in different parts of the questionnaire, is another method of checking the veracity of answers and the honesty of a participant. This is particularly useful for topics on which the respondent may have reason to lie, to cover up something, or to impress the interviewer. This is often the case with social-status and financial questions.
- The tendency of participants to answer all questions in a specific direction regardless of the content of the questions, called **response set**, should be counteracted. This is mainly done by breaking the monotonous sequence and format of questions and response categories. An example of this pitfall and its correction is given below from an attitude questionnaire containing statements on a five-point scale.

	Strongly agree	Agree	No opinion	Disagree	Strongly disagree
Television weakens the sight					
Television develops passivity					
Television curbs creativity					
Television develops aggression					

All four statements express a negative view about television. Participants are thus likely to adopt a certain "set" answer and to apply it to all the questions without analysing them. This could be avoided by reformulating the questions as follows:

	Strongly agree	Agree	No opinion	Disagree	Strongly disagree
Television weakens the sight					
Television develops creativity					
Television reduces aggression					
Television develops passivity					

Here only the first and last statements reflect a negative attitude.

Much more than can be dealt with here could be said about pitfalls and how to avoid them when designing a questionnaire. Interested readers should consult more specialized literature on the topic.

At this stage, one could summarize the guidelines by suggesting that every item should be checked for the following pitfalls.

1. Is the question necessary? How will it be used to address the problem or test the hypothesis?
2. Does the respondent have the information necessary to answer this question? Is the participant willing to do so?
3. Is the question respondent-centred?
4. Will the question be interpreted similarly by all respondents?
5. Is the question neutral or does it favour a particular answer?
6. Is the wording of the question adequate?
7. Is the organization of the questionnaire logical but not monotonous?

The questions

The first distinction to be made concerns the content of questions. A question can seek either *factual information* or *opinion*.

Factual questions request objective information about the respondents, such as their social background or related personal data. Questionnaires usually contain factual questions related to characteristics such as age, sex, marital status, and level of education. It is debatable where factual background (personal) questions should be placed in the questionnaire. In some societies, the placing of enquiries about personal matters (such as level of education and income) at the beginning of a questionnaire is resented and can lead to a refusal to participate.

Factual questions seem easy to answer since they are straightforward and do not influence the respondent. But a common mistake is to allow ambiguity. For example, if a farmer is asked how many animals she has on her farm, she may count livestock only and not mention cats and dogs. This question is ambiguous. The veracity of a factual answer does not only depend on the willingness of respondents to tell the truth but also on their knowledge and memory. A wife asked to determine the income of her husband may not want to disclose it, may want to impress the interviewer by inflating it, or she may have reasons to depreciate it. She may also be ignorant of her spouse's income and just make a wild guess to please the interviewer. A person asked how much he spent

Techniques of Data Collection — Chapter 10

on clothing in the past year may not remember all the details and therefore give an incorrect answer. Because of such difficulties, a researcher must make sure that participants are in a position to answer factual questions.

Sometimes it is possible to check the veracity of factual answers by referring to other sources. In the case of the spouse who is ignorant of her spouse's income, it may be possible to check that income with the spouse directly. However, the researcher must be very careful not to violate the subject's privacy. Checking a person's income with their employer without their express permission would be in invasion of their privacy.

Opinion questions are more problematic, since the respondent is the only person who knows the true answer. There are also many factors which may introduce distortions in the answer. As already mentioned, the respondent may be influenced by what she considers socially desirable. Because racial prejudice is neither morally nor socially acceptable in most societies, a racially prejudiced person would feel uneasy and avoid openly disclosing such feelings. This should be taken into account when formulating research questions. Questions should be stated in such a way that makes answers socially acceptable. For instance, "It is felt by some people that personal interracial contacts are a source of conflict. It is thus felt by some people that personal interracial contacts should be discouraged. Do you support this statement? Yes/No/No opinion." This form of presentation will allow respondents to express their attitudes without much discomfort, since it is implied that they share them with other people. This would not be the case if the question were stated as "Personal interracial contacts should be discouraged. Yes/No". Note that opinions and attitudes expressed in questionnaires do not always reflect actual behaviour.

Information can be gathered in different ways. The participant could be confronted with a statement which must be assessed, or with a question. In the latter case, it could be a direct or indirect question. **Statements** have the property of being more impersonal and allow a shorter formulation. **Direct questions** are also brief and to the point. **Indirect questions**, used especially when dealing with delicate issues, allow the purpose of the question to be less obvious, and give respondents the impression that they state a general opinion, that they do not commit themselves, and they are thus likely to be more honest. The disadvantage is that a greater number of indirect questions is needed to gauge an opinion or a fact than would be necessary if direct questions were used.

e.g.

These three possibilities are illustrated with an investigation into work relations conducted among employees of firm A. For all questions, the respondents have the choice of answering "yes" or "no".

- *Statement:* The manager of firm A lacks democratic skills in his work-relations with the staff.
- *Direct question:* Is your manager democratic in the way he deals with matters of the firm?
- *Indirect questions:*
    - Does the manager of firm A discuss affairs of the firm with staff?
    - Does he take into account the suggestions and wishes of staff?
    - Does he make decisions after consensus has been reached among members of staff?
    - Does he tend to impose his decision on staff?

Another concern is how to present a question in order to obtain a certain type of answer. Here the distinction is between the need for a long, detailed answer, reflecting the individuality of respondents, and a short

© Juta & Co Ltd

answer, chosen among given categories. The types of question considered below are the unstructured or open-ended questions, and the structured ones of great variety such as multiple-choice or check-list, scaled answers and rank answers. To this list one must still add contingency questions and fill-in questions. Each of these types has special functions, advantages and disadvantages. The main distinction is between open-ended (unstructured) questions and structured ones.

Open-ended questions

Open-ended questions leave the participants completely free to express their answers as they wish, as detailed and complex, as long or as short as they feel is appropriate. No restrictions, guidelines, or suggestions for solutions are given. Consider the following questions.

What are your future plans?
....
....
....
....

How do you explain the present situation on campus?
....
....
....
....

What major problems does your country face today?
....
....
....
....

Structured questions

Structured questions indicate a range of possible answers. They give a choice of answers (for example, **multiple-choice questions**) or guidelines on the procedures to follow (for example, ranking questions). Sometimes only two possibilities are given (such as "Yes/No", or "Agree/Disagree"), which allow for very little differentiation. Adding a third, neutral possibility like "No opinion", or "Not applicable" increases the flexibility of the answer somewhat. When many possibilities exist, a check-list is suggested, where the respondent is asked to tick only the most adequate answer or all the suitable answers. Consider the following structured alternative to the open-ended question, "What led you to study at the university?"

Your decision to study at the university was mainly determined by:
☐ Your parents
☐ Your social environment
☐ Your interest in a particular scientific field
☐ Your ambition to have a lucrative profession

When a list is not exhaustive, an additional last choice can be:

☐ Any other reasons (state them)
....

In this last instance the structured question contains an open-ended one which makes the whole question better adapted to all situations.

Some multiple-choice questions have a particular structure, in the sense that the suggested answers are ranked, usually using an ordinal scale. This is the case for questions on opinions and attitudes where a statement is made and the respondents must decide how much they agree with it. The most frequently used scale for such questions is based on three points (such as "I like/no opinion/I dislike"). To obtain more differentiated answers, one can use a five-point scale as in the following example:

> How suitable do you judge the applicant to be for the co-ordinator position?
> ☐ highly unsuitable
> ☐ unsuitable
> ☐ no opinion
> ☐ suitable
> ☐ highly suitable

Ranking questions are used when a set of possibilities is offered and the participant should assess the importance of each of them relative to the others. Here is an example.

> Rank, in order of decreasing importance, the relevance of the following factors in your choice of a profession.
> Rank
> ☐ Money
> ☐ Social contact
> ☐ Type of occupation
> ☐ Social position
> ☐ Intellectual interest
> ☐ Humanitarian relevance

Contingency questions are a special type of structured question, which apply to subgroups of respondents only, namely the ones who have given a particular answer to a previous question. To give a very simple example, when collecting data the following alternative exists:

> Do you have children?
> ☐ Yes
> ☐ No
> If "yes", how many?
> ☐ boys
> ☐ girls

Lastly, **fill-in questions** constitute a transitional type of question, between open-ended and structured, since no format is suggested but only a short format is expected. The following are examples of this type of question.

> Name the feeling you experience when smoking.
> . . . .
> What emotion was painted on her face?
> . . . .

To the first statement, one may answer "excitement and peace", to the second simply "grief". Thus responses are kept quite brief.

Advantages and disadvantages of open-ended and structured questions

The main distinction between the two types of questions is that the open-ended questions are not based on already conceived answers. They are thus well suited to exploratory studies, case studies, or studies based on qualitative analysis of data. Answers may be quite complex and not easily comparable to those of other respondents. Their recording and scoring gives rise to some difficulties. In contrast, structured questions, by restricting the number of possible answers, may produce bias if important categories are left out. Their quality is largely determined by a good pre-analysis and a pilot study or survey using open-ended questions to discover the major possibilities and to classify them. They have the great advantage of being simple to record and to score and they allow for an easy comparison and quantification of the results.

As mentioned earlier, some negative aspects of structured questions, like over-restrictive response possibilities or exclusion of important ones, can be greatly reduced by adding an open-ended option. The two types can be used to gain the confidence and co-operation of participants in different ways. Open-ended questions may relieve the anxiety of participants of giving "false" answers since they can speak freely. But easy, structured questions will also reassure participants who recognize that they are able to answer precise, straightforward questions without difficulty.

As already mentioned in the guidelines, attention should be paid not only to the content of questions and the level of precision that one wishes the answers to have, but also to the interest of the participants by, for instance, avoiding monotony in the questionnaire. Such considerations should influence whether or not one selects open-ended or structured questions and whether one mixes both types of question in a study.

Editing the questionnaire

Suppose that a survey or any type of research based on collection of data through interview or questionnaires has been conducted. Once the data has been collected, the researcher is confronted with piles of interview or questionnaire forms filled in by interviewers or by the respondents themselves. Before even starting to compile and code this data, one has to make sure that each question has been answered and the answer properly recorded. That is, one should check for the *completeness* of the questionnaire. An even more delicate task is to try to check the *accuracy* of the answers. Are there inconsistencies between the answers of different questions? Finally, one should check for *uniformity* in the interpretation of the questions and of the multiple-choice options. These three controls of completeness, accuracy and uniformity constitute the main tasks of the editing process.

The **completeness** of each questionnaire is often essential in research where even one missing answer may demand that the whole questionnaire be discarded. Sometimes, if a question has been omitted by a respondent or, in the case of an oral questionnaire or interview, the interviewer has forgotten to record the answer, it may be possible to enter the type of answer that the respondent would have given, or for the interviewer to recall the general meaning of the answer. In delicate cases, one would even try to contact the respondent directly to ask him or her for the missing information. If the unanswered questions relate to objective information, such as residential area or marital status, the researcher may be able to find the appropriate data by cross-checking with other information sources. Problems may occur when some questions are not answered and it is difficult to decide whether it is due to the unwillingness of the respondent to provide the information or because the question was not applicable to the respondent.

To judge the **accuracy** of the answer is even more difficult. Inconsistencies in a questionnaire may have various causes including, misinterpretation of the question or answer, lack of concentration, carelessness or even purposefully misleading answers. Errors due to carelessness are often easily detected. There is an obvious contradiction between the answer "No" to "Do you have children?" and "Three" to "If yes, how many?" Sometimes the wrong answer is ticked by mistake or the tick is not clearly placed.

As already mentioned, the versatility and accuracy of some factual answers give rise to concern and are difficult to assess. If there is any doubt, one should find other sources to double check the information. Lastly, although precautions will have been taken when constructing the questionnaire to avoid ambiguity in the questions, **uniformity** of the understanding of the questions and answers must be checked. This could result from a misunderstanding between "Not Applicable" and "No Opinion". Similarly, a variation in understanding of "income" or "assets" would result in great differences in amounts indicated by respondents. Although these errors are difficult to correct at this late stage, it is very important that the researcher is at least aware of them when interpreting the results.

Finally, editing can be done in two ways. The first is by question, that is, analysing one or a few questions in all the questionnaires, then another small set of questions, and so on. The second is by questionnaire, that is, analysing one questionnaire after another, going through all answers given by each respondent. The first method allows for detection of inaccuracies in the answers, and lack of uniformity in the interpretation of the questions, but not of inconsistencies within the same questionnaire. The second method will allow better judgement of each individual case as a whole. Moreover, although it is advisable to edit all the collected data, it is sometimes too costly and too time-consuming so that only a sample of questionnaires (or of questions) is edited. This may have a negative impact on the quality of the research.

THE EXPERIMENTAL TECHNIQUES

The experimental method was introduced in Chapters 5 and 7. The main difference between these methods and the ones presented previously, is that data collection through experimental techniques does not rely on what the participant says, but on how he or she behaves. This removes an important source of bias.

In social research, the demands of social reality necessitate the introduction of quasi-experimental designs. Pure experimental research, done in a laboratory, can only be used in a few particular situations, mainly in psychology, and even more rarely in developing countries where the more flexible field experiment is widely applied. The presentation of the experimental method is therefore brief.

The **laboratory experiment** is the most controlled method of data collection. It simulates certain characteristics of a natural environment, but only as far as these do not affect the control and the manipulation of the independent and other variables. The main distinction between this method and all the others is that only the laboratory experiment allows the manipulation of one variable at a time in order to study its effects on other variables.

This concern is expressed by the high level of standardization which guarantees that the conditions be repeated exactly in all details and which ensures a high degree of reliability (see Chapter 11). All conditions are standardized.

1. The presentation of the experiment and the testing situation, the environment, and the laboratory, are the same for all participants in a study (as opposed to an interview which can be conducted in different environments with conditions more or less conducive to concentration).

2. The instructions are rigorously the same, given to the participants by an experimenter who avoids any personal interference with them by remaining neutral.

3. The instruments are strictly the same and are most often produced under copyright to ensure standardization and avoid the slightest modifications.
4. The recording and evaluation of the results are done systematically and usually quantitative measurements are obtained.

Although the greatest care is taken to achieve the highest scientific standards, the laboratory experiment is often quite inadequate for social research. The laboratory environment remains very artificial, notwithstanding efforts to simulate real-life situations. People react to the artificial set-up which modifies their behaviour considerably. Thus, the results obtained cannot be generalized to real-life situations with ease. Moreover, participants often seek to discover how they should behave to "do well" in the experiment and to conform to what they believe the experimenter expects of them.

A remedy for these weaknesses is to conduct the experiment in a natural environment, maintaining as much control of the different variables as possible. Thus, a decrease in scientific rigour is compensated for by a more natural behaviour of participants who are not aware of being subjected to an experiment. In fact, many social phenomena cannot be analysed other than by **field experiment**. The following example contrasts laboratory and field experiments.

e.g.

Co-operation versus competition can be studied in a laboratory, as was done by Mintz (1951). This researcher provoked a certain behaviour in participants by confronting them with the following problem.

Given a jar connected to a source of water allowing the level of the water to rise in the jar, participants have to extricate from the jar cones attached to a string before the rising water reaches the cones. The difficulty resides in the narrowness of the neck of the bottle which does not allow more than one cone to be pulled out at a time. Thus, to avoid jamming the cones in the bottle-neck and losing time, the participants must co-operate and develop a common strategy (Mintz, 1951).

The feeling of emergency and threat which would promote co-operative behaviour or, on the contrary, a very competitive one to save one's own cone, is difficult to awaken in this quite artificial set-up, even when financial incentives or other motivators are introduced.

In a field experiment, many "natural" situations can be devised, using sports events, school life, or incidents in the street. One experiment in which a fire was simulated in a cinema was conducted in order to observe how spectators would react at exits in their attempt to escape. It was perceived that disorganized behaviour, like pushing and queue-jumping was detrimental since, in fact, it slowed down the escape process. In this particular case, the concern of participants was genuine so that no artificial incentives were required. The people involved were completely unaware of being subjected to an experiment and thus the results can lead to valid generalizations.

However, the duplication of this field experiment may cause problems since the sample was a non-probability one (refer to Chapter 8) and very little was known about the participants. In particular, some of them might have realized much later than others the danger of the situation, depending on where they were located, their concentration on what was going on, and other factors. In the laboratory set-up, on the other hand, all conditions are fixed and all the subjects tend to perceive the situation in the same way.

Techniques of Data Collection

THE RECORD METHOD OR UNOBTRUSIVE MEASURES

Collection of data by experiment, interviews and questionnaires is essentially based on an interaction between the researcher and the respondent, the latter reacting to a situation created by the former. The record method, on the other hand, is a non-reactive research method. The information about the respondent is gathered without direct interaction by use of public documents. The researcher will use archival records, published statistics like demographic records of births and deaths, judicial records like court decisions or election results, crime statistics and educational data. One will also refer to institutional publications, data published by the private sector, as well as personal documents, biographies, historical documents, medical and other scientific records.

In all these cases respondents are not aware that they are the subjects of a study and this eliminates some biases. But unobtrusive measures are endangered by many other sources of error. The records used may contain institutional biases. Reports are usually written in such a way as to safeguard the interests of the parent institution and to fulfil some short- or long-term goals. They will present facts to support the efficiency of the institution, or the need for more funds, etc. Thus, the facts presented may be distorted. One very common bias is introduced by mentioning only some facts and by hiding others. For instance, political considerations may result in inflating or deflating the sizes of ethnic groups in a country.

Another source of error is related to erratic record collecting and keeping. Collection of some data may be stopped for political or financial reasons, some records may have been destroyed (by accident, such as fire, or willingly by an overthrown regime to cover up facts) and in some areas no research may ever have been conducted. A third limitation of the record method arises from the secrecy of certain data. Many sources of information exist that are not available to social scientists and some research topics may be prohibited. They may focus on multinational transactions, police records, military issues, court cases, among others. More generally, when a very important decision is taken, the end result is communicated to the public but not the process leading to it, the type of discussions or arguments used or internal conflicts expressed. These constitute important information which is inaccessible to researchers.

Lastly, bias may arise from a lack of information on the actual way in which the recorded data was collected, the sample characteristics, the operational definitions, instruments used, and the bias introduced by the person who collected the data. A population census is a good example in which these types of problem surface frequently.

The record method can be used as the only source of data in a given research, but it has been found more useful to combine it with complementary methods. There is a major difference between data compiled by survey method, using questionnaires for instance, and data presented in records. The latter only give the properties of a group of individuals, an aggregate of much separate information, whereas the former permits the retrieval of data concerning a particular individual.

For example, data related to school performance as presented in ministry records would only indicate the average performance of each school in the country. Data compiled in a survey will still allow for compilation of schools' average-performance rates while at the same time indicating specific performance of individual learners.

It is important that researchers evaluate the instruments and procedures that were used to gather information. How such evaluation is to be done is the subject of the next chapter.

EXERCISES

1. Find the flaws in the following questions and suggest improvements.
   (a) Have you ever falsified information in your income-tax declaration?
   (b) How much did your husband spend on clothes last year?
   (c) Do you believe that television-watching is un-African?
   (d) Are you emotionally mature?
   (e) Is cancer research feasible in Africa and should one strive for it?
   (f) How do you feel about Mercedes-Benz and Peugeot?
   (g) Do you consider your working conditions and wages to be excellent . . . good . . . fair . . . ?
2. Suppose that you would like to find out how much time rural women spend on their various activities, like working in the field, fetching water and wood, cooking, and so on. How would you collect this data? Would it be adequate to use a questionnaire? What method of observation might be suitable?
3. Choose a topic in your field of interest. Suppose that you are to conduct research on the opinions and attitudes of a certain population on the chosen topic. Develop a short questionnaire (10–15 questions) using the types of question presented in this chapter as a guide. Be sure to write a respondent-centred questionnaire, taking into account level of education, language difficulties, emotional barriers and any other factors that arise.
4. Compare and contrast the various techniques of data collection presented in this chapter.

CHAPTER 11

Reliability and Validity of Measurements

Measurement techniques are evaluated in terms of the principles of reliability and validity. Reliability is the extent to which the observable (or empirical) measures that represent a theoretical concept are accurate and stable when used for the concept in several studies. Validity is concerned with just how accurately the observable measures actually represent the concept in question or whether, in fact, they represent something else. Several methods of determining the reliability of observable measures for theoretical concepts are discussed as well as the different types of validity commonly applied to social science concepts.

CHAPTER OBJECTIVES

The learner who has successfully completed this chapter will be able to:

- Evaluate the reliability of measurement instruments and techniques.
- Evaluate the validity of measurement instruments and techniques.
- Select measurement strategies that maximize reliability and validity.

As discussed in Chapter 2, social scientists are required to translate the theoretical concepts in which they are interested into observable measures. This is done by choosing an operational definition of each theoretical concept involved in the research. An operational definition of a theoretical concept explains how that concept is to be measured (empirically) by the researcher. Operational definitions do not, however, tell the researcher whether or not the chosen measures are *adequate* measures of the various concepts.

e.g.

It is hypothesized that factory workers, residing far from their workplace and travelling long distances to reach the factory, experience greater occupational stress than workers who live close to the factory. In this case, the theoretical constructs of "travelling time" or "distance to the workplace" and "occupational stress" need operational definition.

Note that how these constructs are operationalized greatly influences the value of the research. Is living "far or close to the factory" to be determined by the distance in kilometres, or by the travelling time independent of mode and availability of transport? Can one compare thirty minutes travelling on foot when the worker is free to leave home at her own convenience to thirty minutes travelling on a bus, with the stress of catching the bus perhaps two hours early to avoid rush hour and the possibility of missing the bus?

Suppose that the researcher chooses to define workers living far from the factory as those living more than one walking hour from the factory. Similarly, occupational stress may be defined as the score on a specially constructed stress inventory. These two definitions suggest how the concepts are to be measured: by finding out how long it takes each person to travel to work from home, and what their score on the stress inventory is.

By asking how long workers take to get to the factory from home, the researcher may be finding out more about the transport facilities to different areas than about the distance people live from the factory. Similarly, the measure of occupational stress may give entirely different results depending on whether the worker is having a good day or not, or how well she slept the night before.

Unfortunately, virtually no measurement technique in social science is perfect. It is therefore important that researchers always evaluate the measures that they use. This is the purpose of reliability and validity.

RELIABILITY

Reliability is concerned with the consistency of measures. An instrument which produces different scores every time it is used to measure an unchanging value has low reliability. It cannot be depended upon to produce an accurate measurement. On the other hand, an instrument which always gives the same score when used to measure an unchanging value can be trusted to give an accurate measurement and is said to have high reliability. In most cases, the **reliability** of measurement is the degree to which that instrument produces equivalent results for repeated trials.

e.g.

A researcher interested in the health needs of a particular community establishes a list of possible health problems and asks community members to tick off the problems that they think are most important. A week later she repeats the exercise with the same sample of community members and discovers that they tick off a different set of health issues. The check-list approach is not producing consistent results. In this case, the check-list is an unreliable method for assessing the community's health needs. Next, the researcher uses exploratory interviews for the same purpose and finds that these do produce consistent results. The exploratory interview is therefore a reliable instrument. It is possible to speculate that peoples' immediate needs vary from day to day and thus the check-list approach does not produce consistent data. More careful probing, however, reveals a few basic needs from which all others arise.

Thus, the greater the consistency in the results, the greater the reliability of the measuring procedure. Unfortunately, very few instruments ever produce entirely consistent results. The sources of inconsistency in the social sciences are many.

e.g.

A worker who is interviewed about a factory's working conditions after a long day at work or after being refused a day's leave may feel that conditions are very poor. The same worker interviewed during a tea-break may give an entirely different response. Similarly, a group of individuals who are being asked a second time to rate a company's public image may rate it the same as they did the first time, despite changes, just to appear consistent. Equally they may change their ratings merely to "fool" the interviewer.

It is worth emphasizing that in the social sciences there is concern about establishing *regularities* of perceptions, opinions, behaviours, etc. If some regularity is observed in a phenomenon, it is more likely that something meaningful is being measured. Nevertheless, some instruments are more accurate than others and the social

Reliability and Validity of Measurements

researcher must be able to distinguish the reliable from the unreliable in order to achieve the best results. Without going into the mathematical procedures needed to estimate reliability, the following sections provide a description of the various techniques commonly used. These are: test–retest reliability, equivalent forms reliability, split-half reliability, and inter-scorer reliability. Finally, the internal consistency of measures is discussed.

Test–retest reliability

To assess **test–retest reliability**, the same measurement procedure is applied to the same group of people on two or more occasions. A procedure with high test–retest reliability ought to produce very similar results at each testing. The results of a procedure with low test–retest reliability will vary widely. Provided that a researcher can obtain the same people twice to test the procedure, the method is simple. There are, however, several potential problems.

Firstly, other factors may influence the participants between the testings. This problem is due to the effects of history (which was discussed in Chapter 7).

e.g.

A test is developed to measure the extent of racist stereotypes among school children. This test is administered to the same group of participants twice. The second testing falls six months after the first. In the intervening period, however, the country's education policy is changed and schools become racially integrated. In this case, the second testing may produce results very different from the first. This does not mean, though, that the test is unreliable, only that history has changed the respondents' attitudes.

A second similar problem arises due to *maturation* (also discussed in Chapter 7). Maturation refers to changes in the participants which are not due to external events such as those discussed under history.

e.g.

Suppose that a survey on population issues is conducted and the results show that rural adults in an African country favour having a large number of children. After the survey instrument is administered a second time, it may be found that the results are very different. The change may result from experience of the economic hardships arising from having too many children and not from the instrument's lack of reliability.

One should thus be careful when interpreting differences in the test and retest results. They may be the result of factors such as history or maturation, rather than lack of reliability of the instrument.

The third potential problem which must be considered by researchers using the test–retest method of determining reliability is reactivity. **Reactivity** occurs when exposure to the first testing influences responses to the second testing. The first time that participants are exposed to a questionnaire they may find it interesting. However, when the researcher presents the same questions a little while later, they may find it boring and irritating. Also, participants may remember the questions from the first testing and then intentionally provide either similar or different responses on the second testing. Here again there is likely to be disparity between the first and second testing which is not due to the instrument's lack of reliability.

When using the test–retest method, it is important that the researcher find the most appropriate time interval between the test and the retest. Long intervals make the study more vulnerable to the effects of history and maturation. Too short an interval may increase the effects of reactivity.

Fundamentals of Social Research Methods

Equivalent-form reliability

This method of assessing reliability (sometimes called parallel-form reliability) is very similar to the test–retest method but tries to address the problem of reactivity by changing the original test slightly at the second testing. Thus, instead of giving the same test to the same set of subjects on two or more occasions, this method requires the researcher to use an equivalent form of the instrument after the first testing. The following example contains two equivalent forms of a questionnaire designed to measure attitudes to socialism.

Original questions	Equivalent form
Organizing society on the basis of socialist ideology offers the best guarantee for all.	There are minor pronounced inequalities in socialist countries.
Countries organized according to socialist ideology have the same problems with unemployment as countries organized in different ways.	Economies organized on socialist principles are as much affected by unemployment as those organized on capitalist principles.
Socialist penetration of African countries is the best safeguard against international capitalism.	Socialist support of African countries constitutes a protection against the imperialist aims of Western states.

Although the difficulties with history and maturation remain (as for the test–retest method), the problem of reactivity is reduced because subjects are not expected to answer the same questions more than once. The difficulty with the equivalent forms method, however, is knowing whether or not the two versions of the instrument are in actual fact equivalent. Differences between the first and second testing may be due to subtle differences in the questions and may not mean that the original form has poor reliability. Also there are problems with the construction of the equivalent form. This process is time consuming and thus represents an important drain on resources. Literally twice as much work is required for the construction of the research instruments. Moreover, it is often very difficult to construct an equivalent form of an instrument. Most concepts in social science do not have equivalent concepts that can be used as alternatives.

Thus, the equivalent forms method for determining the reliability of a measuring procedure also has both advantages and disadvantages. The researcher must choose the most appropriate test of reliability carefully.

Split-halves reliability

Split-halves reliability is somewhat different to the test–retest and equivalent forms reliability. Rather than testing the consistency of instruments over multiple testings, the split-halves reliability method is concerned with the internal consistency of instruments. As a result, the problems of history, maturation, reactivity and equivalent forms do not plague this method. Therefore, it is more frequently used by social scientists than any of the other techniques. As the name implies, split-halves reliability involves splitting the test into halves and finding the extent of correspondence or reliability between the halves.

Consider the following items from the Subtle Racism Scale (Duckitt, 1990).

1. Given the same education, blacks should be able to perform as well as whites in any field.
2. It would be unfair if greater expenditure on black education were to be funded by the white taxpayer.
3. Given favourable conditions, it is quite possible that black majority rule could

result in a stable, prosperous and democratic South Africa.
4. Only equality between black and white can, in the long run, guarantee social peace in this country.
5. The large-scale extension of political rights to blacks will inevitably lead to chaos.
6. The wealth of this country is almost entirely due to the hard work and leadership of the whites.
7. Although black living conditions should be improved, it is crucial for the stable development of the country that whites retain political control.
8. It is important that drastic steps be taken to ensure a far more equitable division of the wealth of this country.
9. If all races were permitted to mix freely they would probably live in peace.
10. It is almost certainly best for all concerned that interracial marriages not be allowed.

Each of these ten items is designed to measure a subject's attitudes towards people of other races and tries to reduce the effects of social desirability as much as possible. The items can be separated into two groups (halves) according to whether they have an odd or an even number. If the participants respond in a similar way to the two groups of items, high reliability is indicated. In other words, the instrument has high internal consistency. Apart from the odds-evens approach used here, there are other ways of dividing the test items into halves. Each different split will produce slightly different estimates of the instrument's reliability. Some researchers prefer to assign each item to one of the groups on a random basis. This is most useful when there is some reason to suspect that there are systematic differences between the odd and even items. Dividing the instrument into a first half and a second half is not a good technique. This is because subjects will be less alert and interested in the second half of a test and the items and format will appear strange at the beginning of the test. For these reasons most researchers rely on the odd-even split.

Item analysis

A more detailed method for estimating the internal consistency of an instrument is found in **item analysis**. In this case, the researcher is interested in finding out how well the responses to each item correspond to the responses to the other items and to the test as a whole. This helps the researcher to identify those items within an instrument which are not providing useful information about the subjects or which are actually confusing the data. The researcher can then remove these troublesome items from the instrument (replacing them with better items if necessary) to increase the overall reliability of the instrument.

e.g.

If a researcher were to collect a set of questions all relating to racial prejudice and put them together they might form a test of racial prejudice. If this test were administered to a sample of the white South African population, including people who are more and less prejudiced than others, its internal consistency might be measured. If the more prejudiced people tended to respond in a similar way to each item, thus consistently demonstrating high racial prejudice, and the less prejudice, people also tended to respond in similar ways to each item, but consistently demonstrating low racial prejudice, the researcher could argue that the test had high internal consistency. However, if respondents tended to show high prejudice on some items but low prejudice on others (that is, the items are inconsistent) the researcher would be forced to conclude that the test has low internal consistency and is thus unreliable.

The following two questions illustrate how some items may be useful measures of prejudice and others not.

1. How would you feel about having as neighbours people from a different racial background?
2. How would you feel about working with people from a different racial background?

Item 1 is likely to be a more reliable measure of racial prejudice because of the particular relationship implied by the word "neighbours". People who are neighbours are of equal status and power and must interact as such. Item 2, on the other hand, is ambiguous about the nature of the suggested relationship. Some highly prejudiced people may have no objection to working with people of other racial backgrounds, as long as those people are of lower status and have less power than they have.

Most often the researcher will measure the degree of match between each item and every other item in the instrument. Those items which give results contradictory to the others must be discarded. An overall test of internal consistency is also often carried out. This is usually done through the use of a statistic called the **coefficient of reliability**. The value of the coefficient of reliability always falls between 0 and 1. An instrument with no reliability will score 0 and an instrument with very high reliability will score close to 1. For the most part social scientists like to use instruments which have been shown to have a coefficient of reliability of at least 0,7.

VALIDITY

Although both are important to an evaluation of an instrument, validity and reliability are actually entirely different things. The term **validity** was used in Chapter 7 where the internal and external validity of research designs was discussed. This chapter is concerned with the validity of data collection procedures and instruments and, in this context, the term "validity" has a somewhat different meaning. An instrument with very high reliability is useless if it has poor validity. Similarly, an instrument with very low reliability should not be used merely because it has very high validity. Where reliability asked the question "how *accurate* and *consistent* is this instrument?", validity asks questions such as "**what** does this instrument actually measure?" and "what do the results actually **mean**?". Unless the researcher can be sure that the measurement techniques are actually measuring the things that they are supposed to be measuring, the results are difficult to interpret.

e.g.

A school principal is concerned about the standard of teaching in her school. She constructs a spelling test and administers it to all the children in the school. To her surprise the pupils do far better than she had thought they would. A little confused, the principal goes back to her office to think. She begins to wonder if the pupils' spelling ability is really a good measure of teaching standards. It may be that even very poor teachers can teach spelling (especially to children with many opportunities for reading). To investigate further the teaching standards in the school, the principal decides to sit in on a sample of classes every day and observe the teachers in action. After a very few days it becomes apparent that the teachers are relying on rote learning in the class-room, which may work very well for spelling, but which is a very poor teaching method for most other subjects.

In this example, the spelling test was not measuring teaching standards at all, but one particular skill demonstrated by the pupils. As a result, the principal did not find out what she had hoped to. Observation of the teachers'

Reliability and Validity of Measurements

actual practice proved to be a far better measure. In this case the spelling test was not a valid measure of teaching standards, while the observation technique was. The spelling test, however, may have a high reliability, higher even that the observation method which depends on the observation style of the school principal.

There are many different types of validity. The four most important are: content validity, criterion-related validity, construct validity and face validity. Each of these is discussed in more detail below.

Content validity

In many cases, the topics that social scientists are most interested in are very complex and have many different components. In order to measure such complex topics properly, the researcher must find a technique which will provide some information on all its different components. When one or more components is neglected, the researcher cannot really claim to be measuring whatever it is that he or she is interested in.

e.g.

A researcher is interested in the interpersonal skills of a group of hospital workers. However, "interpersonal skills" is a very complex concept and therefore difficult to measure. A good instrument must include questions about how the respondents relate to their parents, their children, their friends, their employers, the patients in the hospital, and the other staff in the hospital. A questionnaire with high content validity would enquire about the participant's behaviour in a wide variety of interpersonal situations. A questionnaire with poor content validity might neglect family relations and focus only upon the interviewee's relations with employers and colleagues, even overlooking communication with patients.

Unfortunately, ensuring good content validity is usually far more complex than it sounds. In many cases social scientists cannot agree about what the essential components of any variable are. The next example describes some of the problems relating to the research of "power".

e.g.

For the purposes of this research, power is defined as a person's ability to make others do as he or she wants them to do. A full list of the different ways of exerting power might include the use of force, threat, persuasion, influence and reward. However, some theorists would argue that the use of force and threat actually demonstrates an absence of power. Others would suggest that the use of rewards is not a form of power, but that threat and force are. In this case it would be very difficult for the researcher to decide what to include in a measurement procedure.

In the case where there is doubt about the definition of a concept, it is the researcher's duty to decide upon an operational definition to guide the research and to substantiate that definition (where possible) on the basis of other research or theory. In other words, the researcher in the previous example might choose to define power as incorporating all the components listed above and should explain why such a broad definition was chosen.

This raises the question of how the social scientist goes about measuring the content validity of a new instrument. In most cases this is achieved by referring to literature relating to the researcher's area of study. If the researcher can show that an instrument measures all the various components of the variable in question, he or she can be confident that the instrument has high content validity. In the absence of relevant literature, researchers sometimes ask other social scientists with experience in the research area to evaluate the content validity of their measurement instruments.

Criterion-related validity

One way to test whether an instrument measures what it is expected to measure is to compare it to another measure which is known to be valid. This other measure is called the **criterion measure**. If the data collected using the instrument in question closely matches the data collected using the criterion measure (which is assumed to be valid), then the researcher may conclude that the new instrument is also valid. Note that the two sets of data must be collected from the same group of subjects. In practice there are two different ways of doing this. When the instrument being tested and the criterion measure are administered at the same time the term **concurrent validity** is used. When the instrument being tested is used to predict a future criterion it is called **predictive validity**.

e.g.

Using concurrent validity to evaluate a screening device

In communities that have been troubled by civil violence, many young adults (the people most likely to be caught up in conflict) often experience severe trauma and require specialized assistance. Unfortunately, it is quite difficult to identify the individuals most in need of help. To this end, a social scientist puts together a check-list of known symptoms relating to trauma as a screening device. In order to test the validity of this screening instrument, he compares the results of the screening test with the results of time-consuming clinical interviews (which are known to be capable of identifying people in need of help). When the results of the screening test match the results of the clinical interview, he is relieved to have found a valid (and efficient) way of identifying trauma survivors.

In this example, the test in question (the screening device) and the criterion measure (the clinical interview) were administered concurrently. Unfortunately, in most cases it is very difficult to find a suitable criterion which can be administered concurrently. Another perhaps more common way of dealing with the same problem is to compare the results of the screening test with an established test with proven reliability and validity.

More often the researcher is forced to wait for some future event against which to measure an instrument. In the next example, the results of the criterion measure are collected substantially later than the data from the instrument being evaluated. The original data is used to predict the results of the criterion measure.

e.g.

A researcher in the education sector has evidence that students' motivation is directly related to their final marks. She develops a questionnaire to measure motivation and administers it to a large group of students. On the basis of her results she is able to predict which students will do well and which will do badly in the final exams. At the end of the year, the students write their final exams and the researcher is able to determine the accuracy of her predictions derived from a measure of their motivation at the beginning of the year.

The most important difficulty with this approach is that, in most cases, the criterion measure may have resulted from a wide range variables, other than the one that the researcher is trying to test. In this case, students who could afford better textbooks or who had parents who demanded three hours of homework a day might do better. Oversimplification of the relationship between

Reliability and Validity of Measurements

variables can result in highly misleading results. Predictive validity should therefore only be used when the researcher is strongly convinced that the variable in question has a clear criterion measure against which a new instrument can be compared.

Construct validity

Construct validity is the most important and most often used of the various forms of validity discussed in this chapter. It is important that a measurement technique be closely linked with known theory in the area and with other related concepts. Where such close links can be demonstrated, the instrument is said to have high construct validity. When the links between the instrument and the related theory are very weak or non-existent, the instrument has low construct validity.

Chapter 10 of this text covers recommended procedures for the construction of questionnaires and interview schedules. The point was made that the researcher who begins by drafting questions is unlikely to create a useful instrument. Rather, the researcher should begin by making a list of the different pieces of information that the instrument is required to uncover and then design questions to secure that information. By following this process the researcher begins to link the items (and thus the instrument as a whole) to the theoretical components of the research topic, thereby contributing to construct validity.

e.g.

Consider the example, used earlier in this chapter, of youths traumatized by civil violence. Trauma of this kind is theoretically and logically linked with a range of other variables. One would expect highly traumatized youths to have been involved in more traumatic events than less traumatized youths. Also, school performance may drop as a result of the trauma. If the researcher can show that what his test measures (level of trauma) relates, as expected, to traumatic events in the subject's history and to changes in school performance, he has begun to demonstrate that his instrument has construct validity.

The following three steps are necessary in establishing construct validity.

1. Identify all of the variables which are strongly related to the variable that the test is designed to measure. This is done on the basis of theory, past research and logical deduction.
2. Measure all the variables involved and determine, through the use of statistical tests, the relationships between them.
3. Interpret and explain these relationships and develop an argument to demonstrate the construct validity (or lack thereof) of the instrument. The more variables other than the one under study that can be shown to interrelate meaningfully, the better the construct validity.

Face validity

Face validity is somewhat different from the other three forms of validity discussed so far. Face validity is concerned with the way the instrument appears to the participant. It is important that an instrument be tailored to the needs of the subjects for whom it is intended. Sometimes instruments may appear insultingly simplistic and, as a result, some participants will not take the social scientist or the research seriously. Other instruments may appear far too difficult to the testees, resulting in their giving up before they begin.

e.g.

A researcher interested in literacy wants to investigate the reading skills of people of different ages in a particular community. To do this

© Juta & Co Ltd

he selects a standard six textbook, fully expecting younger children to find it more difficult and adults to find it very easy. When he presents this text to younger children who find it very difficult, they give up without really trying and he cannot get a meaningful measurement of their reading skill. Similarly, he discovers that adults find the content of the reading matter childish and boring and feel insulted. Again, he cannot find a valid measure of reading skill. This approach obviously has very low face validity. After some careful thought the researcher tries a different approach. He gathers a selection of reading matter suited to a wide range of reading skills. He then gives each age-group a reading test which is comparable to their skill. In this way he gains data about the reading skills of people of all ages in the community.

There are many factors apart from the level of complexity that influence an instrument's face validity. Some personality tests tend to ask the same questions in different ways in order to check that the subject is not responding arbitrarily. When this is not done in a subtle way, subjects may begin to think that the researcher is checking up on them and again react negatively to the instrument.

BALANCING RELIABILITY WITH VALIDITY

Both reliability and validity are important to every instrument. It does not help the researcher to use a highly reliable instrument which has no validity. What is the use of an extremely accurate and consistent technique when one does not know what it is measuring? Similarly, an instrument with high validity is useless unless it can also be shown to be reliable. What does it help to measure something when the measurements are not consistent?

e.g.

Two researchers set out to measure the quality of hospital care in Lagos. Researcher A measures the quality of each hospital's service by calculating the average number of patients discharged in a day. Researcher B interviews one nurse and one patient at random from each hospital on the quality of health care at that hospital. The results that the two researchers come up with are very different, even though they intend to measure the same thing. Obviously something is wrong in the way the researchers are measuring health care.

In this example researcher A has chosen to focus on reliability at the expense of validity. Although she is likely to find very consistent results, the number of patients discharged daily is a very poor measure of hospital care. Some hospitals can treat more patients simply because each patient gets less attention than they would in other hospitals or because of better equipment and management. Researcher B has made the opposite mistake. He has focused on validity at the expense of reliability. Although the perceptions of nurses and patients are probably a valid measure of health care, the results depend heavily upon which nurse and patient are chosen, what kind of day they have had and various other variables.

Unfortunately, social scientists often find that reliability drops as validity increases. For example, exploratory interviews are generally considered to be highly valid because they allow the researcher to discuss issues with the respondent in greater depth. However, exploratory interviews require a good deal of subjective interpretation of the interviewees' responses on the part of the researcher and this reduces their reliability (another researcher may interpret the same responses differently or even get different responses from the participants). A set of rating scales put together in a questionnaire would be far more reliable (rating scales

Reliability and Validity of Measurements

require no interpretation), but is likely to be far less valid since the researcher is not able to check that the respondents understand the questions in the same way as they are intended and is unable to follow up on interesting responses.

The real skill in designing good measurement techniques involves finding a technique that is adequate in terms of both reliability and validity. No technique is perfectly reliable or valid but, unless an instrument can be shown to be well constructed in terms of both these principles, it should not be used in social research.

EXERCISES

1. Try to think of different ways of measuring each of the following variables, then evaluate each technique that you have thought of in terms of its reliability and validity. For each variable choose the technique which you think would be the best.
   (a) the income of families
   (b) a person's employment potential
   (c) a child's social support
2. What do you understand by the terms "reliability" and "validity"? Is a valid measure always reliable? Explain your answer.
3. Discuss the different ways of determining the reliability of measures in social science. What are the limitations of these techniques?
4. Discuss the different forms of validity. Think of examples which explain why each one is important.
5. Select a research article and discuss the reliability and validity of the measures of the variables used in it.

CHAPTER 12

Interpretation of Results and Writing a Research Report

The purpose of this chapter is twofold. Firstly, it discusses how the researcher is to interpret results of research, to check for inconsistencies and for all types of bias and error which could have influenced these results. Only when a researcher has gone through these steps can general conclusions be drawn from the sample to the population and from the special conditions of the particular research to broader frameworks, taking into account previous findings cited in the literature review. Also included is a discussion of how recommendations and further suggestions for more research are made on the basis of the conclusions of a study. The second aim of this chapter is to give some guidelines on how to write a research report, which is basically a way of presenting the whole research procedure in a manner adapted to the interest of the potential reader.

CHAPTER OBJECTIVES

Learners who have completed this chapter will be able to:
- Identify possible sources of error and bias in a study.
- Interpret the results of the data analysis process.
- Draw appropriate conclusions from the findings.
- Present research findings in an appropriate manner.

DATA ANALYSIS

Once data collection and checking have been completed, the researcher should begin the process of analysing the data. This analysis is conducted so that the researcher can detect consistent patterns within the data, such as the consistent covariance of two or more variables. For example, the researcher who finds that higher scores on one variable are consistently found with higher scores on a second variable, can conclude that those two variables are in some way related. Furthermore, the data analysis process allows the researcher to generalize the findings from the sample used in the research, to the larger population in which the researcher is interested.

The process of data analysis itself takes many different forms depending upon the nature of the research question and design, and the nature of the data itself. Quantitative data is often analysed using a range of descriptive and inferential statistical procedures which fall beyond the scope of this book but are covered in detail in the other book in this series. Qualitative data is analysed with techniques especially designed for this form of data. Very often quantitative and qualitative methods of data analysis play complementary roles in the data analysis process.

INTERPRETING THE FINDINGS: DETECTION OF POSSIBLE ERRORS

Based on the quantitative and qualitative data analyses, the research findings are explicitly stated. These findings, as well as the whole procedure leading to them, must be thoroughly and critically reviewed to detect any errors of measurement, bias and mistakes which could have distorted the description of the aspect of social reality under study.

When carrying out a research project, it is essential to recognize that observations of any kind can never be expressed without some error. However, recognition of this weakness does not mean that one should passively accept these errors. On the contrary, every effort should be made to identify, reduce or compensate for them. This is only feasible if all the possible sources and types of errors and mistakes are identified and investigated.

Types of error and mistake

First of all, there are *measurement* and *classification errors*. **Measurement errors** refer to quantitative data which is wrong or inaccurate, whether it pertains to the income of families, the age of children, or the number of votes obtained by a candidate. **Classification errors** are made when data is wrongly identified, that is, put in an inappropriate class. Examples could be the identification of refugees in a certain country as nationals of the host country, or the classification of all children living in a certain house as the offspring of the house-owner. Both types of error can be reduced or eliminated by a more careful and precise handling of the data, for instance, by asking more precise questions.

The second group consists of *constant* and *random errors*. **Constant errors** are systematic, repeated errors throughout the research and they can introduce important biases. The interviewer may record the occupation of a respondent instead of the profession, or systematically underestimate the number of people attending a certain event. A **random error**, on the other hand, occurs on some occasions but not on others; it is thus non-systematic and unpredictable. It may be an overestimation of the number of participants on one day, an underestimation on a second day, then a correct count on the third, so that, on average, random errors compensate for one another over large numbers of data. Thus, random errors are not considered as very serious, while constant errors are very biasing and should be sorted out and eliminated as soon as their source has been identified.

We must also distinguish between *errors* and *mistakes*. Although considered as equivalents in everyday language, these two words have different meanings in research. **Errors**, as those mentioned above, introduce bias and inaccuracies in measurement, but their sources can be detected, their seriousness evaluated and there exist some statistical techniques for controlling or eliminating their effects. The biased formulation of research problems, or difficulties in the way the researcher approaches respondents are examples of error. **Mistakes** or blunders on the part of the interviewer or the researcher are, on the other hand, generally neither predictable, nor detectable in time to permit their systematic analysis and correction. Since they are very often related to the inexperience or the incompetence of the researcher, they should and can be avoided by sound training and long experience with research.

Interpretation of Results and Writing a Research Report

Sources of error

Errors can be introduced at all levels of the research process. Thus, it suffices to analyse each step in order to identify possible sources of bias. The list presented below is not exhaustive, as it only states the main sources without many details. In many aspects, it is a summary of what has been presented in previous chapters. Possible sources of error in research include the following.

1. *Vagueness of the definitions and inaccuracy of the hypotheses*

The lack of adequate operational definitions can lead to an inaccurate description of the population, of the types of information to be collected.

2. *Inadequacy of the design and the planning of the research*

This can arise from failure to identify all possible variables, having too many uncontrolled variables, or having too many sources of invalidity that have escaped detection. Every study comprises many different aspects, any of which may have been overlooked.

3. *Sampling errors and other errors*

These affect the representativeness of the sample. A discrepancy may exist between the actual population out of which the sample has been drawn and the target population to which inferences will be applied. This may be due to the inadequacy of the frame lists or a high number of non-responses. The sample may also not be representative of the population because of the choice of an inappropriate sampling method (for instance, an accidental one) or a very small sample size with no estimate of sampling error. Often, even though the correct sampling method has been chosen, it is not implemented correctly because of the inexperience of the interviewer or unexpected difficulties.

4. *Imperfection in the research instrument*

In experiments, instruments like chronometers may be deficient or not well adjusted to the particular conditions. In the case of interviews and questionnaires, many more errors can be introduced relating to the length of the questionnaire, the venue, the order of presentation of the questions, the content and the type of questions. For instance, leading questions, double-barrelled questions, or questions with incomplete choices of answer and with unfamiliar vocabulary, are particularly likely to induce error.

5. *Interviewer bias*

The interviewer can affect the answers of the respondent through personal characteristics, such as being too lenient, or aggressive, impatient, or partial. The interviewer can also bias the information by recording it inaccurately, either by translating the idea of the respondent into the interviewer's own words and thus interpreting the answers according to his own views, or by writing down only a summary or part of the answer. Unscrupulous interviewers may falsify the answers so as to reflect their own convictions, or even fill in the questionnaires without interviewing anybody.

6. *Respondent bias*

In this category appear not only the biases introduced by unresponsive participants, by uncooperative ones answering at random, but also by respondents who give false information on purpose due to mistrust, fear, conformity or social status pressures. Moreover, one can add here answers based on the misunderstanding of a question or a word, and the difficulty experienced by respondents in expressing themselves.

© Juta & Co Ltd

7. Analyst bias

Here one finds all the errors introduced at the level of processing and coding the answers. Misinterpretations of the answers, in particular of open-ended questions, are frequent, leading to incorrect classification.

The statistical treatment of quantitative data may be defective through the choice of an inadequate test or because of computation errors. Moreover, analysts have many ways of projecting their expectations and prejudices in the computation, comparison and presentation of results.

8. Researcher bias

Throughout the research process the beliefs of the researchers, their political, religious and racial attitudes and other convictions play an underlying role. As human beings, researchers can never be completely objective, particularly when dealing with the social sciences. They have expectations not only on the basis of scientific considerations but also on the basis of their personal views. These surface in their interest in, and choice of, the research topic, as well as in many other steps of the research. They could intentionally choose a particular population, adopt a certain sample, ask (or refrain from asking) some specific questions, deliberately omit to take into consideration some theories or research findings that contradict or question the validity of their approach.

Once all these sources of error have been investigated and the extent and type of possible bias estimated, the findings can be interpreted. In particular, on the basis of a critical study of the procedure, the researcher should be able to explain the inconsistencies in the research results and between these results and the findings of other researchers. The scientist should also be in a position to state the shortcomings and the limitations of the research and take these into account in the evaluation of the findings.

DRAWING CONCLUSIONS

After interpreting the findings it is useful to summarize the aims of the research, compare them with the findings and draw conclusions on how much and in which manner the goal has been achieved. Attention should also be paid to the extent to which the hypotheses have been confirmed, and whether it was possible, for instance, to infer causal relationships between variables.

GENERALIZING RESEARCH FINDINGS

Once the conclusions have been drawn, reflecting some properties of the target population, one can estimate how far these findings could be generalized to a larger population and predict modifications which would have to be taken into consideration when undertaking such a generalization. For instance, one could be interested in estimating how far results obtained on a target population of university students could be generalized to the broader population of students in tertiary educational institutions.

Even more important is the integration of findings within the set of previous research findings and within the theoretical framework used in the research. The first point refers to the comparison of the findings of the present research with the findings of investigations considered in the literature review. Are the present results in accordance with the others? Do they contradict some of them? How does one explain the differences? This critical analysis may help to discover important flaws, misinterpretations, or relevant variables which have been overlooked by either the present or previous researchers.

Unexpected similarities can also help to uncover an important common factor. For instance, many investigations have aimed at assessing whether and how the viewing of

Interpretation of Results and Writing a Research Report — Chapter 12

violence in films affects the behaviour of young children. Seemingly contradictory results have been found: heightened levels of aggression in some cases and a cathartic effect which decreases the level of aggression in others. These opposite findings led to a deeper analysis posing such questions as: In which, circumstances and for what type of children (age, sex, social class) is the effect soothing? What are the characteristics of the films?

The researcher should also try to integrate the final conclusions within a theoretical framework. Do the findings consolidate a certain theory? Do they, on the other hand, put into question some accepted principles? Do they add new perspectives or answer old questions? Do they constitute the "missing link" between theories?

SUGGESTIONS AND RECOMMENDATIONS

Research is mainly relevant if it has implications for the improvement of the human condition. As such, the practical aspects of the findings must be analysed as well. On the basis of the results, suggestions may be made for further investigations to clarify some aspects, to generalize some findings, or to check the importance of some variables and, perhaps, to avoid some pitfalls. One could mention the possible application of the results to other fields. For example, some investigations on emotions could have relevance to the medical profession, in industrial relations, or in education. Lastly, recommendations can be made on the alteration of programmes or policies. These recommendations could be very detailed and practical, such as types of rewards, incentives or punishments to be used in schools to achieve optimal learning motivation.

In action-research, recommendations and suggestions are central to the research process. Concrete plans for the implementation of such suggestions should be formulated by the research participants. These become the action of the action-research process.

TYPES OF REPORT FORMATS

Research reports will be quite different depending on their aims and their readership. Their presentation, completeness and length, their emphasis on one or the other aspect and their level of scientific exposure will accordingly vary greatly. Where the researcher is presenting research findings to semi-literate or illiterate people, it is important that he or she find suitable ways of conveying the research findings. Verbal reports using audio-visual techniques are often essential.

The most detailed, complete and scientific report for research-funding institutions and archives will present all the different steps of research in detail. A report written to be published in a scientific journal will have to show a high level of scientific quality condensed into a few pages. A report written for an agency particularly interested in the conclusions and practical consequences will cut short the technical aspects of the research and emphasize the discussion of the findings. A report to be understood by the average educated readership of a magazine will present the findings in more general terms and will avoid scientific vocabulary. In other words, these different reports will stress one or the other aspect of the most complete research report. Thus, it is sufficient to present here the format of such a complete report.

Note that some organizations specify how research is to be reported. The researcher must make sure that he or she is familiar with the demands of clients, funders or other types of organization. Specific formats are also demanded by particular disciplines. For example, the American Psychological Association specifies exactly how the researcher is to present findings for publication.

ORGANIZATION OF A RESEARCH REPORT

Although no strict rules exist on the structure of a research report, logic and consistency impose a certain order. The guidelines presented below constitute but one possibility. Within each of the main sections the order of the different subsections may vary and some sections may be omitted altogether. On the whole, the guidelines follow the presentation sequence of this book and each subsection refers to a subsection of the book.

The main sections of a research report are: introduction, methods, results, discussion and references. To these can be added an abstract at the beginning and appendices at the end.

Introduction

An introduction includes the following themes.

1. Identification of the research problem

The problem to be dealt with is introduced and the area within which the problem is situated is identified. Authoritative sources, including other scientists, are quoted to assess what is known about the particular issue and what is still unclear and needs further investigation, as well as the relevance of such investigations.

2. Literature review

Only the relevant articles are cited and commented upon. Often it is useful to group the articles into different categories related to particular variables or other conditions considered relevant. Subheadings can be useful. Other types of background information should also be presented.

3. Statement of the problem

The statement of the problem refers to the first two points but contains a more precise approach to the issue and clarifies the purpose of the study. It should be very short and should identify the main variables, defined conceptually at this stage.

4. Statement and rationale of the hypotheses

The wording of the hypotheses is done in a clear and concise way but still using conceptual definitions. This section should provide logical arguments to show that each hypothesis is plausible, reasonable and sound. It should also give empirical evidence to justify the hypotheses. In other words, the reader should be convinced that there are good grounds for stating the hypotheses. Again, such grounds are usually provided by the literature review.

5. Operational definitions of the variables

In this subsection the main variables already mentioned under 3 should be given operational definitions.

6. Operational formulations of the hypotheses

On the basis of step 5 above, the hypotheses are given their final, operational formulation, including their observable indicators or measures.

7. Significance of the study

The relevance of the problem is highlighted considering two aspects: its theoretical and practical implications. Focus is put on each specific hypothesis.

Method

The method incorporates consideration of the following.

1. Subjects (respondents/participants)

In this subsection all issues and information concerning the subjects of the research are examined. Among these are the characteristics of the target population and of the sample, the sampling procedure and the size of the sample.

2. The task and the material or instrument

The type of activity that the participants are asked to perform should be described, as well as the materials used. In some studies the participants might have had to fill in a questionnaire only. In this case, the main characteristics of the questionnaire should be given. In other studies, participants are tested on a certain skill with a particular instrument, or their reactions to a particular situation constitute the observed phenomena. Here again the tasks, the instructions and the measuring instrument(s) must be described.

3. Analysis of variables

Once the tasks are described it is important to state the relationship between these tasks and the manipulation of the independent and moderator variables. Thus, the variables which have been operationalized as required by part 5 of the introduction are reconsidered here in connection with their function as independent, dependent, control and other kinds of variable.

4. Procedures

The description of the task and the different variables is followed by the identification of experimental and control groups, that is, the chosen research design should be specified, including the order of succession of the different activities, their duration and the instructions given to the participants. One can then mention the difficulties and problems encountered during data collection.

5. Data analysis

In this section the process of data analysis is described in detail. As mentioned earlier in the chapter, these processes will depend on the nature of the research question and the type of data.

Results

Essentially, this involves the following two steps.

1. Summary of the results

The main results following from the data analysis are presented here. Tables, graphs and diagrams are particularly effective and should be used to help the reader to understand the data.

2. Analysis of the hypotheses

Each hypothesis is related to the results. The decision to reject or to retain a hypothesis is taken in the light of the respective results.

Discussion

Discussion includes:

1. *Summary of the findings,* based on the tested hypotheses.
2. *Interpretation of these findings,* subject to an analysis of validity and reliability.
3. *Conclusions,* related to the questions raised in the introduction.
4. *Generalization of the research findings.*
5. *Suggestions and recommendations.*

References or bibliography

The list, in alphabetical order, of the names of authors and titles of all books or articles mentioned constitutes the last section of a report.

One of the most frequently used methods is first to give the name of the author(s), then the year of publication, then title of book or article in italics, thereafter place of publication, publisher's name and page number(s).

For instance:

Babbie, E.R. (1979). *The Practice of Social Research*. Belmont, California: Wordsworth.

Tembo, L.P. (1979). The African university and social reform. In B. Turok, (ed.), *Development in Zambia: A Reader*. London: Zed Press, 187–200.

Journal articles are referenced by indicating the name of the journal in italics after the title of the article, as well as by indicating the volume and/or the number of the issue before the page number:

Selltiz, C. (1955). The use of survey in citizens' campaign against discrimination. *Human Organisation*, 14, 19–25.

It is essential that each article or book cited in the text is accompanied by a full reference at the end of the report. Citations in the text appear either in the form, "Babbie (1979) argues that . . ." or, "(Tembo, 1979)".

Researchers must determine the exact reference format required by journals, academic institutions or discipline specific organisations. Where no particular format is required, the ones detailed above will suffice.

Abstract and appendices

Abstracts are frequently required for journal articles and also for other types of reports. Abstracts should be short, usually between 100 and 200 words, and should contain statements about the four main sections, namely problem, method, results and conclusions. Emphasis should be put on the results and their significance, but information on the design and the characteristics and size of the sample is also important. The reader should be in a position to grasp the essence of the whole study by reading the abstract.

Appendices usually contain summarized data and the results of data analysis, both often presented as tables. It is essential to give a number and title to each appendix in line with how they are referred to in the text. Where the instrument of measurement is a questionnaire or any material which can be printed, it may also be added as a separate appendix. Elaborate coding scales are sometimes included at the end of some detailed reports.

REPORTING STYLE

A last word should be said about the style of any type of report. Efforts should be made to submit a clearly written report without unnecessary details and empty phrases. Emphasis should be placed on quality rather than quantity and style must be adapted to the readership.

Interpretation of Results and Writing a Research Report | Chapter 12

EXERCISES

1. Using a questionnaire with scaled answers, a researcher measures the attitude of farmers in a rural district towards family planning. The results indicate a clearly negative attitude. Using the same questionnaire, another scientist replicates this study on an equivalent sample of farmers. The new results show a slightly positive attitude towards family planning. Which type of error could explain this difference? What can be said about the validity and the reliability of the research?
2. Analyse how an investigation can be influenced by a researcher during the planning stages, whether deliberately or unconsciously, at each of the following steps:
   (*a*) selection of a problem for research;
   (*b*) determination of the population and selection of the sample;
   (*c*) design of the research;
   (*d*) construction of the tools of measurement.
3. How might the four steps mentioned in question 2 be influenced by the person who collects the data?

CHAPTER 13

Concluding remarks

Since all human beings are the product of their social environment, they are socialized into and act according to certain cultural values and beliefs of which they are only vaguely aware. It is therefore important to discuss the relationship between the objectivity demanded by science and the impact of the system of values inherent in each individual. Moreover, since research is supported by a society, the nature and the consequences of this support call for analysis. This entails an examination of the role of research-funding institutions.

CHAPTER OBJECTIVES

Learners who have completed this chapter will be able to:
- Discuss critically the questions of objectivity and human values as they apply to research in the social sciences.
- Analyse and manage the various interpersonal and inter-organisational relationships that are part of most social research projects.

THE RESEARCH WORLD

Because introductory texts in research methodology strive to be as clear as possible, they sometimes do not prepare the inexperienced researcher for the complex world of research. Researchers do not work alone. In nearly all cases a range of different people has some kind of stake in the research process. These people include the subjects of the research themselves, other researchers, research funding institutions, various administrations that control access to particular target populations, tertiary education institutions, and publishers. One of the challenges facing the researcher is to develop productive working relationships with all these different groups so that the research may proceed as smoothly as possible.

> **e.g.**
> The Parent–Teacher Association of a school is concerned about the increase in teenage pregnancy at their school. In particular they want to know whether this is a local trend or whether it is also happening in other schools in their district. Finally, they want to identify the best strategy for reducing the number of teenagers falling pregnant. They call in a social researcher for advice and together plan a survey of schools in the area, and an investigation of other attempts to prevent teenage pregnancy. This study will be quite expensive and so they put together a funding proposal to a research donor operating in their area. Having accessed the necessary funds, they find that they must get permission from the Minister of Education in order to conduct research in schools. Having done this they must also explain the project to the headmasters of the schools in which the

research is to be conducted. The researcher also identifies three teenage pregnancy projects in the region, and must liaise with the people in charge of each, in order to discover which strategies are most successful.

Furthermore, many research projects involve more than a single researcher. Because many social research topics are extremely complex and difficult to investigate in their entirety, it is often necessary to break topics down into a series of smaller questions. (This was discussed in detail in Chapter 3). It is often the case that a team of social scientists will embark upon linked research projects, each contributing to a more general topic is a specific way. This is an effective technique which can produce excellent results as long as one common pitfall is avoided. It often happens that the links between the various research topics fall away and that when the results emerge they do not relate to each other in any meaningful way. Thus although five researchers have all studied the same topic, they have defined their research questions and variables in such different ways that the results are not comparable. A much more effective method is to jointly derive a series of research questions which relate to the topic and then to agree upon conceptual and operational definitions of all variables that have relevance to the broader study.

With the ongoing development of the various social science disciplines, areas of overlap are becoming more and more significant. Analysing social reality in terms of varying perspectives is very rewarding but may be complicated. When a team of researchers from different disciplines co-operate on a single research question the term **multi-disciplinary research** is used. The chief value of this form of research is that it helps social scientists to overcome the somewhat arbitrary boundaries that exist between bodies of knowledge within the social sciences. When sociologists, economics and political scientists (for example) work together on a topic they bring to that topic a broader range of experience and theory, than any group of people from a single discipline would bring. In multi-disciplinary research, however, attention to the way questions are asked and variables defined is even more crucial. This is because the various disciplines tend to conceptualise research questions and social concepts in different ways. It is important that social researchers from different disciplines are speaking a "common language" before they embark on a common research problem.

Role players in the research project have their own expectations of what the project will produce, and they will exert influence in different ways. The researcher must be aware of all the different expectations and concerns of this group of people, and make sure that their influence on the outcome of the research is minimized. This is discussed in more depth below.

OBJECTIVITY AND VALUES

Still now some scientists, amongst other people, believe that science is value-free, detached from culture, ideology and politics. Their belief is that science is purely objective. This myth must be discarded and the various ways in which culture, ideology and politics impact upon scientific research must be analysed.

Among social scientists and all the other participants in research projects, culture and ideology play an important role. One discovers easily that they can influence every step of the research process, from the choice of the research topic and the formation of hypotheses to the final interpretation of results. Culture and ideology create implicit and explicit expectations of outcome that permeate the research. Although it is

Concluding remarks — Chapter 13

expected that scientists should set their personal values aside when carrying out research, practice has shown that this is not a reasonable expectation.

e.g.

For example, studies on work motivation in industry can be undertaken in accordance with the interests of the employer who wishes to avoid industrial action which could curb production and profits. Equally, it can be undertaken in the interests of the workers, their well-being and their dignity as human beings. Depending on the approach chosen and the type of data collected, the conclusions may be very different, even if, *officially*, the adopted interest is that of the firm or industry as a whole.

To understand the extent to which research is tied to social politics, one must appreciate the interrelationship between research and society. As mentioned in Chapter 1, the development of knowledge, and of research in particular, is a direct function of the needs of society. Moreover, the emphasis given to different problems and thus the effort to solve them is determined by the people in decision-making positions. Very easily, research becomes a tool in the hands of the most powerful people in society and may be used, either consciously or unconsciously, to promote the needs of those people, at the expense of the needs of less powerful people.

Control over research by the most powerful people in a society is maintained in two ways. Firstly, the resources necessary to conduct social research may be controlled by a particular group. Secondly, the skills necessary to conduct social research may be found only in a particular group. South Africa provides a good historical example of this situation but almost every country in the world has at some time or another faced similar problems. In South Africa, research funds were for many years controlled by the relatively wealthy white population (both English and Afrikaans speaking). This group had particular concerns and beliefs about the world, and resources where allocated to research that coincided with those concerns. At the same time and with few exceptions, very few people from outside this group had access to good quality education and the opportunities to develop competent research skills.

Lastly, the impact of politics, ideology and culture on the application or the use of research findings must be examined. As mentioned before, research is not usually conducted for the sake of pure knowledge but mainly to respond to the needs of society. The social scientist, on the one hand, and the funding institutions on the other, may have quite different views about the relevance of a research topic and its possible application. Social scientists may even be unaware of the ultimate purpose of those funding their investigations. They may be strongly opposed to certain uses to which their scientific findings may be put. Other scientists willingly adopt the aims determined by decision-making or funding bodies.

For example, some psychologists, whether willingly or unknowingly, have been instrumental in developing psychological weapons to boost the morale of invading troops and to discourage and to terrorize the civilian population of a victim society (University of Giessen, 1975).

In spite of all that has been said above and remembering that ethics refers mainly to the methods employed in research (see Chapter 9), it should not be concluded that objectivity and neutrality are foreign to social research. However, the need for awareness of the many ways the search for objectivity is influenced by values, must be emphasized.

© Juta & Co Ltd

THE ROLE OF RESEARCH-FUNDING INSTITUTIONS

Very often, research is expensive and budgets in the developing world are small. Sadly, accurate information does not seem to be highly valued by decision-makers in Africa who would rather spend the scarce funds at their disposal on providing services, even when very little is known about the efficacy or cost-efficiency of those services. The cost and harmful consequences of a poorly researched intervention, without feasibility study or evaluation and monitoring data, is enormous when compared with the cost of carefully designed social science research.

However, given the scarcity of resources available to social researchers, the people that control what funds have a powerful influence on the kind of research that is done. Very often different topics become fashionable at different times and in conjunction with the prevailing and changing concerns of donor agencies. Examples of this include research on women during the UN Women's Decade and research on handicapped people during the Year of the Disabled. Societies experiencing social stress, racial or industrial unrest will allocate funds to find solutions to these problems. But even then, these investigations will be done within a certain political framework. That is, the research is based on certain premises and the results are bound to reflect these premises, ideologies and expectations.

Although a very broad range of structures use the services of social science researchers to address problems and queries on a contract basis, the list of agencies that will embark on research of a broader nature designed to improve society is fewer. These agencies fall into a number of different categories, including:

1. Agencies attached to the governments of particular countries. In South Africa the National Research Foundation fulfils this role for the social sciences.
2. International donors such as those associated with the United Nations and the Organisation for African Unity. These include the United Nations Children's Fund (UNICEF) and many others.
3. Independent philanthropic organisations (sometimes multi-national) usually based in countries in Europe and North America. Examples of these include the Carnegie and Ford Foundations based in the United States of America and the Bernard van Leer Foundation based in the Netherlands.
4. Corporate donors such as large businesses which will allocate resources to social research as part of their social responsibility policies. An example of this might be Shell International which funds a range of different projects.

Every donor organisation specifies criteria for funding. These criteria may relate to the research topic with only a relatively narrow range of topics being considered, or may relate to the nature of the research methods, or the characteristics of the researchers. Although in the past many donors have used their financial power to dictate research topics and methodologies to researchers, the current trend is to allow much more flexibility. At the end of the twentieth century most donors have become extremely sensitive to the problems of dictating research agendas from outside of the developing world and so are much more likely to let local experts and researchers guide their work.

Nevertheless, the prospects for independent unbiased research in countries which must rely on external funding are rather bleak unless social scientists are cautious. The situation can be improved if researchers are conscious of these dangers and confront them. They can be helped in this task by a clear awareness of the real needs of their countries and by the conviction that they will undertake research promoting the genuine development of their countries.

It is the researcher's responsibility to find donors who are interested in the kind of research being proposed and to convince appropriate funders of the usefulness of the project. For this reason the **research proposal** is a crucial document which seeks firstly to convince its readers (including donors) of the value of the research, but also to demonstrate the feasibility of the project and the expertise and experience of the researchers.

HIGHEST QUALITY RESEARCH

The most fundamental of all the ethical guidelines to which the social scientist must attend is that of producing the highest quality research. When social research is conducted without a proper understanding of the underlying principles of scientific enquiry, the results may be misleading and damaging to society. All social scientists have a responsibility to apply the methods of social science correctly and in full, so that society can be assured of the validity of the findings. When biased research is conducted and published the credibility of all social researchers is damaged.

Highest quality research depends upon several factors. Firstly it is essential that all social scientists ensure that they do their job to the best of their ability every single time. Secondly, it is essential that all social scientists are adequately trained so that they possess the expertise to do the job properly. Finally, it is essential that research be made available to peer review, most commonly through publication. This requires full reporting of methods (including mistakes and biases when they occurred) so that each study can be realistically reviewed by other social scientists.

Only in this way can researchers ensure that the reputation and value of social research continues to grow in the developing world, and that the potential contribution to society that researchers have to make, is acknowledged.

Glossary

The aim of this glossary is to provide the reader with a general understanding of a concept or term used in this textbook, rather than to present a precise sophisticated definition. In order to grasp a concept in its complexity the reader should refer to the chapter in which this concept is studied.

Abstract: A brief summary of a study, including research questions, methodology, results and conclusions, found at the beginning of journal articles and other kinds of reports.

Action-research: A form of participatory research which combines social action and research to resolve a specific problem facing a community and to increase human understanding of similar problems and their solutions.

Antecedent variable: That variable that influences the independent variable and in that way indirectly affects the relationship between the independent and dependent variable.

Applied social research: Social research which has the primary aim of finding solutions to specific concerns or problems facing particular groups of people, by applying models or theories developed through basic social research.

Basic social research: Social research which has the primary aim of contributing to the development of human knowledge and understanding of a specific aspect of social reality.

Causal relationship: A relationship where change in one variable (the dependent variable) is shown to result from change in another (the independent variable), and where the direction of such change can be predicted.

Conceptual definition: The definition of a concept in terms of other concepts.

Constant: An empirical property that does not vary.

Control group: The group that is not exposed to the event or treatment in an experimental design, and is compared with the experimental group. Note that because the control and experimental groups result from the use of randomization or matching, they are equivalent before the event or treatment.

Control Variable: That variable that is controlled (eliminated or neutralized) by the researcher, to avoid it influencing the relationship between the independent and dependent variables.

Correlational relationship: The relationship between two variables where change in one variable is accompanied by predictable change in another variable. The variables are said to "covary". Correlational relationships are not necessarily causal relationships.

Correlational research: Social research with the primary aim of establishing correlational relationships between variables.

Cross-sectional design: A research design where all data is collected at a single point in time. Since this term does not relate to a specific design, it is also referred to as a "cross-sectional study".

Dependent variable: The variable which is observed and measured to determine the effect on it of the independent variable. It is that factor which varies as the researcher manipulates the independent variable.

Descriptive research: Social research with the primary aim of describing (rather than explaining) a particular phenomenon.

Diagnostic evaluation: Research designed to increase the effectiveness of interventions by identifying neglected areas of need, target groups and unresolved problem areas.

Directional hypothesis: A hypothesis which specifies in what way (direction) the dependent variable will vary in response to a determined variation of the independent variable.

Dummy table: A table of results constructed before the data is collected to assist the researcher in designing appropriate measuring instruments for the research.

Evaluation research: Social research designed to investigate whether a particular project or intervention has met its stated objectives and how the effectiveness of that project might be improved.

Experimental design: The most rigorous type of research design which depends upon randomization or matching for the construction of equivalent groups.

Experimental group: The group that is exposed to the event or treatment in an experimental design, and is compared with the control group.

Explanatory research: Social research with the primary aim of establishing causal relationships between variables.

Exploratory research: Social research which explores a certain phenomenon with the primary aim of formulating more specific research questions or hypotheses relating to that phenomenon.

External validity: A measure of the extent to which research findings can be generalized to a0 broader population.

Extraneous variable: That variable which, if not controlled, will obscure (confound) the observed relationship between the independent and dependent variables. It is thus sometimes called a "spurious" or "confounding" variable.

Feasibility study: A study designed to determine whether a particular strategy or intervention is likely to reach its stated objectives.

Field experiment: An experiment conducted in everyday social reality where the artificiality of a constructed setting is reduced at the expense of a loss of control of extraneous variables.

Focus group: A semi-structured group interview conducted by a skilled facilitator.

Formative evaluation: Research designed to find solutions to any problems that emerge during a particular intervention.

Hypothesis: A tentative, concrete and testable explanation or solution to a research question.

Independent variable: That variable which is measured, manipulated, or selected by the researcher to determine its relationship to an observed phenomenon, the dependent variable.

Inference: The process of generalizing findings from a sample to the broader population from which the sample was drawn.

Internal validity: The extent to which a particular research design excludes all alternate explanations for the research findings, or in simple terms, whether the independent variable is really the cause

Glossary

of the variation of the dependent variable.

Interval scale: A scale of measurement characterized by regular units of measurement but no absolute zero, on the basis of which units are classified by quantitative value.

Intervening variable: That variable which is determined by the independent variable but influences the dependent variable, and is often difficult to manipulate or measure.

Interview: A data collection technique based on a series of questions relating to the research topic to be answered by research participants.

Laboratory experiment: An experiment conducted under artificial conditions which allow the researcher to control many extraneous variables but which may not be typical of everyday social reality.

Literature review: An integrated summary of all available literature relevant to a particular research question.

Longitudinal design: Research designs where the data collection is spaced over a period of time. Since this term does not relate to a specific design, it is also referred to as a "longitudinal study".

Matching: The process of creating equivalent groups by balancing the effects of variables other than the independent and dependent ones. This is often achieved by identifying matched pairs of units and distributing them between the control and experimental groups. Note that groups constructed in this way are called "dependent groups".

Moderator variable: That variable that is measured or manipulated by the researcher to determine the manner in which if affects the relationship between the independent and dependent variable.

Nominal scale: A scale of measurement where units are classified in terms of two or more qualitatively different categories.

Non-directional hypothesis: A hypothesis which states that the dependent variable will change in relation to changes in the independent variable. However, the way (direction) of this variation is not specified.

Non-probability sampling: Sampling techniques where the probability of each element of the population being included in the sample is not known.

Observation: A data collection technique based on the direct observation of participants' behaviour.

Operational definition: The definition of a concept in terms of the way that concept is to be measured or observed. This form of definition is based on the observable characteristics of a concept and indicates what to do or what to observe in order to identify those characteristics.

Ordinal scale: A scale of measurement where units are classified in terms of rank ordered categories.

Participatory research: Research based on the principle of an ideal complementary and equal relationship between researchers and the community.

Pilot study: A small study conducted prior to a larger piece of research to determine whether the methodology, sampling, instruments and analysis are adequate and appropriate.

Population: The complete set of events, people or things to which the research findings are to be applied.

© Juta & Co Ltd

Population parameter: A numerical value which summarizes some characteristic of the population.

Pre-experimental designs: A set of research designs characterized by very few requirements but which do not approach the rigour of experimental and quasi-experimental designs.

Primary data: Data collected with the primary aim of answering the research question posed by the researcher.

Probabilistic explanations: Explanations of social reality expressed as statements of likelihood (probability), rather than certainty.

Probability (random) sampling: Sampling techniques where the probability of each element of the population being included in the sample can be determined.

Qualitative research: Research conducted using a range of methods which use qualifying words and descriptions to record and investigate aspects of social reality.

Quantitative research: Research conducted using a range of methods which use measurement to record and investigate aspects of social reality.

Quasi-experimental designs: A set of designs of similar rigour to experimental designs but with less rigid requirements which are more easily met by the social researcher.

Questionnaire: An instrument of data collection consisting of a standardized series of questions relating to the research topic to be answered in writing by participants.

Randomization: The processes of creating equivalent groups by ensuring that each unit of the study is distributed by chance (randomly) to a certain group (experimental or control).

Random (probability) sampling: Sampling techniques where the probability of each element of the population being included in the sample can be determined.

Ratio scale: A scale of measurement characterized by regular units of measurement and an absolute zero, beyond which the scale is meaningless.

Reductionism: The research method of considering only the essential necessary properties, variables or aspects of a problem.

Reliability: An estimate of the accuracy and internal consistency of a measurement instrument.

Research design: The set of procedures that guides the researcher in the process of verifying a particular hypothesis and excluding all other possible hypotheses, or explanations. It allows the researcher to draw conclusions about the relationship between variables.

Sample: The group of elements drawn from the population, which is considered to be representative of the population, and which is studied in order to acquire some knowledge about the entire population.

Sampling: The technique by which a sample is drawn from the population.

Sampling Error: Margin of error in the way the sample represents the population due to inadequate or inappropriate sampling.

Scales of measurement: Different systems used to measure or classify units, enabling comparison.

Secondary data: Data used in a specific study, although collected by a different researcher for the purpose of addressing a different research problem.

Statistic: A numerical value which summarizes some characteristic of the sample.

Glossary

Summative evaluation: Research designed to determine the extent to which a particular intervention has met its stated objectives.

Unit of analysis: The person, object, or event from which data is collected, and about which conclusions may be drawn.

Validity: The degree to which a study actually measures what it purports to measure.

Variable: An empirical property that is observed to change by taking more than one value or being of more than one kind.

Bibliography

American Psychological Association (1982). *Ethical Principles in the Conduct of Research with Human Participants*. Washington DC: American Psychological Association.

Babbie, E. R. (1979). *The Practice of Social Research*, Second Edition. Belmont: Wadsworth.

Barlow, D., Hayes, S. and Nelson, R. (1984). *The Scientist Practitioner: Research and Accountability in Clinical and Educational Settings*. New York: Pergamon.

Barnett, V. (1991). *Sample Survey: Principles and Methods*. London: Edward Arnold.

Beach, D. (1996). *The Responsible Conduct of Research*, New York: VCH.

Blalock, H. M. (1972). *Social Statistics*. Tokyo: McGraw-Hill.

Blalock, H. M. & Blalock (Eds.) (1986). *Methodology in Social Research*. New York: McGraw-Hill.

Bless, C. & Kathuria, M. (1993). *Fundamentals of Social Statistics: An African Perspective*. Cape Town: Juta.

Brown, L. D. & Tandon, R. (1983). Ideology and Political Economy in Inquiry: Action Research and Participatory Research. *Journal of Applied Behavioural Science*, 19(3), 177–194.

Bulmer, H. (1987). *Social Research in Developing Countries: Surveys and Censuses in the 3rd World*. New York: John Wiley and Sons.

Campbell, D. T. (1988). *Methodology and Epistemology for Social Science: Selected Papers*. Chicago: University of Chicago Press.

Campbell, D. T. & Stanley J.C. (1966). *Experimental and Quasi-experimental Designs for Research*. Chicago: Rand McNally.

Carmines, E. G. & Zeller, R. A. (1979). *Reliability and Validity Assessment*. Beverly Hills: Sage Publications.

Casley, D. & Lury, D. (1981). *Data Collection in Developing Countries*. Oxford: Clarendon Press/Oxford University Press.

Collins, K. (1999). *Participatory Research: A Primer*. Cape Town: Prentice Hall.

Cook, T. D. & Campbell, D. T. (1979). *Quasi-experimentation: Design & analysis issues for field settings*. Chicago: Rand McNally.

Cronbach, L. J. (1982). *Designing Evaluations of Educational and Social Programs*. San Francisco: Jossey-Bass.

Dawson, S., Manderson, L. & Tallo, V. L. (1992). *The Focus Group Manual*. World Health Organisation.

Denzin, N. K. & Lincoln, Y. S. (Eds.) (1994). *Handbook of Qualitative Research*. Thousand Oaks: Sage.

Duckitt, J. (1990). *A Social Psychological Investigation of Racial Prejudice among White South Africans*. Unpublished doctoral dissertation, University of the Witwatersrand.

Edwards, A. L. (1970). *Experimental Design in Psychological Research*, Third Edition. London: Holt, Rinehart and Winston.

Festinger, L. (1953). *Research Method in Behavioural Sciences*. New York: Holt, Rinehart and Winston.

Forcese, D. & Richer, P. (1973). *Social Research Methods*. New Jersey: Prentice-Hall.

Gay, L. R. (1981). *Educational Research: Competencies for Analysis and Application*. New York: Charles E Merrill.

Goode-Halt, D. (1984). *Methods in Social Research*. New York: McGraw-Hill.

Bibliography

Greenwood, D. J., Whyte, W. F. & Harkavy, I. (1993). Participatory action research as a process and as a goal. *Human Relations*, 46, 175–192.

Haslam, S. A. and McGarty C. (1998). *Doing Psychology: An introduction to Research Methodology and Statistics*. London: Sage.

Horowitz, I. L. (1974). *The Rise and Fall of the Project Camelot*. Manchester: MIT Press.

Kaplan, A. (1963). *The Conduct of Inquiry: Methodology of Behavioural Science*. New York: Harper and Row.

Kerlinger, F. N. (1973). *Foundations of Behavioral Research, Second Edition*. New York: Holt, Rinehart and Wilson.

Kpedekpo, G. & Arya, P. (1981). *Social and Economic Statistics for Africa*. London: George Allen and Unwin.

Lang, G. & Heiss, G. D. (1994). *A Practical Guide to Research Methods, Fifth Edition*. Lanham: University Press of America.

Lazarus, S. (1985). Action research in an educational setting. *South African Journal of Psychology*, 15, 112–118.

Leedy, P. D. (1989). *Practical Research: Planning and Design, Fourth Edition*. New York, Macmillan.

Lincoln, Y. S. & Guba, E. G. (1985). *Naturalistic Inquiry*. Beverly Hills: Sage.

Mason, E. J. & Bramble W. J. (1978). *Understanding and Conducting Research*. New York: McGraw-Hill.

Miles, M. B. & Huberman, A. M. (1984). *Qualitative Data Analysis: A Sourcebook of New Methods*. Beverly Hills: Sage.

Miller, D. C. (1991) *Handbook of Research Design and Social Measurement, Fifth Edition*, Newbury Park: Sage.

Mintz, A. (1951). Non-adaptive group behaviour. *Journal of Abnormal and Social Psychology*, 46, 150–159.

Mitton, R. (1982). *Practical Research in Distance Teaching: A Handbook for Development Countries*. Cambridge: International Extension College.

Moganu, E. T. & Rumish, D. W. (1994). *Prospects for Tuberculosis Control in Botswana: The HIV Factor*. Presented at the TB 2000 Conference, Pretoria.

Nachmias, D. & Nachmias, C. (1981). *Research Methods in the Social Sciences, Second Edition*. New York: St. Martin's Press.

O'Donohue, W. S., Curtis, D. and Fisher, J. E. (1985). Use of Research in the Practice of Community Mental Health: A Case Study. *Professional Psychology: Research and Practice*, 16, 710–718.

Pausewong, S. (1973). *Methods and Concepts of Social Research in Rural Developing Society*. Munich: Weltforum-Vertaz.

Peil, M. (1982). *Social Science Research Methods: An African Handbook*. London: Hodder and Stoughton.

Posavac, E. J. & Carey, R. G. (1989). *Program Evaluation: Methods and Case Studies, Third Edition*. Englewood Cliffs, NJ: Prentice Hall.

Prewitt, K. (1980). *Introducing Research Methodology: East African Application*. Nairobi: Institute for Development Studies.

Selltiz, C., Wrightsman, L.S. & Cook, S.W. (1976). *Research Methods in Social Relations, Third Edition*. New York: Holt, Rinehart and Wilson.

Solso, R. L. & Johnson, H. H. (1994). *Experimental Psychology: A Case Approach, Fifth Edition*, New York: HarperCollins.

Strachan, P. and Peters, C. (1997). *Empowering Communities: A Casebook from West Sudan*. Oxford, Oxfam UK and Ireland.

Susskind, E. C. and Klein D. C. (Eds.) (1985). *Community Research: Methods, Paradigms, and Application*. New York: Praeger.

Taylor, S. T. and Bogdan, R. (1984). *Introduction to Qualitative Research Methods: The Search for Meanings, Second Edition*. New York: Wiley.

Tolan, P., Keys, C., Chertok, F. & Jason, L. (Eds.) (1990). *Researching Community Psychology: Issues of Theory and Methods*.

Washington: American Psychological Association.

Tuckman, B. W. (1976). *Conducting Educational Research, Second Edition.* New York: Harcourt.

University of Giessen (1975). *Psychologie: eine Form Bürgerlicher Ideologie. Aufsätze zur Kritik Psychologisher Theorie und Praxis.* Plankstadt: Sendler.

Walsh, J. A., Wollersheim, J. P., Bach, P. J., Bridgwater, C. A., Klentz, B. A. & Steblay, N. M. (1985). Program Evaluation as Applied to the Goals of a Psychology Department Clinic, *Professional Psychology: Research and Practice*, 16, 661–670.

Webb, E. J., Campbell, D. T., Schwartz, R. D., Sechrest, L., & Grove, J. B. (1981). *Nonreactive Measures in the Social Sciences, Second Edition*, Boston: Houghton Mifflin.

Winter, R. (1987). *Action-Research and the Nature of Social Inquiry: Professional Innovation and Educational Work.* Aldershot: Avebury.

Index

A

Absolute zero 98
Abstract 144, 153
Accidental sampling 92
Acquiring knowledge 1
Action-research 56, 59, 153
   contract 58
   developing countries, in 60
   implementation 59
Actions 64
Aims
   formulating in measurable terms 53
   identifying 52
Analysis, unit of 64, 157
Anonymity 100
Antecedent variable 29, 153
Appendices 144
Assistance, requesting 56
Assumptions 3
Authority 1
Availability sampling 92

B

Background information 15
Bias
   analyst 140
   interviewer 139
   researcher 140
   respondent 139
   selection 80, 94
   sources 78
Bibliography 143, 159

C

Case study 67
Causal relationship 26, 153
Chance factors 94
Classification errors 138
Cohort studies 66
Community projects 45
Community-centred research 45
Completeness 120
Conceptual definition 31, 153
Conclusions 140

Conditions 64
Confidentiality 101
Constant 26, 153
Construct validity 133
Content validity 131
Control group 153
   design
      post-test only 75
      pre-test/post-test 68, 74
Control variable 29, 153
Correlational relationship 153
Correlational research 42, 153
Criterion-related validity 132
Critical mass 19
Cross-sectional design 153

D

Data 97
   analysis 137, 143
   collection 53
      according to research type 99
      basic concepts 97
      ethical considerations 100
      record method 123
      techniques 103, 112
      unobtrusive measures 123
   nature of required data 40
   primary 156
   secondary 156
Definitions, vague 139
Dependent variable 27
Description 3
Descriptive research 41, 154
Design 63, 156
   experimental 67, 73, 154
   inadequate 139
   intact group comparison 69
   longitudinal 155
   pre-experimental 67, 156
   quasi-experimental 67
   time-series 71
Diagnostic evaluation 49, 50, 154
Directional hypothesis 154
Discussion 143
Dummy table 154

E

Ecological fallacy 65
Empirical referents 33
Empirical testability 18
Equivalent-form reliability 128
Errors 138, 139
    classification 138
    constant 138
    measurement 138
    random 138
    sources 139
    types 138
Ethical considerations 11, 100
Evaluation 49, 55
    formative 51, 154
    research 49, 154
    study, designing 53
    summative 52, 157
Experiment, field 154
Experimental design 67, 73, 154
Experimental group 154
Experimental mortality 79
Experimental techniques 121
Explanation 3
    deductive 5
    probabilistic 5
Explanatory research 42, 154
Exploratory research 41, 154
External validity 80, 154
Extraneous variable 154

F

Face validity 133
Factorial designs 76
Facts 8, 97
    and theory — problem, hypothesis and model 10
Feasibility 18, 47, 154
Field experiment 122, 154
Filter questionnaire 115
Findings
    generalizing 140
    interpreting 137, 138
Focus group 110, 154
Formative evaluation 50, 51, 154
Formulation of problem 25
Funnel questionnaire 115

G

Generalizing findings 140
Group design, contrasted 70
Groups 65

H

History and maturation 78
Hypothesis 10, 154
    analysing 143
    directional 34, 154
    formulation 25, 33
    inaccuracy 139
    non-directional 34, 155
    operational formulation 142
    rationale 142
    statement 142

I

Independent variable 27
Individuals 65
Inference 154
Instrumentation 79
    accuracy and consistency 130
    constructing 53
Intact group comparison design 69
Interest 19
Internal validity 80, 154
Interpretation of findings 137, 143
    detection of errors 138
Interval sampling 88
Interval scales 99, 155
Intervals, equal 98
Intervening variable 29, 155
Intervention 3
Interview 104, 155
    non-scheduled 105
    scheduled 105
    semi-structured 107
    structured 108
    techniques 106
    unstructured 107
Item analysis 129

J

Judgemental sampling 92

K

Knowledge
    perceptual 8
    rational 8
Knowledge acquisition 11
    authority 1
    empirical method 2
    mystical method 2
    non-scientific methods 1
    rationalistic method 2
    scientific method 2

Index

L

Laboratory experiment   121, 155
Laws   3
Literature   20
   review   19, 142, 155
Longitudinal design   66, 155

M

Magnitude   98
Mailed questionnaire   109
Main effects   76
Matching   73, 155
Maturation   78, 127
Measurement   97
   errors   138
   scales   98, 156
Mistakes   138
Model   10
   building   10
Moderator variable   28, 155
Monitoring   48

N

Natural causes   4
Natural sciences, distinct from social sciences   7
Needs assessment   45
   survey   46
Negotiation   57
Nominal scales   98, 155
Non-directional hypothesis   155
Non-participant observation   103
Non-probability sampling   155
Non-response error   94

O

Objectives
   formulating in measurable terms   53
   identifying   52
Objectivity   4
   and values   148
Observation   15, 103, 155
One-shot case study   67
Open-ended questions   119
Operational definition   31, 142, 155
Operational formulations of hypotheses   142
Ordinal scales   98, 155
Organizations   65
Orientations   64

P

Participant observation   104
Participants   143
Participatory research   56, 155
Personal interest   16
Pilot study   52, 155
Planning   58
   inadequate   139
Population   84, 155
   parameters   84, 156
   well-defined   85
Practical concerns   16
Practical value   19
Prediction   3
Pre-experimental designs   67, 156
Previous research   16
Primary data   156
Probabilistic explanations   156
Probability   5
Probability sampling   156
Problem   10
Problem conception   15
Procedures   143
Project evaluation   49
Project monitoring   48
Promulgation of results   12
Proof
   co-variance of A and B   42
   non-spuriousness of the co-variance   43
   stable time-order   43
Purposive sampling   92

Q

Qualitative research   156
Quantitative research   156
Quasi-experimental designs   67, 70, 156
Questionnaire   104, 156
   constructing   113
   developing   113
   editing   120
   filter   115
   funnel   115
   mailed   109
   self-administered   105
   structure   115
   techniques   106
Questions   116
   factual   116
   open-ended   118, 119
   opinion   117
   structured   118, 119
   wording   114
Quota sampling   92

© Juta & Co Ltd

163

R

Random sampling 156
Randomization 73, 156
Ratio scales 99, 156
Reactive effects 79
Reason 2
Recommendations 141
Reductionism 65, 156
References 143
Regression towards mean 78
Regularities 126
Relationship between variables 25
Relevance 12
Reliability 126, 156
   equivalent-form 128
   measurements 125
   test–retest 127
   and validity 134
Replicability 6
Report formats 141
Reporting 53
   style 144
Reputability studies 66
Research
   aims 40
   basic and applied 38
   classifying 37
   community projects 45
   explanatory 41, 42, 154
   findings, generalizing 140
   focus 64
   funding institutions 150
   highest quality 151
   inadequate planning 139
   instrument, imperfection 139
   object of 40
   problems
      identifying 16, 142
      sources and identification 15
   qualitative 38, 156
   quantitative 38, 156
   report 137
      material or instrument 143
      organization 142
      task 143
   scientific 5
   sources of topics 15
   types 37
Research design 63, 67, 77, 156
   validity 80
Research world 147
Respondents 143
   needs, interests and problems 114
Response set 115

Results 143
Review
   purpose 20
   techniques 21
Rights of research participants 100

S

Sample 84, 86, 156
   dependent 93
   independent 93
   related 93
   representative 86
   size 93
Sample statistics 84
Sampling 83, 93, 156
   accidental 92
   advantages 84
   availability 92
   cluster 90
   concepts 85
   errors 94, 139, 156
      related problems 94
   interval 88
   judgemental 92
   multi-stage 90
   non-probability 92, 155
   probability 87, 156
   purpose 83
   purposive 92
   quota 92
   random 156
   replacement, with or without 93
   simple random 87
   stratified random 89
   systematic 88
   types 83
Scales of measurement 98, 156
Scientific method
   properties 3
   social reality 7
Scientific research 5
   steps 12
Secondary data 156
Semi-structured interviews 107
Significance of study 142
Simple observation 103
Social artifact 65
Social research
   applied 153
   basic 153
   objectives 39
Social sciences, distinct from natural sciences 7
Sources 20
Split-halves reliability 128

Index

Statement of the problem   142
Statistics   84, 156
Structured interviews   108
Structured questions   118, 119
Subjects   143
Suggestions   141
Summary of findings   143
Summative evaluation   50, 52, 157
Systematic   4
Systematic sampling   88

T

Test effect   69, 79
Testable   34
Test–retest reliability   127
Theoretical value   19
Theory   8, 15
   relating to facts   9
Time dimension   66
Time-series design   71
Topic area   17
Tracer studies   67
Transmittability   6

U

Unit of analysis   84
Unstructured interviews   107

V

Validity   80, 130, 157
   content   131
   criterion-related   132
   external   80, 81, 154
   face   133
   internal   80, 81, 154
   of measurements   125
   and reliability   134
Values   148
Variable   25, 26, 157
   analysing   143
   antecedent   29, 153
   control   29
   dependent   27, 154
   extraneous   154
   identifying   26
   independent   27, 154
   intervening   29, 155
   moderator   28, 155